DATE DUE			

PN 1992.8.A3S48 2003

AUDITIONING AND ACTING FOR THE CAMERA

Shepard, John W.

televison acting: motion picture acting

Smith and Kraus
Career Development: Auditioning Series

AUDITIONING
and ACTING for
the CAMERA

Proven Techniques
for Auditioning and Performing in
Film, Episodic TV, Sitcoms, Soap Operas,
Commercials, and Industrials

John W. Shepard

CAREER DEVELOPMENT SERIES

Smith and Kraus

Published by
Smith and Kraus, Inc.
177 Lyme Road, Hanover, NH 03755
www.smithkraus.com

First edition: March 2004
9 8 7 6 5 4 3 2 1

Cover and text illustration by David Droxler
Cover and text design by Julia Gignoux, Freedom Hill Design

Library of Congress Cataloging-in-Publication Data

Shepard, John Warren, 1952–
Auditioning and acting for the cameras: proven techniques for auditioning
and performing in film, episodic TV, sitcoms, soap operas, commercials,
and industrials / John Warren Shepard. — 1st ed.
p. cm. — (Career development series)
Includes bibliographical references.
ISBN 1-57525-275-9
1. Television acting. 2. Motion picture acting. I. Title. II. Series.

PN1992.8.A3S48 2003
791.45'028—dc22
2003054449

DEDICATION

To Ashley Carr, for his inspiration and mentorship;
Barbara Minges, for her patience and support;
and, most importantly, to all my students — I can only hope
that I have taught you as much as you have taught me.

ACKNOWLEDGMENTS

I gratefully wish to acknowledge the efforts of a number of people without whom this book would otherwise not have been written. Foremost among them is Evelyn Chen, a tireless and brilliant editor who guided me through every phase of this process. Other invaluable assistance was provided by Peter Zapp, Marisa Smith, Mary Rawson, David Droxler, Kate Mueller, Julia Gignoux, Matthew Gitkin, Naomi DeVries, Ronald Allan-Lindblom, Rick Hamilton, Fredi Olster, Blythe and Matthew Shepard, and the representatives of the Pittsburgh chapter of the American Federation of Television and Radio Artists as well as the Screen Actors Guild in Los Angeles.

Contents

CHAPTER 1

"ACTION!" (NOW WHAT?)

"Action!" is a formidable command when you are standing in front of a camera that's focused on you. Whether it's for a commercial, an industrial film, an interactive CD-ROM, a situation comedy, a soap opera, an episodic television program, or a motion picture, it's given as a cue from the director. But it's more than just a cue. When an actor hears "Action!" it's his or her job to give an interesting and believable performance.

Just as acting in a Shakespeare play requires abilities different from those needed for a realistic American play, each genre in television and film requires special acting skills. The genres of commercials, industrials, sitcoms, soap operas, episodic television, and film are stylistically distinct from one another. Each demands a different approach from the actor; one that respects the genre's inherent characteristics.

In Shakespeare, for instance, you need to pay attention to the demands of the language and become adept at verse, prose, and rhetoric. In American realism, you need to be sensitive to the subtleties of subtext and mood and be able to successfully incorporate them into a performance. The genres of film and television require similar kinds of knowledge. You wouldn't necessarily bring whimsicality, which might be appropriate for situation comedy, to a soap opera, or audition for a commercial in the same way you would for a film. A truly professional actor needs to perceive the stylistic differences of the genres and know how to adapt easily to all of them. The purpose of this book is to help you learn to adapt to any genre you might find yourself working in.

Each chapter represents a different genre. Within each chapter the demands of the particular audition procedure, what employment options to expect, and how to conduct yourself on the set once you've gotten the job are discussed. I have also devised principles for each genre to help you. However, this book is not merely theoretical; practical exercises accompany each chapter. Hopefully you are studying somewhere (studio, classroom, or lab) where you have access to equipment and can practice these exercises.

No matter how much you know, however, the reality is that it's hard to get a job as an actor. Whether it's in film, on television, or on stage, at any given moment approximately 95 percent of all actors are out of work. And that percentage only represents professional actors who belong to one or more unions. It doesn't include aspiring actors who are studying, paying their dues, and not getting paid toiling in low-budget and student films, as well as university and community theater, or those dreaming of becoming a star. Since getting work is so difficult, it's vital to know what to do to get the job. Therefore, a crucial goal of this book is to help you understand the process of auditioning for on-camera employment.

To act on camera, you must have some basic acting skills. To grasp the subtle distinctions of each genre, an actor needs to know some acting vocabulary and some rudimentary acting techniques. You will receive some of that essential training in this book. However, to act effectively on camera, you need training, either studying in an acting class or working onstage. In the same way that one learns to walk before one learns to run, an actor should learn to act for the stage before anything else. Nearly all great film and TV actors were trained to act for the stage first.

Even if you've never acted before or had any formal training, you may still find this book useful. History is full of brilliant film performances by actors who had never acted before. However, if you want to have a career and be able to work in a variety of media, you need the appropriate training. The techniques learned for acting onstage are indispensable for acting in front of a camera. In addition, acting demands a huge commitment to studying humanity and to hard, conscientious work, plus amazing discipline.

Although acting is acting no matter where it's done, one technique an actor must learn is to be aware of the size of his or her performance and how much the audience will be able to see it. To do this, let's look at the difference between acting onstage and on camera.

WHAT IS THE BASIC DIFFERENCE BETWEEN ACTING ONSTAGE AND IN FRONT OF A CAMERA?

It's all a matter of scale. For our purposes scale includes closeness versus distance and large versus small. The biggest difference between acting onstage and acting in front of the camera is the *size* of the actor's performance. This includes physical size, of course, but it also includes vocal dimension and emotional breadth.

When actors are onstage, they are taught to fulfill the technical demands of their craft by being heard and seen by an audience. It's not uncommon for actors to perform in both an intimate theater that holds 100 people and a large theater for 1200 people. The actor must adjust his vocal, physical, and emotional volume so that it's appropriate for the space. Obviously, the bigger the theater the louder and more physically and emotionally expressive the performance has to be. The opposite is true for a small theater. The very nature of theater is its communal arrangement — actors and audience all share the same space, no matter how big or small.

The biggest challenge a stage actor faces on camera is learning to condense the scale of her performance. Because the space is much more restricted, the actor's scale has to be smaller. Not only does the actor need to adjust technically by diminishing her vocal and physical projection, but she must also learn to emotionally temper what she is doing. The camera minutely records the actor's vocal, physical, and emotional life; therefore, an actor has to be subtler in conveying character.

That is not to imply, however, that when actors are in front of a camera they are void of vocal, physical, or emotional life. One of the biggest mistakes many actors make when they start acting on camera is that they go to the opposite extreme. Many actors think (or are taught to think) that they mustn't do anything at all when they are in front of a camera. That's not true. What's happening with a character is just as important on camera as when the actor is onstage.

However, instead of projecting it the actor must internalize it. When you're performing onstage, you are playing for an audience of many; when acting on camera, you are playing for an audience of one.

Vocally, working on camera is easy. Since you are always miked, you never have to worry about projection. Of course, that takes some getting used to. Many stage actors overproject when they are wearing a microphone. (Maybe that's because the urge to perform and reach out to an audience is firmly embedded in an actor's psyche.) The first lesson, then, is to know that when you are wearing a body mike, or are being picked up by a boom (a microphone on a long pole usually held over the actor's head by a crew person), you can speak and be clearly heard without having to project your voice any more than you normally do.

Your physical considerations don't need to change when you're on camera, with one notable exception — you must pay attention to the framing of each shot. Basically, the actor needs to know what kind of camera shot is being used. When you know what the camera's frame is, you know what the camera is seeing. If the camera is shooting a wide or long shot, more of your body will be seen. A wide frame is equivalent to performing onstage in a large theater. Conversely, the closer the shot, the narrower the frame, and the less of your body will be seen. A narrow frame (such as a close-up) is equivalent to performing in a small space. Knowing what the frame is will govern what you can physically do within each shot. For instance, it doesn't matter what you're doing with your hands if the shot is a close-up of your face. Conversely, if the shot is a long master shot of a group of people, that wonderfully subtle physical tic you created might not be picked up. Ultimately, it's the actor who is responsible for knowing his frame. (I deal with this extensively in chapter 4 on situation comedy, where you'll also find illustrations of different kinds of camera shots.)

When it comes to emotional scope, what an actor can do on-camera is far more complex than what he can do onstage. This is one reason why so many great actors leave the stage to act in film and television. For an actor in a theater, depending on the type of play and the space, it may be necessary to project emotion. The one thing you never want to do on camera is to project emotion; it will just come across as overacting. If you aren't honestly feeling something, the camera will know. If you aren't honestly feeling something, it's best not to feign it. You can sometimes get away with lying onstage, but you can never lie when you're on camera. The camera is like a microscope: it can see into your soul.

Because the camera demands such truthfulness, some assert that acting on camera is more honest than working onstage. But there are many wonderful aspects about acting onstage that you don't get on camera. In the theater actors develop a relationship with the audience and receive immediate feedback. Each performance is unique and can never be repeated, no matter how many times a play is performed. And doing a play creates a sense of community. (Those are the reasons *I* love working onstage.)

However, the appeal of working in front of a camera is immense. Television and film are universally attractive; they represent the popular concepts of success and fame. Everyone in this country has been raised to some extent on the fantasy of film and television; it's natural that if one becomes an actor, one does so to be a part of that dream. Part of the media's allure is its power to influence the way people think and behave. The sheer number of people who watch a performance on film or television is huge compared to the number of people who attend theater. (More people have seen me act in one episode of a TV series than have seen me act onstage over a twenty-five-year career.) Working in film and on television is lucrative — not only can actors make a lot of money, but so does anyone associated with the industry. Because you can repeatedly show a single performance on DVD, videotape, and film, it's a money-making machine.

Whether it's your intention to appear in musicals, plays, or in any of the genres of television or film, there is no guarantee of success. However, it is my contention that if an actor is going to make a living, she must know how to work on camera. Because of the proliferation of cable stations, the Internet, and the digitalization of the entertainment business, for an actor to have a viable career she must be able to navigate her way in front of a camera.

WHAT DOES IT TAKE TO BE A PROFESSIONAL ACTOR?

It's like the old joke: A guy on a street asks a passerby, "How do you get to Carnegie Hall?" The other guy says, "Practice, practice, practice." As far as I'm concerned, becoming an actor is no different. You need to study and work hard. I would go so far as to add that a little prayer for luck wouldn't hurt. However, one of my favorite quotes is from Thomas Jefferson. When asked what he thought about luck Jefferson replied, "I believe in luck. I work hard for it every day." To get lucky, you must work hard and not waste opportunity. Let that be your mantra for becoming a professional actor.

On a more literal level, though, a professional actor in the film and TV industry is generally someone who belongs to one of the actors' unions. There are three major unions in this country that oversee the acting profession: the Screen Actor's Guild (SAG), the American Federation of Television and Radio Artists (AFTRA), and Actors' Equity. Since Actors' Equity only has jurisdiction over professional stage work, this book just discusses SAG and AFTRA.

WHAT ARE SAG AND AFTRA AND WHAT'S THE DIFFERENCE BETWEEN THEM?

SAG and AFTRA are labor unions created to protect the wages and working conditions of their members. They also represent their members by negotiating contracts with employers. These contracts include issues ranging from how much money an actor makes to how much time off he needs between call times. Employers who honor these contracts are known as signatories of the unions. Most of the producers working in film and television are signatories of SAG and AFTRA. Producers who are not signatories are not bound to the rules of the union contracts; therefore they don't have to pay the appropriate scale, and working conditions are not regulated.

Although a recent vote to merge SAG and AFTRA was narrowly defeated, at some point they will merge. Until then, the difference between SAG and AFTRA is that SAG has jurisdiction over everything that is filmed (hence *screen* actor's), and AFTRA has jurisdiction over everything that is videotaped or on radio (hence *television and radio* artists). For example, commercials are generally filmed, as are some industrials and certain sitcoms, and as a result, fall under the jurisdiction of SAG. SAG's domain also includes all motion pictures and most episodic television. (When I say episodic television, I'm referring to one-hour dramatic series — "E.R.," "N.Y.P.D. Blue," "Law and Order," and so on. TV miniseries and movies of the week would also fall in that category.)

Anything videotaped would fall under AFTRA's authority. This includes some commercials and industrials (as long as they are taped), videotaped situation comedies, and all soap operas. One of the big differences between the two unions is that while SAG only represents actors, AFTRA does not. Only those actors who have contractually appeared on film are members of SAG. This now includes extras, also known as background performers. Because AFTRA covers everything that is videotaped or on radio, its members aren't only considered actors; they are also deemed "on-air personalities." Besides sitcoms and soap operas, game shows are also videotaped; therefore, the hosts are members of AFTRA — so are news anchors and reporters on local, cable, and national news programs. Sports announcers on television as well as on radio are also members of AFTRA.

HOW DO YOU GET INTO THESE UNIONS?

I get asked this question a lot. Basically, it's a catch-22 situation. To be eligible to join a union, you must have a contract (a job). However, to get a job (and thereby have a contract), you usually need an agent — and to get an agent you must be in a union. It seems like a no-win situation, and in a sense that's what the unions want you to believe. (Don't forget that it's part of the unions' responsibility to protect their members — who are mostly unemployed at any given time. One way they protect their members is to make it difficult for non-members to join.) However, there are ways to circumvent this.

AFTRA, for instance, currently has an "open door" policy — anyone is welcome to join as long as he or she pays the initiation fee (which can be considerable). Then, one year after *receiving a contract* for a principal role, you are eligible to join one of the sister unions — SAG or Actors' Equity. (The distinguishing characteristic of a principal role in both SAG and AFTRA is that a principal role has lines and an extra doesn't.) This method of joining is reciprocal among all three unions. The bottom line is that you must have either a SAG contract or wait a year after receiving a principal contract from one of the sister unions to get into SAG. Besides having a contract for a principle role, it is currently possible to join SAG by being hired three times as an extra. "Background vouchers" are obtained from the Assistant Director on the days when you're hired to prove employment.

This rule is subject to change at any time by SAG's elegibility committee, so the safest way still to join SAG is to secure employment via a principle role.

I could spend an entire book going over strategy regarding how to get into the unions. However, it is not this book's intention to do that. Many resources offer you that kind of information. For information about SAG, visit their Web site at www.sag.org, or call their national office in Los Angeles at (323) 954-1600. AFTRA's Web site address is www.aftra.org; the phone number for their national office in New York is (212) 532-0800.

If you are determined and willing to work hard and give this business your undivided attention, you will at some point be able to join one or all the unions. The overriding goal is always to get the job.

It's certainly true that there are actors who are paid and do professional quality work but are not members of SAG and AFTRA. A lot of excellent professional-level work is nonunion. However, because most of the work that you're going to want to pursue falls under the authority of the unions, I mostly deal with union jobs in this book. At some point you'll have to join, but until then, you should get as much experience as possible. Whether it's by doing student films or low-budget nonunion work, keep working on perfecting your craft; because once you do join the unions, there is no turning back. When you become a member of SAG and AFTRA, you can only accept union work, and the penalties for union members doing nonunion work are severe. So until you're ready (and qualified) to join, my advice is to do what you can to become a better actor. Don't let the goal of getting into the union exceed the goal of becoming a better actor.

HOW DO YOU GET AN AGENT?

Again, this is a subject that demands more attention than this book gives it. Lots of great resources on this subject fill up bookshelves at local bookstores. (I deal with this issue more in chapter 2.) Though an agent is important in New York and other cities, it's not vital to have one. You can work for yourself, especially when it comes to getting stage work. On the other hand, it's almost impossible to get anywhere without an agent in Los Angeles.

Managers are becoming more important today, as well. Basically, managers handle an actor's career the way agents used to. That is, they deal with a smaller and more select group of clients (actors), take a very keen interest in them, and personally try to cultivate their individual careers. (The biggest distinction between agents and managers is that agents represent a much larger clientele and give less personal attention.) Besides nurturing careers, managers try to secure agents for their clients. Agents and managers work together in getting auditions for their clients and negotiating salaries. Managers make 15 percent of an actor's income; agents make 10 percent. When you get too busy to handle your own career, you will eventually need a manager — until then, stick with an agent.

The one thing you'll need that will help you get an agent is a good headshot. (I deal extensively with this topic in the next chapter.) I also recommend that you only pursue agents that are franchised by both unions. (This way you can be assured that they will be helping you seek only union work.) Being franchised means that the agency has signed a contract with the unions agreeing to protect their clients' interests according to the union rules. You can get a list of franchised agents by visiting each union's Web site.

To get an agent, you will have to market yourself. This may include inundating agencies with mailings of your pictures and résumés, as well as notes reminding them of plays, films, videos, or TV programs that you're appearing in. Leave no stone unturned; use every connection you have to meet agents. You'll need to cultivate relationships and charm the agent's receptionists and junior agents. In other words, you'll have to do everything you can think of to get an agent to notice you and become interested in representing you.

One of the most important things an actor should keep in mind about the film and television industry is that it's a business. In many ways, actors are self-employed. Think of acting as going into business for yourself. Although it seems that actors work for agents, the opposite is really true: Agents work for actors. A better way to think about this relationship is that actors and agents are partners. In seeking representation, actors are looking for business partners — partners who will help them deal with the business. When looking for an agent, find someone who you would feel comfortable being a business partner with — someone who can help you market yourself and who is good at negotiations.

While you're looking, just make sure that you don't compromise your beliefs. Use your instincts. If someone asks you to do something that you're not comfortable doing or behaves in a way that you don't like, move on; you wouldn't want to be represented by him anyway. Remember this: You never pay an agent unless he gets you work; agents can only get paid if they get actors work.

GENERAL ACTING TECHNIQUES

You're going to need a few general techniques to work effectively in film and television: naturalness, the ability to listen, concentration, spontaneity, and proficiency at improvisation. These skills are common to all on-camera work and, in fact, are basic skills needed to be a good actor. I deal with each of these qualities within each genre. First, let's discuss the central idea of each one.

What do you mean by naturalness?

As I mentioned earlier, you cannot get away with lying on camera. The camera resembles a lie detector in that it can discern the difference between truth and deception. If your performance is honest, the camera will reveal that; and if it's dishonest, the camera will expose it. You must ingratiate yourself with the camera, and the best way to do that is to be natural.

To me, naturalness means unaffected honesty. If you are self-conscious in front of a camera, you will not be able to behave naturally. Acting on camera requires that you be at ease and able to behave with complete candidness. I truly believe that the most successful actors on film are those who have a high degree of self-awareness. It's not about self-confidence; many excellent actors are timid. Although self-confidence sometimes helps, it's the self-aware actors who are most natural. They are generally more comfortable with who they are, and therefore worry less about what other people (and, by extension, the camera) think. The quality of being fully who you are without caring what others think is not only a measure of naturalness, it's also an attractive trait. Audiences tend to enjoy watching people like that because most people care too much about what other people think.

The ability to be natural on camera also requires that you are both willing to be watched and enjoy it. Call it a form of exhibitionism, but actors must want the camera to look at them. But there is a distinction between wanting to be watched and showing off. Wanting to be watched easily relates to self-confidence; showing off is a need for validity and usually springs from self-consciousness. Showing off also implies pretension, and at its worst, overacting. Showing off is acutely self-conscious because it is self-serving — and the camera will always pick up on that. Good acting obligates the actor to share what she is doing with another character. Acting is not done in private. Not only does an actor share what she's doing with another character, she shares her performance with a camera or an audience in a theater. A desire to be watched is also about that kind of sharing. This is why shy people can be successful actors.

Why is listening important for an actor?

How do you feel when someone doesn't listen to you? It probably doesn't make you feel very good. Whether you admit it or not, you probably think less of people who don't listen than of people who do. In many ways, listening is an act of kindness because it's something we give freely to someone else. Listening is also verification; when you do it, you prove to the person doing the talking that what he is saying is worthwhile. This is an essential quality for an actor. Since acting is about sharing something with someone else, listening is the first step in making that happen.

Think about it this way — for an actor, listening is perhaps the most important skill because it automatically places the listener in a position of vulnerability. To fully convince another character (and an audience) that you don't know what's going to happen next, you need to be vulnerable. When you truly listen, you are forced to give of yourself to another person. When you do that, you ultimately have no control over the situation, and you have no idea what the other person is going to say. Therefore, a result of honest listening is ingenuousness on the part of the listener — and not only is ingenuousness a sign of vulnerability, it is riveting to watch because it opens the actor up to the audience.

Every great performance contains vulnerability. I once heard a memorable definition of a movie star as someone who is heroic and, at the same time, vulnerable. I think there's a lot of validity to that. Think about your favorite film actor; often she is someone you identify with on some level. Though we tend to get a vicarious thrill from her courageousness, we adore and empathize with her even more when she, like us, doesn't have all the answers. It's this antithesis that attracts an audience. The first step to achieving that vulnerability is to listen.

Listening is also important because of the many reaction close-ups that are shot when acting on camera. Too often actors concentrate more on the shots when they are speaking and overlook the shots when they are not. Reaction shots are extremely important; as you watch television and films, notice the amount of time that is spent on them. If you watch closely, I bet you can tell when someone is listening and when he's not. I also imagine that you're going to like the performance of the actor who listens more than that of an actor who doesn't. Because of the importance of reaction shots in relation to listening, I discuss this extensively in the sixth principle in chapter 6.

One of the best techniques for listening (which is very helpful when working on camera) is something that a wonderful teacher, Paul A. Ford, taught me many years ago. He called it the "Five-Step Reaction." It is a simple sequence that breaks a reaction down into its basic components. It's a listening technique because a genuine reaction is always the natural by-product of active listening. I urge you to learn the Five-Step Reaction and practice it in your daily conversations.

Step 1: Hear. The first thing you need to do when being addressed is to give your attention to someone when he or she is directing a comment to you.

Step 2: Listen. Once someone has your attention, you must actively acknowledge what he or she is saying by listening to him or her. (If you're already engaged in a conversation, it becomes a four-step reaction; you can eliminate the first step and start with this one.) It's crucial to understand the distinction between *hearing* and *listening*. Perhaps the best way to distinguish the two is to bear in mind that *hearing* is fairly passive and *listening* is always active. All of us go about our daily lives hearing extraneous white noise like traffic, television, and the radio playing in the background. Many of us have also perfected and learned to substitute an "appearance of listening," when actually we may only be *hearing*. This is usually learned in school, as students are highly accomplished at letting hearing stand in for listening, when in fact, they are a million miles away. *Listening* is much more active and requires concentration on what the speaker is saying. Listening is maybe the most important element in a conversation.

Step 3: Form an opinion. This is the most crucial of the five steps and can only be executed successfully when one is listening. Before you respond to someone, you need to have a basic idea of what you want to say. This can only happen when you've formed an opinion about what the other person is saying. Forming an opinion is a natural extension of listening. The opinion the actor forms before he actually speaks will directly affect his performance during the reaction shot.

Step 4: Want to speak. You may notice in your own conversations that once you've formed an opinion about what you want to say, you usually have an urge to speak. Generally, this happens before you actually get an opportunity to do so. (You might also refer to this step as a moment of interruption because this is where an interruption usually happens if it's going to.) Since this step may take place before the person who is speaking finishes and because most conversation is civil to a certain point, there is usually a delay between this step and the next one, which is . . .

Step 5: Speak. This is the moment of truth. This is the culmination of the four previous steps. If you've successfully completed them, then this step is the payoff when you actually get to say something.

Think about these steps as rungs on a ladder. You can only move up the ladder one rung at a time, and each rung must be earned. You'll find that the steps sometimes happen simultaneously; that's OK. Here's an example of when that might occur (although this is fairly simplistic, give it a try): Alex is playing a video game when Danforth comes home from the grocery store. The italics indicate Alex's Five-Step Reaction.

Danforth	Alex
1. Hey Alex!	1. *Hears.*
2. Look,	2. *Listens.*
3. I know you're busy, but I need some help	3. *Forms an opinion.*
4. in carrying in the groceries.	4. *Wants to speak.*
5. Give me a hand.	5. *Speaks:* I'm busy!

Now take a script from a movie or a play and have two people prepare a short scene and break it down in the same way. If you are in a situation where you can videotape it, go ahead and see if the Five-Step Reaction works. You'll want to get a close-up of the person going through the five steps. When you play it back and watch it, see if you can tell if the actor really seemed to be listening. Were you able to see the wheels turning?

What about concentration?

Concentration is a necessary skill for acting of any kind. Concentration includes remembering your next line, accounting for your actions as well as your objectives, and ignoring all the distractions around you. Believe me, concentration looks a lot easier than it is. Because we live in a society where we are constantly besieged by stimuli, in many ways we have lost the ability to concentrate on something longer than thirty seconds. As a result, this elemental acting skill has now become a specialized talent. If you are working in the television and film industry, you will need to maintain your concentration over long periods.

If you can imagine threading a needle during an earthquake, you have a fairly good idea of the kind of concentration you're going to need on the set. This may be an extreme example, but it's not too far off the mark. With all the activity that occurs during filming, it is essential that an actor learn to be calm in the middle of such tumult. Whether it's filming on location or for a commercial where a great deal has to happen in a short time, a lot of frenzied activity surrounds the actor on the set. The excitement includes crew members rushing back and forth moving equipment, the pressure of working on schedule when trying to shoot the required number of pages for the day, and making sure to get the right shot before the weather turns. Despite all this hectic activity, actors must do their jobs with ease and skill — or at least appear to do so.

And, of course, there are the distractions! Besides activity on the set, extras in a crowd scene, and even the onlookers watching, can be a formidable obstacle to the inner calm that is needed. If you waste your energy indulging in these diversions, I guarantee that you'll exhaust your ability to concentrate.

Filming is also a very slow process. It can take twelve hours to shoot two and a half to three pages of a motion picture. For an actor, this means a lot of waiting around. Waiting around will sap your energy and concentration and will leave you worn out by the time your important coverage is to be shot. As it is, the job of acting requires so much energy that you can't afford to waste it unnecessarily on anything that is not the task at hand. I deal with specific examples of this in Principles 1 and 2 in chapter 7 on film.

What does spontaneity have to do with camera acting?

Spontaneity is more than just being impetuous — it's the ability to think on your feet, to seize inspiration, and, like running with the bulls, to race with it. You can't be rigid as an actor, especially when it comes to acting in front of a camera. One of the best qualities that successful film and television actors possess is adaptability. That includes the ability to easily assimilate script changes, to adjust to the different shots, to preserve continuity over long periods (continuity is a continuous logical flow of action that must be maintained despite an inconsistent shooting schedule), and, most important, to know how to creatively use inspiration when it hits during filming. When you're on camera, it's not enough to reproduce what you've rehearsed; you must live it as if for the first time. And, like life, you never know what's going to happen next.

In each of the genres, you will have to deal with script changes. You may get new lines days, hours, or even minutes before you shoot a scene. The capacity to be spontaneous is the only thing that will help you handle this. Many actors get so attached to dialogue they've already memorized that it completely throws them to have to make a change. The same goes for adjusting to the different shots. In movies and episodic television where filming is done with only one camera, you must be able to maintain a fresh performance when the camera is turned around (a term for setting up and shooting the scene from the opposite direction). It's in those moments when your perspective changes that the ability to adapt is crucial. (I deal extensively with this in chapters 6 and 7 for episodic television and film.) Actors must also be able to jump back into a particular scene many days later, recreating and retaining the integrity and spirit of the earlier performance. If you can't instinctively and naturally accomplish that, you won't get too many jobs. Finally, you must be able to generate and incorporate inspiration into your performance when it hits during filming. The greatest actors come alive most when they're performing; it's at those moments that they soar the highest. Many extraordinary things can happen when the camera is rolling.

Cultivating spontaneity is important for all acting work. Think about your daily life and imagine the moments when you are most spontaneous. How does it feel when you are? Try and discern ways that you fight spontaneity and think about what happens when you do. Make a list of how you think you are spontaneous and what you think you could do to be more spontaneous. Developing your improvisational skills will help you become more spontaneous.

Why do I need improvisational skills?

Improvisation is the ability to react extemporaneously to whatever comes your way. If you've ever talked your way out of a speeding ticket or handled a situation completely by your wits, you have the capability to become an expert improviser. Improvisational skills can help manifest your spontaneous nature. In a way, improvisation gives form to spontaneity. Think of it this way — if spontaneity is the stimulus, then improvisation is the response. After all, what good is spontaneity if you can't effectively put it to use? It's like having the spontaneous urge to articulate something but not finding the voice to say it. Having the ability to improvise gives you that voice.

I've heard some actors say that since they speak another person's words, they shouldn't have to be adept at improvisation. (SAG makes it illegal to ask actors to improvise during an audition for a commercial.) I admit that there is some validity to that point. My response, however, is that if actors are only to act others' words, that makes them merely interpreters and not artists. I believe that actors are artists not because they make up dialogue, but because they create action, which is revealed as character. This is where improvisation comes in. Sure, actors are paid to say someone else's lines; but sometimes under specific circumstances, actors have the ability to improve on specific moments within a script. Often, improvisational moments happen when there is no dialogue written, and the actors create something that is perfectly suited for a particular situation. Therefore, the art of actors not only reveals itself in the words they say, but in their choice of action, the way they say lines, and the behavior of their character.

However, when it comes to changing words and lines, improvisational moments certainly occur more frequently in a movie or in an episodic television drama than they do in a play. Unquestionably, creating new dialogue happens more often in soap operas since many of the principal characters actually change and supplement the writers' lines. Don't get me wrong, I don't advocate your going around randomly changing lines, but in the case of soap operas, the writers expect the actors playing those long-running characters to know what might be more appropriate to say at any given moment. After all, the writers figure that the actors know the characters' better than they do. I've been in many situations in episodic television and motion pictures where, because of the way the scene was written, it was begging for the actors to improv their way through it — and the fact that the actors did made it a better scene.

The bottom line is that even if you never change or add a line throughout your career (which is highly unlikely), having the talent for improvisation will help you immeasurably. Improvisation requires you to think constantly and to put those thoughts into motion. I also believe that being a gifted improviser will assist you in knowing how to say the lines in the script. What's more, being adept at improvisation will assist you when directors keep the camera rolling after a scene has supposedly ended to see what might happen. (This happens a lot.) If you're left standing there with nothing to say, you're not going to be very interesting. After all, it's the actor's job to create interesting action for the audience's enjoyment; having improvisational skills will help you enormously in doing this.

I deal extensively with improvisation throughout every chapter in this book. Many of the exercises ask for a certain degree of improvisational dexterity. If you don't feel like you're very good at improvising, don't despair. By incorporating the exercises into your study of acting you will become better at it.

SUMMARY

This book will help you learn how to audition and act in commercials, industrials, situation comedies, soap operas, episodic television, and film. To be successful in these genres (as well as on location) you must give each the focus it deserves. Each genre represents a distinct style. An actor must possess the knowledge of how best to approach each of these styles. While this book provides a foundation, learning how to act on camera requires a solid background in acting for the stage.

The biggest difference between acting onstage and in front of a camera is the scale of an actor's performance. Scale includes *dimension* — close versus far, large versus small, and so on — and *size* — vocal, physical, and emotional projection. Generally, an on-camera actor must reduce the scale of her performance. An actor is miked and, with the exception of overprojection, never needs to worry about volume. Physical considerations include knowing what kind of shot the camera is getting and the framing of that shot. Because of the camera's intimacy, the emotional scale is important. You don't ever want to project emotion on camera, but at the same time you can never get away with falseness.

Two unions have jurisdiction over professional actors in film and television. The Screen Actors Guild (SAG) governs all work done on film, and the American Federation of Television and Radio Artists (AFTRA) covers all work shot on videotape.

It's important to remember the business aspect of being a film and TV actor. Getting an agent is like looking for a business partner. You have to be skillful at marketing yourself. To get a job you must have an agent and to get an agent you must be in the union. Despite this seemingly no-win situation, if you keep studying and working, with persistence you'll eventually get all these things.

Five basic techniques are essential for acting on camera. They are crucial elements discussed throughout this book, and appear in many guises. They are:

1. *Naturalness.* In many ways this is accepting honestly who you are and wanting to share that with others.

2. *Listening.* This is an essential quality that creates vulnerability. Think of the Five-step Reaction: Hear, Listen, Form an opinion, Want to Speak, and Speak.

3. *Concentration.* Because of all the activity and distractions, this is a vital skill.

4. *Spontaneity.* An actor must be able to adapt to script changes, different shots, and continuity issues. You can only accomplish this if you're spontaneous.

5. *The ability to improvise.* Improvisation gives spontaneity form. The better you are at improvising, the better camera actor you will be.

CHAPTER 2
COMMERCIALS

Commercials are as intrinsic to commercial television as apples are to apple pie. Programs appearing on free television have always needed sponsors to pay the bills, and corporations, wanting exposure for their products, have always been happy to provide that valuable service. Because of this symbiotic relationship, advertisers have been making commercials for corporate sponsors since the beginning of television entertainment.

Though all commercials today are filmed in advance, they began as live interruptions of live television programs. Back then, programs were even named after sponsors. The popular weekly drama "Philco-Goodyear Playhouse" was sponsored by the battery and tire manufacturer of the same name. Certain sponsors became synonymous with certain television programs even as spokespersons became associated with specific products. Ronald Reagan was famous for being the spokesman for Borax, the sponsor of the TV serial "Death Valley Days." Commercial sponsors first represented themselves with spokespeople who pitched their products. Sponsors wanted the audience to believe that these spokespeople were proxies for the corporation. Although these spokespeople were usually celebrities who, though they used their own names, were acting, the sponsors didn't want the audience to think that these people were merely actors hired to sell the products.

One of the first television commercials that portrayed actors as someone other than spokespeople was for Texaco, and it became an instant success. In it a chorus of actors dressed as gas station attendants sang, "We are the men of Texaco!" They were, of course, selling Texaco's service station products. However, they weren't doing it as spokespeople; they represented real Texaco service station employees. This commercial was not only selling the viewers something, it was entertaining. Since then actors have represented the "real" people that populate most TV commercials. Even though television commercials have come a long way in the last fifty years, their main objective is still to sell products and entertain.

WHY COMMERCIALS?

To an actor, the most important aspect of commercials is the amount of money he can make acting in them. In 2001, out of a total of $1.6 billion earned by SAG actors that year, $563 million was made from commercial contracts. Aside from television contracts, SAG members earned more money from commercials than any other type of contract! In 2001, television contracts represented $614.7 million, theatrical motion pictures came in at $449.5 million, and industrials/interactive contracts were $14 million.

Because of the potential income, commercials can subsidize an acting career. I don't know too many actors who would choose to do temp work, wait tables, or a myriad of other "survival" jobs if they could be free to pursue acting work without having to wonder where the next paycheck was coming from. Depending on the type of commercial, working one or two days can make you enough money to keep you from having to do any other work the rest of the year — or longer, if you're lucky.

So how does the $563 million break down for SAG actors? A commercial actor is paid a session fee for the actual shoot. According to the newest SAG commercial contract, the minimum payment for an on-camera principal is $500 for the day. The actor's agent negotiates the actor's fee, which is always negotiated at a higher price than minimum. (Union rules stipulate that actors cannot make below the minimum, therefore agents have to negotiate at least 10 percent higher than the minimum to make their 10 percent commission.) But the real money in commercials comes from the residuals.

Residuals are the payments actors receive for appearing in commercials running on television. It's similar to the royalties authors receive every time someone buys their book or musicians receive when someone buys their CD. Most of the money earned in commercials comes in the form of residuals. Depending on the type of contract, actors can receive a residual payment every time the commercial airs. In 2001, SAG actors made $302.6 million in residuals; in other words, 54 percent of all the money made in commercials was earned solely because a commercial filmed at an earlier time was running somewhere on television.

The residual payment can be anywhere from $6.63 to $500 *per use*. Depending on when and where a commercial is shown, every time it airs the actor gets a residual payment. If the commercial is showing during prime time and airing across the country, the actor can make approximately $90 per showing. Think about the commercials you see repeatedly during your favorite shows. You do the math regarding how much the actor is being paid. Of course, the amount of money an actor makes also varies depending where the commercial is shown, what time the commercial is shown, and if it's on network television, local television, or cable television. I have known actors who worked two days shooting a national commercial and because of residuals ended up making $40,000 in a year for that one commercial.

But maybe it's time for a reality check: not all commercials that are shot get on the air, not all commercials end up getting shot, the national commercial you booked can be canceled, it can take up to one hundred commercial auditions to actually book a commercial, and so on. What's important is that you know how to audition for commercials and how to act in them once you get the job.

WHY DO RESIDUALS SOUND TOO GOOD TO BE TRUE? (AND WHY THEY'RE NOT)

Although residuals sound like the icing on the cake for actors who have already put in a day's work, they generally represent a kind of payback for the effort and sacrifice it takes to have an acting career and spend so much time being unemployed. Literally, however, residuals are the compensation actors receive for giving *exclusive* use of their looks to the sponsor of the commercial.

Actors receive residuals because the advertising industry made a rule that states that an actor appearing in a commercial *cannot* do a commercial for another sponsor that sells the same type of product.

From the sponsor's point of view, it makes sense. If Coca-Cola is going to pay an actor to appear in one of its commercials, it wants the audience to associate that actor with Coca-Cola. Coke doesn't want that actor to appear simultaneously in a Pepsi commercial. This is called exclusivity, and it applies to *all* competitive products. But though the actor appearing in a Coca-Cola commercial cannot appear in any other soft drink commercial, he *can* simultaneously appear in a Gap commercial, since Gap doesn't sell soft drinks.

There are also cases where a corporation wants an actor exclusively to represent its product and will stipulate in the actor's contract that he cannot appear in any other commercial of any kind. This is called a buyout contract. It is rare, but this kind of contract compensates the actor so handsomely that he wouldn't want to appear in any other commercial. Frequently, a buyout contract pays the actor millions of dollars for the actor's exclusive image. A good example of this was the successful IBM campaign many years ago in which an actress impersonating Charlie Chaplin appeared in all of IBM's advertising. Her contract was a buyout. As a result, she was exclusively associated with IBM and could only do commercials for it. But my guess is that she probably made millions of dollars, so she didn't really care. Another more recent example was the Pepsi campaign in which Hallie Eisenberg represented Pepsi in all its advertising. This was certainly a buyout and not only made her a lot of money but also fueled her acting career.

Because of the enormous expansion of advertising options in cable television and the Internet, issues of fairness regarding residuals and exclusivity have changed over the last couple of decades. In fact, these issues came to such a head that by 2000 there was a huge SAG commercial strike concerning residuals and exclusivity that lasted months.

In the past, most people watched only network television — the big three (ABC, CBS, and NBC) and their local stations. For actors, the big advertising money was always made on network television. When still in its infancy, cable was confined to very small markets; therefore, it wasn't able to reap the highly profitable advertising dollars reserved for the networks. Before the proliferation of cable television and the Internet, advertisers did not pay appropriate residuals (or any residuals at all) to actors appearing in ads that ran on local stations or on cable. Certain contracts for local markets and cable channels existed (and still do) that let sponsors pay actors a one-time fee for appearing in commercials. In the early days of the Internet, residuals weren't paid at all. But all of a sudden because of the explosion of interest in cable and the Internet (and therefore the increase of advertising revenue from those media), actors weren't getting their fair share of the money this advertising represented. In these situations, the exclusivity rule worked against the actor.

For example, let's say that an actor makes a commercial for a favorite fast-food restaurant that is only going to appear on cable. Because of this, the actor makes little or nothing on residuals. Then the commercial becomes popular, and everyone starts associating the actor with that commercial. This happens all the time; an actor becomes semifamous for appearing in a popular commercial. Now on every audition the actor goes to, the advertisers recognize this actor from the popular fast-food commercial. Well, the advertisers don't want the general public seeing this actor, who is associated with another product, in their commercial, even if the other product isn't competitive. In this case, the actor cannot get another job and at the same time is not making the kind of money he deserves from the now-popular commercial running on cable.

Commercial actors depend on residual payments for their living. Remember, between one-half and two-thirds of the money made in commercials is made in residuals!

Now that you've got a basic idea of the history of commercials and some of the complexities of the business, let's get down to business: understanding commercial auditions, getting an audition, and, more important, doing the job. Knowledge is power, and the more informed you are about how the process works, the better prepared you'll be. If "acting is doing," let's prepare to do it!

WHAT DO I NEED TO GET AN AUDITION?

The first thing an actor needs is a commercial agent. The agent should be franchised with SAG, which means that the agent has signed a contract with SAG promising to abide by all SAG rules. Don't forget that since SAG is an actor's union, its first priority is to protect the actor. A list of franchised agents can be acquired from SAG. SAG's main switchboard in Los Angeles is (323) 954-1600; in New York it's (212) 944-1030. The SAG Web address is www.sag.org. SAG franchised agents will occasionally work with actors who are non-SAG.

You'll also need a headshot, a professionally done photograph of you (make sure it looks like you), and a résumé (although your résumé is not as important when it comes to commercials). Books have been written about headshots, and I could spend a long time discussing them, but here are two key points: 1. A good headshot will help you get an agent. 2. A good headshot will get you commercial auditions. *So invest in great pictures!*

Prices for photographers to shoot your headshots can vary anywhere from $50 to $1500. You should be able to get a fairly good one for $200 to $500. A lot of aspiring actors are understandably reluctant to spend that amount of money up front for a photograph — especially when there's no guarantee the photo will get them a job. Many actors decide to have a friend or relative shoot their headshots with a handy 35mm camera. If the friend or relative is a good photographer, this may work. But to agents and casting directors, the difference in quality is similar to buying a cup of coffee from Starbucks versus a vending machine. You want to be perceived as a professional. In the business world, the first thing a businessperson gives you is his business card. I like to say that an actor's business card is his headshot and résumé. If you want to have an acting career, then you must be prepared to deal with the *business* of acting. Actors are in business for themselves, and like any other business, it demands an upfront investment. Try opening any business without capital, and see how far you get. If you think about headshots that way, you'll probably be more willing to spend the money to get it done right.

Be reassured, though, that you are the one in control when shopping for headshots. You should go about it as you would any major purchase. Since you wouldn't go out and buy the first car you see; don't hire the first (or most expensive) photographer you meet. You should shop around for photographers just as you would for any sizeable purchase. Make appointments to meet photographers and look at their books or portfolios of their work. If you notice that they shoot people like you well, then they are probably going to shoot you well also. For instance, if you're a blond female and you notice while looking at a certain photographer's book that his pictures of blond females are really great, then you might think about hiring this person. One thing I recommend is that you feel *comfortable* with this person. Never lose sight of the importance (and investment) of the headshot; and considering that most people are self-conscious about having their picture taken, what's most important is that the photographer makes you feel comfortable.

A warning regarding agents and headshots.

Once you have an agent, the agent will more than likely ask you to invest in new pictures. Do it. However, be cautious if you meet an agent and she tells you she would like to represent you, but you'll need to get new pictures first, and she insists you go to a particular photographer. In this situation, the agent and the photographer are in business together and will split the money you spend on the pictures, when the agent may not actually be interested in representing you. A lot of agents will recommend photographers they know are good, but ultimately the decision is yours. In this business it's important to remember caveat emptor: Buyer beware.

WHAT HAS HAPPENED EVEN BEFORE I GET THE AUDITION?

Besides having an agent and a good headshot, it's important to understand the steps that have led up to your getting the commercial audition. Knowing the procedure can take some of the mystery out of it and ease some of the anxiety of waiting.

The corporation selling the product hires an advertising agency to make the commercial, and it's the ad agency who hires the director and the production team and, ultimately, the actor. First, however, the ad agency hires a casting director to select the actors who are going to audition. Once the agency has created the spot (commercials are called spots), then it tells the casting director what type of actors are needed for the commercial. The casting director then sends what's called a breakdown (a description of the types of characters needed for the commercial) to all the agents in town.

The agents then submit headshots of the actors they represent that they feel are right for the type of characters needed for the commercial. The casting director then goes through the pictures and selects who she wants to audition for the commercial. Imagine the enormity of this. There are hundreds of SAG-franchised commercial agents in Los Angeles alone. If every one of them submits two or three of his or her clients for each role in a particular commercial, the number of pictures the casting director receives is overwhelming. The casting director couldn't possibly audition every one of those submissions for the commercial. So when you do get an audition, you need to remember how much has gone into it and the hurdles that have already been cleared to get you into the audition.

I HAVE MY FIRST AUDITION! WHAT DO I DO NOW?

Once you have the audition, your agent will tell you where you are going, what time your audition is, and, most important, the type of character you're auditioning for. (I discuss types in Principle 2.)

Get as much information as you can from your agent when he gives you the call for the audition, but also be prepared to get a lot of that information yourself. For instance, plan on arriving fifteen to twenty minutes early for your audition. You'll need to do some paperwork and discover if there's copy (the written script for the commercial).

What do I wear to the audition?

Besides information on who, what, when, and where, the most important information you can get from your agent is what to *wear*. Make sure you understand how to dress according to the role by checking with him. Because he has access to the breakdown, your agent will have specific information that you'll need regarding the character. Usually your agent will tell you, "You're a young business-executive type, wear a suit" or "You're a young mom, dress accordingly." If you're unsure how a typical young mom dresses, ask your agent to be specific. There's a difference in the way a young mom dresses when she's changing diapers and when she's taking her child to the doctor. What the product is and what the sponsor wants to accomplish in the commercial should govern the way you dress. One of the biggest mistakes you can make is to show up at the audition and not be dressed appropriately.

I know commercial actors in Los Angeles who drive around with about four or five different changes of clothes in their cars just in case they get a call for an audition before they can get home. If you find yourself auditioning for the same type of character, such as a doctor, nurse, fireman, waitress, and so forth, you might think about investing in the uniform of that profession (doctor's coat, nurse's uniform, fireman's helmet, waitress's uniform). Appreciate that casting directors want you to look right for the part. After all, they've called you in to audition, and you are a reflection of them. If you look foolish, they look foolish — and they don't want to look foolish. So if you show up dressed inappropriately, they may tape you at the audition, but I guarantee that you'll be erased before the next actor comes in to audition. I've seen it happen. You'll also be lucky to be called in again for another audition at that office.

Is there anything I shouldn't wear?

You should avoid wearing certain things when you are auditioning in front of a camera, and almost all commercial auditions are taped. You should never wear white on video. White fuses onto the tape and leaves an imprint, commonly known as a "ghost." I'm sure you've seen ghosts on television while shooting home videos. A woman wearing white is standing talking to someone else, and when she leaves, her ghost lingers after her. White also tends to reflect light and wash out the actor's face. Black should not be worn because it absorbs light and makes the actor look pale. Thin pinstripes or small complex patterns are also not a good idea because they tend to move and have a life of their own. What you should wear are bright primary colors: deep reds, yellows, and blues. Greens and purples are also good. If you're in class working in front of a camera, I suggest you experiment with your wardrobe and try wearing different colors. Just for fun, and to satisfy your curiosity, prove to yourself the pitfalls of wearing whites, blacks, and pinstripes.

OK, so now you know where you're going and you know what time your audition is, what you're auditioning for, what kind of character you're auditioning for, and what to wear. The big day comes; you arrive early and . . .

WHAT DO I DO NOW?

One of the reasons you want to arrive early to the audition is that there will always be paperwork for you to do. You'll have to complete a fact sheet for the casting director that includes your name and phone number, agent's name and phone number, sex, age range, height, weight, and special skills. Never list special skills on this sheet or your résumé that you can't really do. For instance, if you speak a few words of Spanish, don't say that you are fluent in Spanish. You may be asked to demonstrate during the audition, and the directors don't have time for people who need to warm up ("Give me a few minutes while I practice") or who aren't proficient. You do not want to embarrass yourself at your audition.

Very often a Polaroid or digital photograph will be taken of you and stapled to the information sheet. Don't panic! Everybody looks horrendous in a Polaroid. The purpose of the Polaroid is to capture how you look at the moment, and it is more convenient than getting another one of your headshots. I imagine they started using Polaroid pictures because too many actors didn't look like their headshots.

You will also have to sign in on the SAG sign-in sheet. SAG uses these sign-in sheets to cross-check members, check demographics of members who are auditioning, and to make sure that the casting director is not holding actors too long. (You also sign out when you're done.) Casting directors are only allowed to keep actors at an audition for a certain period (usually one hour) before they have to start paying an overtime fee to the actor. (However, I caution you against pursuing this clause with SAG. Unless the casting office has been appallingly neglectful about your time, be aware that if you do make a claim against it, you will probably never be called in for another audition at that office.)

When you arrive, find out if there's copy and a storyboard. If there is, study them. However, don't feel you need to memorize the copy — unless, of course, it consists of one word or a simple line of dialogue. If there's a lot of copy, memorize the first line and the last line and be able to deliver those to the camera during your audition.

Be careful about when you sign in; once you sign in, the casting directors are free to call you in to audition. Only sign in if you're ready to go or you know they are running behind and you can't stay long. For example, let's say your audition is at 2:30, and you arrive at 2:15. You notice on the sign-up sheet that they are running about thirty minutes late. If you have another audition to get to or have to get back to work, you might want to sign in before you start filling out the paperwork. But if they aren't running late and you sign in immediately at 2:15 and then spend the next fifteen minutes doing the paperwork, you won't have a chance to look at the copy and prepare before they call you in to audition at 2:30.

WAIT A MINUTE . . . WHAT'S A STORYBOARD?

A storyboard is a frame-by-frame drawing of what the commercial is going to look like (see figure 1). It's the ad agency's concept of the commercial. You don't have to duplicate it exactly, but you should respect the vision of the person who created the commercial. The advertising people who create ad campaigns make a lot of money, and besides needing to justify their income, their ideal is to see that the final commercial is similar to the initial conception. It's been said that if you can look like the character in the storyboard, you have an advantage over the competition. However, I've also learned that the ad people and the director want actors to tell them what the commercial is about. There's validity in both sentiments. The point is you want to follow the storyboard *and* be original.

ARE THERE ANY LAST-MINUTE THINGS I NEED TO KNOW BEFORE I FINALLY GO IN?

In the moments before your audition, you must keep focused on what you want to accomplish. This requires preparation. One of the greatest threats to an actor before an audition is *distraction*. Be careful. Some people in this business make it a point to try and make you do a bad audition. I call them ringers.

This is how they work: You're at an audition. You've filled out the paperwork, looked over the storyboard, signed in, and started preparing for your audition. All of a sudden someone is sitting next to you and starts talking to you. He might say something like, "I saw you in that Volkswagen commercial. What a great job!" Of course, you're flattered. You think, "What a nice person" and feel that you've just made a friend. Or he might ask you a question or tell you about another audition that you would be right for. Odds are, this person is your competition, and he wants to distract you and prevent you from preparing for your audition. I've seen it happen. It's happened to me.

Fig. 1. The storyboard.

1. Shot of sleepy man in bathroom.

Announcer: Monday mornings got you down?

2. Sleepy man slowly puts toothbrush to mouth.

Announcer: Well, put a little *Fresh* on your brush . . .

3. Shot of sleepy man now becoming energized while brushing.

Announcer: . . . and we'll get you right back up.

4. Shot of product.

Announcer: *Fresh.* The freshest way to start your day!

You're engaged in a wonderful conversation and suddenly your name is called to go in to audition, and you realize, "Whoops — I forgot to prepare." Ringers are usually experienced commercial actors who have been doing this a long time and don't need as much preparation as you. They typically prey on beginners.

Once you start going to a lot of auditions, you'll see a lot of the same people. They are probably your type and right for the same commercials that you are. Just avoid turning auditions into a social hour. The people who socialize usually don't get the job.

WHAT HAPPENS WHEN I GO INTO THE AUDITION?

Once you're called into the audition, you'll be put on videotape. A casting assistant usually does the taping. You'll be asked to "slate," stating your name and sometimes your agent and other information. (This is Principle 3, which I discuss at length later in this chapter.) Listen and follow any direction the casting person might give you. There is nothing worse than an actor who is programmed to show what he has prepared for the audition come hell or high water and is unwilling to take another's direction (see Principle 9).

However, the casting person will sometimes let you do a couple of takes — the first one being what you've prepared and another take after she's given you some feedback. Don't expect this, though. In a lot of cases, the directors are running behind and want to get people in and out. My advice in all these situations is to make a good impression with the casting person in the audition, even if you know she's an assistant. In this business, today's assistant is tomorrow's casting director.

Make sure when you're in the audition that you are as prepared as possible. As a professional actor, you are expected to do your job — and much of an actor's job is about getting the next one. It's a career in which you spend most of your time in search of more work — so make auditioning an integral part of your job. Take your job seriously, and then you'll be hired to do the fun stuff! As you prepare for your audition, it may help you to remember the commercial principles that appear later in this chapter. They are meant to help you audition for commercials and assist you in knowing what to do once you get the job.

WHEW, I'M DONE . . . WHAT HAPPENS NOW?

Let's say you've had the audition and followed the principles. The best thing you can do is to get on with your life and try to forget the audition and go to the next one. Maybe you'll get a callback. A callback is another audition. Casting is a process of elimination and callbacks are part of that process. Getting one means you've made it through round one and are that much closer to getting the job. There can be numerous callbacks, and SAG stipulates that actors are paid a nominal fee after the first two. But unless the directors really can't decide, they generally conclude the casting after one or two callbacks.

WHAT SHOULD I KNOW ABOUT CALLBACKS?

Callbacks are vital. It is at the callback that you'll usually meet the director for the first time. Sometimes the advertising people will also be there. You should keep two significant things in mind about your callback.

First, make sure you wear the same clothes that you wore at the first audition. Directors tend to make visual associations when actors audition. Usually they make a note that they liked the "girl in the red sweater" and will call her back. There are famous stories about directors wanting to know why the "actor that wore the green shirt" didn't come to the callback — only to be informed that, indeed, the actor had shown up.

Second, make sure you repeat the performance you did at your first audition as closely as possible. Don't forget what got you the callback in the first place. A lot of actors go home kicking themselves after an audition thinking they should have done something different with their audition. The actor then comes to the callback primed to do her new and improved version. Afterward, the actor beams at the director as if to say, "Now wasn't that better?" — and the director sits there with his mouth open, wondering what happened. You should always strive to give the best audition you can and walk out confident that you did the best job you could.

Am I given direction at the callback?

Unless you've really done the perfect audition for the part, you will be given direction at the callback. This is a good thing. Some actors are afraid of direction at auditions thinking that they've done something wrong. This couldn't be further from the truth. Being given direction is a sign that the director likes you and may be interested. *Make sure you follow the direction.* Even if you think the direction is stupid. Many times directors give irrelevant direction just to see what the actor does with it. Their purpose is to see if the actor can follow it. Directors want to work with actors who know how to take direction and who can improve on it. Often the director will ask the actor to improvise; be ready to do so. Improvisational skills are important for commercials and are discussed in Principles 7 and 9.

I GOT THE JOB! WHAT HAPPENS NOW?

Now let's discuss what happens *after* you get the job. Besides congratulating you, your agent will tell you how much she's negotiated for your session fee and what type of contract it is. (She will have probably done this when she sent you out for the commercial, or at least by the callback.) She'll tell you when you're scheduled to shoot the commercial, and she'll remind you that you are now exclusive to this sponsor and cannot audition for any competing products. (Before she sent you out on the audition, she will have cleared you to make sure that you are free to do a commercial for this product.) You'll get a call from the production company shooting the commercial to be scheduled for a costume fitting. A day or two before you shoot, you'll get a call time, which is the time you're to report to the set.

WHAT DO I DO ON THE DAY OF THE SHOOT?

Make sure you're on time! Commercials cost hundreds of thousands of dollars to shoot, and you don't want to start off on the wrong foot by showing up late. I guarantee that you won't work in this business if you're chronically late for auditions and call times. Actually, all it takes is *once* for it to be considered chronic. If you were paying thousands of dollars a minute to make a commercial, you wouldn't appreciate actors being late for work, especially given the attitude in the industry that actors are easily replaced. And because of the number of talented actors out of work at any one moment, it is true: They are easily replaced.

You'll report to makeup and costume on the day of your shoot, and you will usually get two call times: one for makeup and costume and another to be on the set. Make sure you are as prepared for the shoot as you were for the audition. If you have lines, memorize them. Don't wait for the day of the shoot to do that. Also, though it will be fun to be on the set, be wary about making the entire day one big social hour. When you have the job, you don't need to worry about ringers, but until you get a lot of experience, you don't want to waste energy on partying. Make sure you know when it's time to work.

Most important during the shoot, of course, is to follow directions and try to improve on them. You may have a director who will guide you and is open to your ideas, but the bottom line is to never forget who is paying you. Believe me, word spreads in this business, and when you are exemplary on the set, people find out. Behave on the set in such a way that they'll want to hire you again.

One of the greatest challenges about working in front of a camera is the repetition. When shooting a commercial, be prepared to repeat each take many times. This will be discussed in more depth in later chapters on episodic television and film acting, but the skill involved in commercial acting is that each take has to be fresh, exciting, and spontaneous. This takes a lot of energy, so you need to conserve your energy on the set. Multiple takes for a commercial are draining.

THE PRINCIPLES OF COMMERCIALS

Now that you know the basics about what to expect at a commercial audition and on the set, let's examine the specifics. I've devised eleven principles to keep in mind when you are both auditioning for and performing in commercials. Think of them as guideposts to follow. Some are theoretical and others are more practical; each should be employed according to your need. Following each principle is a set of exercises. Feel free to incorporate the principles and exercises into a curriculum for study or simply for your individual edification.

1. Commercials require energy because they are the most theatrical of all the film and television genres.

By *theatrical* I mean "showy" or "presentational." Some forms of musical theater are a good example of what I mean by theatrical. They directly acknowledge and cater to the audience and make no apologies in doing so. This kind of theatricality also implies an absence of subtlety. This is not a qualitative judgment but simply a recognition that it exists.

For anyone studying acting for the camera, this principle is important because it makes sense to start with commercials. If an actor is trained for the stage and has little experience in front of the camera, one of his biggest challenges is to scale down his work. Beginning with commercials enables the inexperienced camera actor to ease his way into the precision needed to work in front of a camera.

So it's OK to be somewhat theatrical in commercials. Watch them. Notice how jarring it can be when the network switches to a commercial during an episodic drama. The mood created in an intense scene is shattered by an over-the-top commercial. You might think advertisers are insensitive, but they simply want your attention. Lately, more advertisers are trying to maintain the mood of the program that is on. For instance, sometimes you'll see funny commercials during situation comedies and, of course, sports commercials during sporting events. However, demographics (the sex, age, race, geographic location, and socioeconomic standing of the audience) are the most important considerations to sponsors of commercials. They gear the commercial to the audience they've been told is watching that particular program. For example, drug commercials appear frequently on the evening news because older people (the ones most likely to take the drugs) are a large segment of the audience. Commercials geared toward young stay-at-home moms are more likely to be shown during daytime television.

It has been said that television programs merely fill in the time between commercials, and since commercials pay for free television, in many ways the sponsors call the shots. But advertisers are aware that commercial breaks are also breaks for the audience. These are the moments when everyone leaves to go to the kitchen or the bathroom. So they try to get your attention and keep it. One way they do this is to record the sound louder for commercials. How many times have you turned down the volume on your TV set when the commercial comes on? Advertisers are clever about getting your attention. They make advertisements entertaining and highly theatrical. By incorporating suspense, humor, and good storytelling techniques, advertisers get our attention and motivate us to watch the commercial to see how it's going to end. The more aware the commercial actor is about this need for entertainment and theatricality, the better off she will be.

Not only does theatricality require energy, but characters in commercials are also sunny, positive, and incredibly *active*. It takes energy to be consistently upbeat and to do things with gusto. Think about the commercials you've seen for food products. When the characters in a food commercial eat, they do it vigorously. When the characters are changing a tire, they do it energetically. A commercial has a lot of information that has to be given in a short amount of time. Think about moments in your life when you've had to communicate information quickly. Likely it took lots of energy.

Commercial characters are always relentlessly pursuing a goal. Most of the time the goal is simple: to sell the sponsor's product. But to convince someone to do something (like buy something) takes a lot of energy. The many how-to-sell books on the market cover common themes such as the power of persuasion, never take no for an answer, play the numbers in a numbers game, and so on. It takes Herculean energy to do all those things. It's simple — consumers don't buy from people who give up. It's as if we as consumers want to test the seller's belief in his product. Almost instinctively we say no, just to see if the salesperson has enough conviction in what he is selling to keep after us. Although that is often not enough to get us to buy something, we will always appreciate his tenacity.

Most important, energy is contagious. We like energetic people and we enjoy watching people who are energetic. We tend to buy from people who are excited about their product rather than people who are bored by their product. If salespeople are having fun and are excited about what they are doing, we are inclined to want to share in that fun. The subliminal message that advertisers are sending in commercials is twofold: Someone really enthusiastic about a product must have a reason to be enthusiastic about it, and if you buy this, you'll have as much fun as these people and your life will be as fulfilling as theirs.

- Watch commercials and notice their theatricality. How much more theatrical are they than the program you're watching? How much are they trying to emulate the style of the program that's on?

- Watch commercials and notice how advertisers try to get your attention and keep it.

- Try to persuade someone to do something that he or she doesn't want to do. Try "selling" something to two people using two different methods — one with energy and one without. See which method works better.

- Find an exceptional salesperson at your favorite store and surreptitiously watch the tactics she employs to get customers to buy something. See if you can gauge the energy that it takes for her to make a sale.

2. Be yourself in commercials.

Commercial advertisers are looking for the uniqueness that is *you!* One of the biggest mistakes actors make when auditioning for commercials is thinking they are playing a character different from themselves. Assume that once you've got the job, you've been cast for who you are. The people that hired you trust that you will re-create who you were when you auditioned. If you come in and play a character different from what the directors have already seen and liked, they'll probably get anxious and either direct you to re-create what you initially did or get someone else. This is why there are a lot of callbacks. They want to see if you can successfully repeat the same brilliant audition many times under pressure. Considering it costs hundreds of thousands of dollars to make a commercial, you can be sure they want to protect their investment by casting the right person.

But let's assume that for now we're talking about getting the job. One of the most important principles in acting for the camera is to learn the skill of being comfortable with who you are and to honestly assess your own performance. The people who get work in commercials tend to have an excellent sense of self and of how that self is perceived by others. They know how they come across on camera and capitalize on that. Ultimately, the most important thing you can do in a class on camera acting is to tape your work and learn to watch the playback objectively.

Learn not to stray too far from who you are. One of the most important things to remember for commercial auditions is that you have been called in for how you look based on your headshot. If you have an audition for a commercial, it's because you look a certain way in your picture (or the casting director already knows you and thinks you're right for the commercial). Live up to the smiley person in that picture. Sure, it may be a bad day for you: You might be depressed and not feel up to the audition. But if you're a professional actor, you will put that aside and represent the person in the picture that they've called in for the audition. If you think, "I'm just not right for this commercial," you're invalidating the judgment of the casting director who gave you the audition and invalidating the person you were on the day of your headshot. In other words, if your headshot is a picture of you, then you're expected to bring that person into the audition. Someone perceived a quality in you that fits a particular commercial, so learn to trust him! That's his business and he's good at it; trust him to do his job as he is expecting and trusting you to do yours.

Learning your type is another important aspect of this principle. *Type* is basically a marketing term indicating the type of character category you fall into. For instance, do you resemble an executive type, a young-mother type, or a blue-collar type? Discovering your type is probably the most important thing you can do to become a successful commercial actor.

So let's talk about your type. One of the biggest questions I'm asked by students is, "What type am I?" Two things best define your type: your sex and your age. A lot of other things go along with that, like race, complexion, and the physical traits of hair color, eye color, hair length, height, weight, and what you wear. Some of those things you can do something about, some you can't. Watch commercials and observe what products people like you are selling. That is an example of demographics. Advertisers tend to categorize their audience. If it's a diaper commercial, they're not trying to sell diapers to the infants who wear them; they're selling to the young mothers that are *buying* diapers. Procter & Gamble, one of the leading diaper makers in the country, studies its prospective customers. The manufacturer might decide that 90 percent of its target consumers for diapers are women between the ages of twenty-two and thirty-five, which are the peak years of women bearing children. So those are the types Procter & Gamble is looking to cast in its diaper commercials.

To determine different possible types, let's categorize starting with age and sex. See if you can find one or two possible types that fit you under each age category.

FEMALE

Under 25
young romantic
student
girl next door
sports/outdoorsy
punk /exotic
young spokeswoman

20 to 40
young mom
glamour
woman next door
country/outdoorsy
young executive
spokeswoman

40 to 60
executive/professional
older glamour
woman next door
character
spokeswoman

60 and older
older executive/professional
grandmother
retired
older character
older spokeswoman

MALE

Under 25
student
jock
outdoor
young romantic
party/punk
young spokesman

25 to 40
young executive/professional
young father
rugged outdoorsy
young blue collar
young character
spokesman

35 to 60
executive/professional
guy next door
older blue collar
character
spokesman

60 and older
older executive/professional
grandfather
retired
older character
older spokesman

These are just a representation of types that exist. There are certainly more, and obviously, it is possible to be more than one type. For example, a twenty-five-year-old female could certainly be a young mom and a spokesperson, or a country/outdoor type as well as a woman next door. A sixty-two-year-old man could certainly be both retired and a grandfather type (and often is), or an older executive as well as an older spokesperson type. My advice is that you try not to be too many types. Successfully defining yourself means avoiding being all things to all advertisers or all casting directors. This is a hard concept for actors to learn because they are taught to believe they can play a variety of roles and are convinced that they could be *any* type if given the chance. Try to limit yourself to those types you *fit best*. Become so analogous with your particular type(s) that casting directors automatically think of you when they need that type.

Of course, what you look like is going to help you determine which of these types you fit. If you're a twenty-three-year-old male who is one hundred pounds overweight, you are probably not going to be considered a jock or young romantic type, even if you are a champion surfer and have dozens of girlfriends. You've heard the phrase "image is everything." Well, advertisers probably invented that phrase. You not only need to act the part but, more important, *look* the part! Occasionally advertisers will "go against type," meaning that they consciously go in a direction contrary to the norm. However, they usually only go against type for comic effect. I can almost guarantee that if you see an overweight twenty-three-year-old as a young romantic type, it's for comic effect.

Again, my advice is to *watch commercials!* Look for people in commercials who share certain physical traits with you. Assuming that you are an honest judge of what you look like, ask yourself, "What kinds of commercials do I see people like me in?" For example, fast-food restaurants tend to cast a lot of young people, especially as counter people. That's because most of the people who take your order are young and this is their first job. As it happens, a lot of fast-food customers are young, too. So if you are eighteen, you could expect to be used in a lot of fast-food commercials. If you have bad teeth, you are probably not going to be used in toothpaste or gum commercials. If you look like a model, expect to be cast in makeup commercials. If you really can't define your type after watching commercials, ask people whose opinions you respect. Avoid asking your immediate family, lovers, and closest friends because their opinions can be as subjective as yours. Ask your commercial agent what type you are; agents are the ones who are "typing" you in the first place. Look objectively at yourself and balance who you are and what you look like. That is going to be unique to everyone, and when you determine those attributes, then you will be a type that is singularly you.

At one time it was widely believed that most of the advertisers on Madison Avenue felt that if they could sell to the people in the Midwest, they could sell to anyone, anywhere. For some reason, they believed that most people who live in the Midwest have blond hair and blue eyes. So in most commercials everyone had blond hair and blue eyes. For instance, I have dark hair, and because of this, I was always told that I was an urban type; everyone knows that most people who live in cities have dark hair and dark eyes! Fortunately, you now see much more diversity in commercials and a much better representation of the human race. Some even say that more change is needed and that types should be relied on less in the first place. A goal we should strive for is that all actors learn to be so successful marketing themselves that we replace the artificial types that I've listed with individual types: i.e., the Katy Garcia type, the Matthew Clinton type, the [put *your* name here] type.

EXERCISES

- Make an honest effort to find out how people see you. Ask friends, teachers, coworkers, and so on. Ask them to pick from the list that I provided. If you ask people who don't know you intimately (as you should), remember that their response will be based mostly on appearance. In other words, their opinion will be based on how you present yourself when you're around them, what clothes you wear, how you wear your hair, and so on. This is a good indication of your type. If you're not satisfied with that type, you need to change the way you present yourself; this can include changing your weight, hairstyle, wardrobe, and any number of things.

- Watch commercials and determine which ones are trying to sell you something. Notice the type of actor they are using. Is this a type you could be?

- Get in front of a camera as much as possible. If you're in a camera-acting class, get as much time as you can in front of the camera. Buy yourself a camcorder and tape yourself practicing commercial copy, or better yet, reading out loud. But under no circumstances, "act up" in front of the camera as you might be inclined to do in a home movie. Get used to seeing yourself on camera without mugging or overacting. Your objective is to honestly critique yourself while you watch yourself on camera.

3. The slate in auditions is as important as the audition.

For the audition, this is probably the most important principle. The slate in a commercial audition is, very simply, stating your name into the camera before the audition begins. Often, they will want you to slate your agency if you have one. Sometimes, they'll want you to slate your name, agency, and height, as well. If you are a minor or look very young, they may also ask you to slate your age. They may ask you to slate and then turn profile left and profile right. The slate part of the audition can incorporate any part of these. I've even seen casting directors have a mini-interview during the slate. The slate is important because it's the only part of the audition that distinguishes you from everybody else auditioning. The slate is your only chance to be you and make a first impression, and in auditions, as in life, you have only one chance at making a first impression.

In a hypothetical audition situation, you are called into a studio where there is a casting assistant, a VHS camera, and a VCR for playback. (They are starting to use digital equipment, but you get the idea.) The casting assistant will ask you to stand on a mark on the floor about six feet from the camera. (If there's no mark, stand approximately six feet from the camera.) The assistant will ask you to slate and then cue you to start the audition. The camera shot for a typical slate is head and shoulder (see figure 2). Sometimes they'll film your slate, and then turn off the camera and give you a chance to rehearse. So the audition consists of two parts: the slate and the audition. This is true for everyone who auditions.

At the end of the day or the end of the casting session the tape is sent to the ad agency. If it's a national commercial, then it usually goes to New York. So if you're auditioning in Los Angeles or Chicago, the

Fig. 2. The slate.

tape is usually delivered overnight to the agency. In New York, the ad executives on that account sit around and watch the tape to decide who is going to be called back. Now if there are a hundred people who are auditioning for the same commercial and everyone's audition is conducted this way, you are probably starting to get the idea of why the slate is so important.

Because of the nature of the business, the auditors make up their minds in the first fifteen seconds. The slate can make or break you. Put yourself in their position. If your job were to sit there for days on end and watch tapes of dozens of people auditioning for the same commercial, you might be inclined to use the fast-forward button on the VCR. The ad agency executives watch your slate. If they don't like your slate, no matter how good the audition is, they are probably not going to watch it. If they don't like what they see on your slate, they're going to fast-forward through it. Your goal is to keep them from doing that.

Some dos and don'ts regarding slates:

DO be friendly. Remember that they are spending a lot of money to make the commercial. They want to work with friendly people.

DON'T be overly friendly or needy. They *know* you want to be cast. They don't want to be begged or made to feel like you're about to sell them time-shares in Florida.

DO be professional. It's a *business*, behave that way.

DON'T be sarcastic. It would not behoove you to try something cute like momentarily forget your name on the slate. (You laugh, but it's done.)

DO look straight into the lens. If the commercial calls for you not to look into the lens, *always* look into the lens on the slate. (Unless directed otherwise.)

DON'T try to have a conversation with the ad executives in the slate. Unless you're asked a question during the slate, keep the slate limited to what they've asked for. Although it might be tempting, don't try to endear yourself to ad executives whom you don't know. For instance, let's say you're auditioning for a Maxwell House coffee commercial, don't try, "Hi, my name is Shane Brennan and I drink Maxwell House every morning! I *love* it!" Or don't say something like, "Hi, my name is Meghan Amplas. How's the weather today in New York?"

DO smile. Remember that a smile is one of the best ways to disarm someone. It is also the easiest way to show someone you're friendly.

DON'T force a smile. If you can't smile naturally, you might be better off doing something other than acting in commercials.

DO play an objective during the slate. You'll need to practice this, but try things like "to charm them," "to make them feel good about themselves," "to wake them up" (without yelling). Try different objectives. But make sure you don't overact your objective. Remember you want them to watch what you do with the commercial.

DON'T behave or come across as if you wish you were someplace else, or that it's a hassle being there. Whatever you need to do to psyche yourself up about the audition, do it. Don't forget that the camera sees into your soul.

DO incorporate a lot of energy in the slate — as long as you don't overdo it and come across forced. Send a lot of good energy with your slate.

DO have confidence in yourself. If you can't have confidence in yourself during the slate, why should they think that you're going to be confident acting in the commercial or on the set?

DO act the part if necessary. This applies to specific character work. For instance, if you're auditioning for something that calls for a southern accent, or you've made a choice that a southern accent would be appropriate, and you do a brilliant southern accent, by all means use it in your slate. Let them think that you're the real thing.

There are many more dos and don'ts. Remember that a slate is your only chance to make a first impression: Your goal is to get them to watch your audition. Try to be unique with the slate, but make sure that you remain professional. Never forget that the advertising business is a *business*. They are looking to hire professionals.

EXERCISES

- Tape yourself auditioning for commercials. If necessary, transcribe copy from television. Make sure that before every audition, you slate.

- Tape everyone in class one at a time as they slate. After their name they should state the three best or unique qualities about themselves. This exercise allows your individuality to come forth. During the playback, try not to judge if one actor was good and another bad. Every actor has to connect with his or her own individual unique qualities. Rather than judging good or bad simply try to identify who stood out and try to determine why. What did that actor do to stand out from everyone else? Imagine you are at the ad agency looking at these tapes as auditions. Judge for yourself who you would choose to represent your product. Who do you like and why? What do you like about them? It's not about what you did that was good or bad, but what about you viscerally appeals to the viewers. You'll discover that the best way to impress is to simply be fully yourself. You may not get the commercial, but that has nothing to do with you and everything to do with them. It all has to do with what they are looking for. At any given audition that may not be you; but if you continue to be yourself at commercial auditions, at some point you will be what they are looking for.

4. Always be aware of selling the product.

This principle may seem like a no-brainer, but you'd be surprised at how often actors forget that they have to *sell* the corporate sponsor's product. Never forget who is paying the bills, or better yet, who is paying your salary! The corporate sponsor always has the last word on everything about the commercial.

As long as you remember who is paying the bills, you'll be all right. If you are hired to appear in a commercial, you are, in essence, an employee of the corporation that hired you. However, this principle works best when you are *auditioning* for the commercial. Always make sure you know who is sponsoring the commercial and what the commercial is about.

If you are auditioning for a McDonald's commercial, it's best to know what McDonald's does. McDonald's is one of the most recognizable corporate names in the world: a fast-food giant that serves up great burgers and fries. It may sound like I'm doing a commercial for McDonald's, but if you're auditioning for a McDonald's commercial, it's best to remind yourself of those things. You should do a little research on the sponsor and know what it does. Most of the time your agent will tell you who the sponsor is, and you'll recognize the sponsor. But let's say your agent sends you out on a commercial for a regional bank in the Midwest and you live in New York. You might want to do a little homework to find out about the company and familiarize yourself with their product.

It's also important to specifically *figure out what the sponsor's objective is* for the particular commercial that you are auditioning for. You must try to understand its objective in making the advertisement. Ask yourself, "Why is the sponsor making this specific spot? What is the sponsor trying to say, and to whom is it saying it?"

For example, years ago I was cast in a McDonald's commercial.

The company was introducing pizza and created an ad campaign to tell people about it. Actually, McDonald's was testing pizza in select markets to see if it would be successful (it wasn't) and did a test spot for those specific markets. At the time I was thrilled at the prospect of doing a McDonald's commercial. (You can make a lot of money doing a fast-food ad.) If the test for the pizza had been successful, I would've appeared in a national spot, touting the new McDonald's pizza.

Getting a McDonald's commercial surprised me, however, because I wasn't the company's characteristic type. But what helped me get it was I believed I knew why they were making the commercial, what they were trying to say in it, and who they were talking to. Because of my dark hair, I am considered an urban type and sometimes an Italian type. I'm not Italian and not necessarily urban, but remember — it's all about how you look. I figured an urban Italian type, who might be considered a pizza aficionado, could give credibility to McDonald's pizza. It's as simple as that. I played up the urban Italian aspect of myself at the audition. I added a slight New York Italian accent when I read the copy, and I gave them my idea of an urban Italian type. I got the job because I inferred the sponsor's objective for the ad and fit the type that helped the sponsor accomplish that. So even if you are extremely familiar with the sponsor and what it does, make sure you analyze the sponsor's reasons for making the commercial.

So let's say that you have an audition for McDonald's. The first thing you need to do if you have any lines, and if you ever have a chance to say "McDonald's," is to make sure you *highlight* the name of the sponsor. "Welcome to *McDonald's*. How can I help you?" Always give the name of the sponsor emphasis when you say it. It separates the name of the sponsor from the rest of the copy. After all, the sponsor is paying the bills. You'd like your name emphasized too if you were paying a bundle to have a commercial made. You also might want to add a slight pause before and after the sponsor's name: "Welcome to *(Pause.) McDonald's. (Pause.)* How can I help you?" The idea is to get the people watching the commercial to remember the name of the product. I urge you again to watch commercials; the name of the sponsor is always highlighted and slightly isolated when it is said. Notice, too, how many times the name of the sponsor is flashed in the commercial. Count how many times you see the word *McDonald's* the next time you see a McDonald's commercial.

Also look for key words in the copy like: *new, improved, limited offer, while it lasts, only, just, right now the price is, guaranteed,* and so on. If a sponsor is telling viewers something different about its well-known product, then it's important to stress that. Sure, we know what Coca-Cola is, but if the sponsor is having a special promotion, you need to stress that in your audition. Let's say your line is: "For a limited time, six-packs of Coke are only $1.99!" You might want to emphasize it like this: "For a *limited time,* six-packs of — *Coke* — are *only $1.99!*" If you stress these words, the end of the line is naturally going to be emphasized. That would be appropriate as the message is to tell people that six-packs are $1.99. Coca-Cola wants to create urgency by saying "for a limited time," and of course you always want to highlight the name of the sponsor.

When selling a product, it's important to actually use it. *In food and beverage commercials, the number one rule is to eat and drink!* I can almost guarantee that you will always see people eating and drinking in a food or beverage commercial. A notable exception is commercials for anything alcoholic. It's against the law for alcoholic beverages to be consumed in television commercials.

Always look at the product. When you look at it, you focus on it and so does the audience. *Always keep your eyes open* whenever you express joy eating or drinking in a commercial. This is contrary to how most of us react when we taste or smell something good. Normally, we close our eyes. But don't forget that on camera the eyes are the windows to the soul. The audience wants to see your eyes.

Coffee commercials are classic examples of this. A person comes downstairs in the morning in his bathrobe to pour his first cup of coffee. First he *looks* at it, then *smells* it, and finally *drinks* it. And what happens after he takes a drink? He reacts with a *pleasurable smile* and the inevitable exhaled *"ahhhh"* suggesting "that's good." They always do that. Try it yourself. The truth is we *never* have that reaction after drinking our first cup of coffee. How often do you take your first drink of coffee and sigh "ahhhh"? Think about all the commercials where you see someone drink and then react with "I needed that" or "Wow, that was refreshing," or "I can't believe it tasted that good!" Their objective is to make you thirsty! If they succeed, you will get thirsty and immediately go out and buy that product. Remember the steps: *Look at it, smell it* (usually just for coffee or tea), *drink it* (with your eyes open), and *react with a pleasurable smile and some kind of vocalization like "ahhhh" or "mmm."*

The same goes for food. Sponsors want to send the message that eating their product is enjoyable and fun — and the actor is the one that sells that message to the public. Actors in commercials always eat with enthusiasm. If there's no food at the audition, pretend. Make sure you take your time and luxuriate in it. Most actors make the mistake of rushing their eating. For some reason they think that they aren't very interesting while they eat. But don't forget that you are selling the product, and if it's a food commercial, the product is the food and the best way to sell food is to eat it. The process is basically the same: *Look at the food, smell it* (if appropriate), *bite it, chew it* (make sure your eyes are open), *swallow it, smile,* and *react with an "mmm"* or something equivalent. You may want to lick your fingers. A lot of times you'll see actors talking with their mouths full because they just can't contain their excitement about telling you how good what they've just eaten is. Do anything that will help you sell the food by making it appealing and the audience hungry. (As a side note, you might be interested to know that when shooting a food commercial that requires you to eat or drink, you will be given a "spit bucket." It would be impossible to take that big bite out of a hamburger over a series of takes and actually swallow it. You take a bite, and as soon as the director yells "cut," you spit it into the spit bucket.)

Again, the idea is to sell the product and one of the ways you do this is by using it. When was the last time you saw a commercial for a car and no one drove it? Or a commercial for a camera and no one took a picture with it? Or for lipstick when no one wore it? The more you can show, express, educate, or just delight in the product, the better off you will be.

EXERCISES

- Watch commercials and write down each one's objective. Try to figure out why they made that particular commercial, what they are trying to say with it, and to whom are they trying to sell their product or services.

- Write your own commercial copy for a food product. Put it on tape and show it to someone. Does your eating the product make your audience interested and hungry, so they want to go out and get one of their own? Try different ways to enjoy the food and see if one method works better than others. Try the same exercise and include different products: drinks, phones, computers, makeup, clothes, and so on. The idea is to see if you've piqued the interest of your audience by incorporating the use of the object in your commercial. *Remember that sensory involvement will help — look at the product, touch the product, smell the product, eat or drink the product, listen to it, and so forth.*

- Write your own commercial copy, or transcribe it from television, using catchwords and phrases like *new and improved, for a limited time only, guaranteed,* and so on. Rehearse the copy making sure that you emphasize those words and phrases. *Remember that those words and phrases are all selling points!*

- Write your own commercial copy, or transcribe it from television, and rehearse stressing and isolating the sponsor's name.

5. Always make positive choices.

It might be wise to define the word *choice.* A choice is simply a decision about any number of things. An actor is constantly making choices regarding how to say a line, how to stand, how to move, and even choices on how to dress. Not making choices usually results in bad acting. So making choices is vital. Generally, it's the quality of choice that separates the professional actor from the nonprofessional actor. The most important choices made in commercials are how you are going to present yourself in the audition and on the set after you get the job.

The corporate world is very careful about how it presents itself to the public. Corporations do almost anything to keep their images clean. Corporations will change the way they conduct business based on public attitude. Because corporations rely on other people's money to do business, they care what people think, especially corporations that sell their product directly to the public. Businesses don't stay in business if they don't have earnings; and if they don't conduct business well, they don't have earnings.

How many times have you vowed never again to shop at a store where you were ignored? Likely you stopped going because you had a bad experience with a rude employee. I'll bet there is a store you shop at regularly because you are treated well by a particular employee. Actually, a lot of us only shop at particular places *because* a certain employee works there and that employee is positive and feels good to be around. I mentioned earlier that we buy from people who are energetic. Well, we also tend to buy from people who are positive and make us feel good about ourselves. How many places have you worked where you have been exhorted to "smile"? That's not an accident. The smile is a universal greeting that immediately disarms others. Smiles are infectious. When someone smiles at us, most of us smile back. We may not be sure why we do, but most of us want to believe in the inherent goodness of others.

To smile, then, is the first positive choice an actor can make in auditioning for and acting in commercials. It's simple to do, and it accomplishes a lot. It immediately shows vulnerability and sends an affirmative message. It is my guess that people who smile a lot are also more content and have greater self-esteem. Corporations want those kinds of people representing them and their products.

There's one more aspect of this principle I would like to discuss. I have seen actors audition for a commercial and make negative or catty choices with the innocent aim of being funny. Granted, a lot of negative humor is very funny. But be careful. Corporations don't like to be associated with negativity and nastiness, even if it's for the harmless intention of making someone laugh. This is difficult because a lot of commercials walk a fine line in this regard; truthfully, a lot of commercial copy seems negative. My advice is to find the positive energy even in seemingly negative copy.

Let me give you an example: In reality, if you worked in a donut shop and had to get up at 4:00 A.M. every day to get to work and make donuts, you'd likely feel unfriendly and not disposed to be cheerful. If you were to play such a character in an audition for a commercial, you might choose to play the character cranky. You might even be directed to play it that way. Even if it seems like the funniest thing in the world, if your choices are bitingly realistic (even if you think it's funny), you're sending a negative message. Somehow you must choose to play it with reality, follow direction, and still keep the *choices positive*. If you remember the commercial I am referring to ("Time to make the donuts!"), the actor not only did a brilliant job of playing the reality of his situation, but he kept his choices positive. Watching the commercial we knew that he liked his job and that we would enjoy buying donuts from him.

- Transcribe copy from a television or radio commercial, or write your own, and practice reading the copy while you smile. Tape the exercise twice: once smiling and once not smiling. When you play it back, see which of the commercials sends a more *positive* message.

- Using new commercial copy, tape it without thought of choices. Now analyze the copy and incorporate as many positive choices as you can and tape it. When you play both of them back, notice the difference. Ask yourself which version is more inviting. Better yet, ask a neutral party which one of the commercials makes him want to buy that product and why. If he chooses the positive one, ask if that had anything to do with his decision.

- Watch commercials and judge their positive messages. Notice the ones that make you smile and why. Do the commercials that make you smile make you feel more positive? If so, does that positive feeling make you feel good about the product?

6. Commercials present a problem and a solution.

Very simply, commercials create a problem that needs a solution. The product is almost always the solution. Whenever you analyze commercial copy, or the sponsor's intention behind the commercial, you must detect the inherent problem and solution. The problem/solution of a commercial is the equivalent of dramatic action or dramatic conflict for the commercial — and it's generally quite easy to discern. Think of all the commercials you've seen that adhere to this principle. *Problem:* "I wonder why girls just never seem to like me?" *Solution:* "It could be your breath, here try this mouthwash!" *Problem:* "My skin is always so dry and flaky." *Solution:* "Hmmm, I wonder if this face cream would help?" (And of course, it does.) *Problem:* "I'm starving to death!" *Solution:* "Welcome to Pizza Hut." I could give hundreds of examples, but I think you recognize the typical commercial format. What's important is that you learn to identify the problem and, more important, the solution.

How many times have you heard something like: You can't fix it if you don't know what the problem is? Well, commercials exist to answer that question for you. It's the job of a commercial to illuminate your problem, sometimes illuminating problems you never knew existed, and to offer the appropriate solution: the product.

When there were such things as door-to-door salesmen, vacuum cleaner salesmen would sometimes throw dirt on the floor as soon as some poor unsuspecting housewife opened the door. This ploy would create an immediate problem, which the salesman then had to fix by demonstrating his product — the vacuum cleaner he was selling. Well, television commercials do the same thing. They create a problem that the product can correct. As a commercial actor you need to be sensitive to finding the problem and selling that. Remember that you can only sell a solution (the product) if you've successfully sold the problem (the need for the product).

A lot of commercials are subtle about creating problems. In the examples I've given, the problems are obvious. But commercials are not always so blatant about stating the problem. What makes commercials ingenious is their ability to create a problem where none existed. A beer commercial is a good example. Where is the problem in a group of people having fun just hanging out and drinking beer? Here the fundamental problem is one of peer pressure. The message is, "If you don't drink this beer, you're probably not having as good a time as these people; therefore there's something wrong with you and you're not cool." Years ago Pepsi created a highly successful advertising campaign called "The Pepsi Generation." Everyone who drank Pepsi in those commercials was young, vibrant, and beautiful. To impressionable youth watching the commercial the problem and solution were clear: If you're not drinking Pepsi, you're not one of the Pepsi Generation. If you want to be like these people, you'll drink Pepsi too.

Every commercial has a problem and a solution that solves the problem, and the solution always revolves around the product. Don't make the mistake a lot of actors make, assuming that it's your charming personality or beauty that gets the girl or boy. What gets the girl or boy is the mouthwash or the underarm deodorant or the mint that you're chewing. *Never put yourself above the product.*

Make sure that you acknowledge and play the transition from the problem to the solution. There has to be a clear difference between the guy whose problem is an upset stomach and the same guy after he has taken the antacid tablet. The sponsor wants you to act out the change their product makes. We've all seen the typical before and after examples used in commercials. This is just a more obvious way to articulate the idea of problem/solution. Usually when someone has a problem, he can be concerned, frustrated, upset, or angry. But when he finds the solution, everything changes. He becomes happy, relieved, more content, and so forth. The solution, as most solutions are, is always a good thing. The commercial actor has to reflect that change.

EXERCISES

- While watching commercials, see if you can explicitly state a problem in every commercial. Notice how the problem is portrayed. Is it obvious? Is it subtle?

- Notice the solution in every commercial you watch. How effectively does the solution address the problem? Notice how dependent the solution is to the problem presented.

- In front of a camera, tape yourself performing commercial copy that you've written or transcribed from television. Before you tape it, make sure you acknowledge the problem and solution. In the performance, practice "selling" the problem as much as the solution.

- With the same commercial copy, rehearse the transition from the before (the problem) to the after (the solution). Pay attention to the positive nature of the solution.

7. Spontaneity is vital in commercials.

The great architect and teacher of improvisation, Viola Spolin, once said, "Spontaneity is the moment of personal freedom when we are found with a reality and see it, explore it, and act accordingly. In this reality the bits and pieces of ourselves function as an organic whole. It is the time of discovery, of experiencing, of creative expression." The reason spontaneity is so important in commercials is the same reason it is important in acting. An actor must always appear to be doing it for the first time. There can never be the sense that the script is rehearsed and prepared.

Let's look at the last sentence of Spolin's quote: "It is the time of discovery, of experiencing, of creative expression." This is a guideline for how to apply spontaneity in commercials. As we discussed in Principle 4, in a commercial you must *discover* and *experience* the product. The spontaneity results in how your *creative expression* is manifested. How you "creatively express" is your job as an actor and why you are going to be paid handsomely for acting in commercials. What you do after you see, smell, and taste the cup of coffee is your creative expression and that is going to be unique to everyone.

What's important is that your creative expression is distinctly your own. This is something that I can't teach you. No one can teach you how to be creatively expressive. What I can do is to help you trust in yourself and trust in your imagination. Spontaneity is different for everyone, and everyone has the potential to be spontaneous. Start trusting yourself to know that your response to any kind of stimulus is going to be unique and interesting. Too many actors make the mistake of creatively expressing something based on what they've seen other actors do in commercials! Learn to take your cues from yourself and what you see in other people. Just make sure that the other people you're watching aren't auditioning for the same commercial you are.

EXERCISES

- Go about your daily life and spontaneously react to situations in your life that you usually take for granted. For instance, when doing a mundane chore that you've done a million times, like washing dishes, pretend that this is the first time you've ever done it.

- Imagine that you've just landed on Earth from another planet and pretend that you are learning for the first time everything that you do as part of your routine. Really *discover* the everyday things you do as if for the first time, *experience* them as if for the first time, and make a mental note of how you *creatively express* your reaction to this experiment.

- In a group of people, try the improvisation: "What are you doing?" Person A begins an action, jumping rope for instance. Person B asks, "What are you doing?" Person A *must* say something *other* than jumping rope. "Building a doghouse," Person A might say. At which time, A *stops* jumping rope, and B *must* start building an imaginary doghouse. Person A then asks Person B, "What are you doing?" and so on. Keep it going until one person can't come up with something. Response speed is important as is making the action as different from the response as possible. Keep in mind that this improvisation forces you to be absolutely spontaneous. This is also a great warm-up, and if you are doing this in a camera-acting class, by all means, tape it.

8. Learn to play the obvious with unique choices.

To fully understand this principle you might want to go back and read Principle 2: Be yourself in commercials. Remember that we're dealing with Madison Avenue and the huge advertising industry, so you need to be concerned with "type"; and because the advertising industry wants to sell to as many people as it can, it ends up being rather generic in its appeal. Therefore, you must have the widest appeal when you audition for a commercial, and at the same time, you should be unique. Your challenge is to fit the advertiser's generic mold and be different at the same time. The reason this principle is important is because the advertising industry doesn't want you to deviate from its stereotypical image of the commercial. They want you to "be normal." Still they *love* it if you portray that image in some interesting or unique fashion.

Think back to the memorable Charmin ad campaign where Mr. Whipple exhorted his customers: "Please don't squeeze the Charmin!" Now this situation is not normal. But the sponsor still wanted to appeal to a large audience. Imagine auditioning for this commercial. All you have at your disposal is the storyboard and the line, "Please don't squeeze the Charmin." Your task is to make this unique situation normal. What do you do? The choices are innumerable. It could be done angrily, petulantly, demandingly, controllingly, or any number of ways. Yet the actor who was cast brilliantly chose to play it fussily, and at the same time he was extremely likeable. Suppose the actor who made the choice to be angry ended up getting the commercial. I'm not sure that Mr. Whipple snapping at his customers to not squeeze the tissue would have ever made us think he was endearing or likeable. Or imagine even if the actor had chosen to play it fussily, and then obsessively grabbed the tissue to put it back on the shelf. We might have found that funny but not necessarily charming or agreeable. What he did do was to ask the customer not to squeeze the Charmin in an overly concerned, comical manner after which he clutched the Charmin as if to protect it and smiled as if he had done something heroic. We found the actor and the action funny. The actor ended up finding the perfect blend of the obvious and the unique, and he and the campaign went on to make a successful and unforgettable commercial, not to mention a lot of money.

As I was trying to explain this principle in a class, one of my students illustrated this principle by commenting, "Oh, they want you to be quirky, not kinky." This may be the best way to describe this principle. The advertisers don't ever want you to be enigmatic in any way. But they want you to be eccentric. So remember that even if the commercial is meant to be funny, you can never become so distorted that the audience is afraid of you. Be quirky but never kinky!

EXERCISES

- Make up a commercial around this line: "Leave me alone with Mrs. Butterworths." (Mrs. Butterworths being a pancake syrup.) Try different ways to do this commercial making sure that you are making unique choices and being "normal" at the same time. If you are filming this exercise, notice the different ways it can be done. Make sure that you and your classmates aren't trying to make it funny in any kind of negative way. Note the ways it can be done in a quirky way without becoming kinky.

- Prepare the following non-gender-specific commercial copy: "I fell in love last night. I mean really in love. I felt the glow, the tingle, the goose bumps. It happened over dinner. A beautiful dinner with soft music and candlelight. And wine, oh, what a wine! And somewhere after the stuffed mushrooms and before the chocolate soufflé, I fell head over heels in love — with Paul Masson. I never knew it could be like this." (For those of you who don't know, Paul Masson is a wine.) Make sure you capture the humor and the surprise ending without ever letting it get bizarre. Videotape the exercise and notice the many different ways it can be done. When you play the copy back, discuss the differences and why some choices worked better than others did.

9. Be open to changes in auditions and on the set.

Most of the time, commercial auditions are improvisational and most of the time the actual shoot incorporates some improvisation. However, SAG rules prohibit producers from asking actors to do improvisation at auditions — and so, there's your conundrum. Your employer wants you to do what your union prohibits. I'm afraid the reality is if you want to be successful in commercials, you had better learn to improvise. Be open to modification. If you get too locked into your audition plan, you could well end up losing the job. Let's say they like you but the director wants to give you a piece of direction or asks you to improvise; for example the director might ask you, "Try it this time as if you were free falling out of an airplane." If you can't do it, he may no longer be interested in you.

Now that I've encouraged you to improvise away, I'll admit it's also true that the writers from the ad agencies are inevitably wedded to their "magnificent" copy and want you to perform it *exactly as written.* Therefore, while many if not most commercial work includes improvisation, the contradiction is that they don't really want you to do it unless you hand them the next V-8 head slap. At the same time, *be ready to improvise.* It's just that there is more concern for the copy in commercials than there is in, for instance, soap operas. In soaps, actors can almost say whatever they want. In commercials, producers and ad agency executives get very protective and territorial about what they've written. They do not like actors changing one word. The best way to reconcile this arbitrariness is to prepare what they want but be ready to vary it at a moment's notice.

To illustrate how arbitrary the whole business is, I'll tell you a story that sounds apocryphal, but my friend swears is true. As a quick review, remember that the corporate sponsor hires the ad agency, which hires the casting director, which hires the actors. A small fortune goes into auditioning actors, but the corporate sponsor always has the final word.

A major corporation was looking for a spokesperson for one of their frontline products. The company was in need of a series of effective commercials to promote this product and needed a strong spokesperson to anchor the commercials. Whoever was chosen would have it made, financially, for the rest of his or her life. (Recall buyout contracts, under whose terms the actor cannot make any other commercials for the term of the contract.) Well, the team looked high. They looked low. They looked in New York. They looked in Los Angeles. They looked in Chicago. They searched the country, then finally found the actor they were looking for. The ad agency loved him. The director loved him. Even the midlevel corporate people loved him.

They all thought they had the perfect actor. The only hurdle left was the CEO of the corporation, who had the final say. They brought the videotape into the executive's office, who watched it, shook his head, and said simply, "That's not the guy." His team was stunned and asked, "What do you mean?" "Nope," he said. "That's not the guy." "Why not? We've looked everywhere. We've seen thousands of people. He's perfect! He has it all. *Why not this guy?*" The CEO responded, "Because he reminds me of my nephew and I *hate* my nephew." The point is, this business is arbitrary; it has little to do with talent, and nothing to do with art. We can only hope that the poor actor of the story never knew how close he'd gotten to landing that job.

EXERCISES

- As a warm-up to get energy going, with a class or a group of people, try this improvisation: Jeepers Peepers. Everyone sits or stands in a circle with his or her head down and eyes closed. On the count of three, everyone looks up at the either the person on the left, right, or directly across from him or her. If eye contact is made, both must scream and step out of the circle. Repeat. Tape the exercise and play it back.

- With a class or a group of people, try this improvisation: Commercial. Two or three improvisers ask the audience for a fictitious product. The improvisers act as an ad agency writing a slogan, copy, or a jingle demonstrating what the product does. Once finished, the same group or another group should present the final commercial. Tape the finished commercial and play it back.

- With a class or a group of people, try this improvisation: "Yes, and . . ." Divide the group into smaller groups of three to four people. Each group should decide on a product it is doing a commercial for. Improvise the commercial copy making sure that every line of dialogue begins with the words "Yes, and . . ." The goal is to absolutely support your partners' suggestions and to be supported, as well as develop your improvisation skills. Tape it and play it back.

10. Sex sells.

Even if it's for gum. Even if it's for motor oil. Regardless of what it's for, sex sells. Certain philosophies believe that there are three things that govern human behavior: sex, greed, and fear. Examples of commercials that push your greed buttons are investment firms, anyone offering bonus gifts, and anything that appeals to your desire to accumulate. Insurance ads, home security devices, and anything dealing with the unknown are a few of the ways that fear manifests itself in commercials. But sex is prevalent in commercials. In fact, sex is prevalent in *all* advertising. Pick up any magazine; check out ads on the Internet and billboards. Sex appeal is visceral, and it's been proven that shopping can be a visceral experience.

We can all quickly think of many examples where the advertiser uses sex as a tool to try to sell us something. Soap commercials, hair products, beer commercials, toothpaste, cologne, and jewelry commercials are a few examples. But most of the time it's done in a subtler manner. Anything tactile is potentially sexy. Anything sensory is sexy. The eyes are sexy. Hair is sexy. The mouth is sexy. And of course, gorgeous people are sexy. You'll see all these employed in commercials. When you watch commercials, look for how advertisers try to engage you on a subconscious level. Baby oil is sexy because the selling point is that the product makes your baby's skin soft (soft skin is sexy). Airline and car commercials are sexy because the selling points are speed, adventure, and travel (which are sexy). They even try to make computer ads sexy by incorporating dancing people and cute couples (which are sexy). I've already discussed in Principle 4 how the advertising world makes food and beverages sexy in commercials. All the commercial actor can do is to remember this when he auditions for commercials.

Sometimes, of course, being sexy in an overt, obvious way can get you work. Much of the time, however, being sexy has much more to do with a certain kind of connection with the camera. The difference is between you *yourself* trying to be sexy and finding the *other* person sexy. That is the difference between seducing the camera and simply trying to be sexy. It's a connection that most successful actors have with the lens. They are seducing whoever is watching. It's what we commonly refer to as charisma, personal magnetism, sex appeal, or charm. A good camera actor brings this to everything he does — to every performance. One friend tells the story that, out of the hundreds of commercial auditions he went on in New York, when he let go of all concern for being good and simply looked into the camera and connected, he landed the job.

To some extent, it's probably true that selling itself is seduction. It's not something that can be satisfactorily explained. It's certainly not easy or simple to explain. Sex appeal might not even be the most accurate way of describing it. Of course, it is also true that sex, for its own sake, sells. I suppose one must never lose sight of that simple fact. Being sexy in a cheap way definitely has been proven to sell. For commercials, however, stay far away from anything that smacks of cheap sex. Madison Avenue doesn't want to associate their products with *anything* cheap, least of all sex.

EXERCISES

- Tape your slate twice. The first time try to be overtly sexy and the second time try to seduce the imaginary person watching. When you play it back, notice the difference between the two and try to discern which one is more effective. Discuss what works versus what doesn't.

- Distribute various commercial copies to the class. Have everyone prepare an audition. Look to incorporate sex appeal in each of the copies. Tape the audition and make sure to include the slate. On the playback discuss the effectiveness of sex appeal as a selling tool. Did the ones where sex appeal was obvious work better than the ones that were subtler? Discuss why or why not.

- While watching commercials, observe the advertiser's use of sex and sex appeal. Try to discover why the advertiser is using it and what its objectives are in doing so.

11. Always be aware of and look for the tag.

The tag is usually at the end of the commercial and sums up everything you've seen. You could also call it the lure or the hook at the end. Sometimes the sponsor will put the tag at the beginning as well as at the end to tie everything together. You'll probably recognize some of these tags: "Coke, just for the taste of it!" "McDonald's, we love to see you smile." "Wow, I coulda had a V-8!" "Ruffles have ridges." "Be a Pepper." "Maxwell House, good to the last drop." Often the tag will accompany a picture of the brand logo (Gap, Nike) or a picture of the product. Think about these examples and decide what's significant about the tag. If you said that the tag revolves around the product, you're right! *The tag is always centered on the product.*

The real importance of the tag is that it's the final image or message of the commercial: It's the last thing you'll see or hear. The sponsor wants to make certain the viewer remembers its product. You may remember the tags I've given, but I bet you don't remember the commercials themselves—only the tags. Take the sponsor's name out of the tag, and I bet you'd still be able to remember the product: "_____, we love to see you smile." "_____, just for the taste of it." It's all about association. The sponsor's objective is to get the audience to associate its product with the commercial — and the last image of the commercial is the most important.

The commercial actor needs to be aware of the importance of the tag and must be able to capitalize on it. If the tag is verbal, the actor can bring a visual association to complement the tag. The tag should be the most heartfelt part of the commercial. Smile during the tag; try making the tag sensory, and, as long as it's appropriate, try something funny or provocative with the tag. And in the audition, always memorize the tag so you are free to look into the camera. For the tag "Wow, I coulda had a V-8!," the actor hit his forehead with the palm of the hand when speaking the tag. I assume that the actor who was initially cast in the commercial came up with the gesture for that tag. The gesture ended up becoming synonymous with the tag. In this case, the actor's gesture augmented the association of the verbal tag.

But the tag can serve two purposes. I've heard commercial directors say that they look for actors in the audition to tell them what the commercial is about. So the most successful commercial actor not only creates something with the tag to help teach the sponsor what their commercial is about but also uses the tag in the audition to get the job. Let's face it, if the tag is to help the audience remember the product with an image, then the actor auditioning for the commercial has to develop a tag as an image to help the sponsor remember the actor. I guarantee that if you create an exciting and memorable tag for the product, the sponsor will remember you. The important thing is to take a risk and try something, even if you think it's silly or goofy. Remember, though, that it's not appropriate to cast a poor light on or to be negative about the product.

Tags don't have to be complex to be effective. Sometimes the simplest tags work best. Think of the gum commercial where the actress runs her tongue over her teeth indicating how refreshing the gum tastes. (Remember that tags work best if they are also sensory.) Let's use an example of a known tag, "When you care enough to send the very best." We recognize the memorable Hallmark tag. If you were to see this on a copy at an audition, what would you do? Even something as simple as a wink and a nod to the camera might be enough to get a callback or even the job. You need to figure out what the sponsor wants to say with the last image of the commercial. If you want to relay a sense of confident encouragement, a knowing wink and a supportive nod might be the most appropriate gesture. If the copy preceding the tag is humorous, you might try laughing through the tag as if you had thought of a funny moment in the past when you didn't care enough to send the best. You might choose to be in the act of sealing the envelope, and just before you do, you say the tag as if encouraging us to stop and think about what we send before it's too late. More than likely the storyboard for the commercial will indicate how you should do the copy, but frequently the tag is up to you. The creative way you do it will determine how effective you are in the audition and whether you get the job.

EXERCISES

- When you watch commercials, look for the tags. Notice how often they are verbal and how often they are visual. Notice what makes some tags more memorable than others. Try to guess how much the actor had to do with making the tag effective.

- Prepare an improvisation of a commercial based on one of the following tags. (You can also use your own tag.) Ask yourself what commercial would be appropriate for the particular tag line you choose. Be sure to incorporate the tag line at the end of your improvisation.

"Diet Coke — you're going to drink it just for the taste of it." (Coca-Cola)

"If you don't look good, we don't look good." (Vidal Sassoon)

"At McDonald's we do it all for you." (McDonald's)

"At Dellwood we put our hearts into everything we make." (Dellwood Dairy)

"Secret, strong enough for a man, but made for a woman." (Secret deodorant)

"He needs the deodorant that works overtime." (Old Spice deodorant)

"Federal Express, when it absolutely positively has to be there overnight." (FedEx)

"Orange juice from Florida; it isn't just for breakfast anymore." (Florida Citrus)

"Underalls make me feel . . . like I'm not wearing nothing!" (Underalls pantyhose)

"No cat walks away from Friskies buffet." (Little Friskies)

"M&M's melt in your mouth, not in your hand." (M&M candy)

"I'm stuck on Band-Aids, and Band-Aids stick on me." (Band-Aid)

"If you want someone's attention, whisper." (Emeraude perfume)

"I can't believe I ate the whole thing." (Alka Seltzer)

"This is a good place for a Stick-Up." (Stick-Up room freshener)

"Nervous is why, you need Soft and Dry." (Soft and Dry deodorant)

"Three Musketeers; it's fluffy, not stuffy." (Three Musketeers candy)

"At Kentucky Fried Chicken, we do chicken right." (Kentucky Fried Chicken)

"Last cold Bayer, this cold Comtrex." (Comtrex cold medicine)

"Is it live or is it Memorex?" (Memorex tape)

"Please don't squeeze the Charmin!" (Charmin toilet tissue)

"Nobody plays more music than 98.7, KISS FM." (KISS FM radio station)

"Crisp and clean — and no caffeine." (7-Up)

"Ring around the collar."(Wisk)

"I want my MTV." (MTV channel)

"Don't get mad — get Glad." (Glad Bags)

"Escape the greasies." (Agree shampoo)

"You can roll a Rollo." (Rollo candy)

"WPLJ Rocks!" (WPLJ radio)

"Kiss me; I got the Signal." (Signal mouthwash)

"I was flat . . . 'til I went fluffy." (Prell shampoo)

"Got milk?" (Milk Association)

"White Cloud *is* softer." (White Cloud tissue)

"Scotch-choo!" (Scott tissue)

"Bet ya can't eat just one?" (Lay's potato chips)

"Get Wise." (Wise potato chips)

"Flash 'em the Coppertone tan." (Coppertone)

"It's not too sweet." (Canada Dry)

COMMERCIAL EXERCISES

Now that you know what you're doing, let's put it to practical use. We'll start out with "singles' copy." Singles' copy is not copy for single people. It's a monologue, one person doing the talking even if there are other people in the commercial. It also might be called "spokesperson's copy."

Prepare the following copy (feel free to use your own), and treat it as if you were either auditioning for it or actually shooting it. Make sure you incorporate as many of the principles as you can. If you are using it as an audition exercise, make sure to incorporate a slate. Videotape it with one camera and shoot it in a medium close-up from the chest up. If you're in a class situation, everyone should do the same copy. Don't discuss how to do the commercial before you prepare. Treat this as if it was a real situation and you are on your own.

TACO BELL

Now at Taco Bell! The new taco pizza!!! You've heard of the Mexican pizza, now try the new taco pizza at Taco Bell!!! The same great Taco Bell taste, but with a new added zing! Rich, thick, mozzarella cheese, and a fabulous Italian marinara meat sauce spread thick over a toasted pita bread crust. Wow! What a great taste! And for a limited time only 59 cents for two. Hurry now to your nearest Taco Bell and bring a friend . . . heck, bring everyone you know! This deal is too good not to share. Taco Bell's new taco pizza. Olé amoure!!!

Play it back and discuss it. Make sure that you can pause the tape after each take.

- Did you analyze who the sponsor is and what the sponsor is selling?
- Did you highlight the name of the sponsor? Did you stress for a *limited time only 59 cents?*
- Did you get caught speeding during the line: "Rich, thick mozzarella cheese, and a fabulous Italian marinara meat sauce spread thick over a toasted pita bread crust?" That is a mouthful, which I call a speed bump. You should make a notation on your script that prepares you for it. Try a couple of slashes (//) to warn yourself to slow down.
- Did you eat the product? Two good places to do that were right before, "The same great Taco Bell taste . . . " and at the end of the copy — and look right into the lens!
- Did you have your first and last line memorized so that you could look directly into the lens?
- Did you smile?
- Did you play the *urgency* of the commercial?
- How did you handle "Olé Amoure!!!"? As the tag it's the last image anyone is going to see of your audition (or commercial) and it should be memorable.

How did you do? Did you have fun? Hopefully you learned something by watching it in playback.

This next one is a "doubles' copy," which is a scene between two people. Transcribe the following commercial copy onto a sheet of paper so that you can hold it, the same as you would at an actual audition. This is exactly what a commercial copy at an audition might look like. This is for Denny's.

Open on medium shot of	(ANNOUNCER)	Excuse me.
busy business person	(PERSON)	Look, I'm kind of
walking across screen		in a hurry.
	(ANNOUNCER)	We understand.
		You're a busy
		person, right?
	(PERSON)	Right.
	(ANNOUNCER)	So you don't always
		have time to sit down
		to a meal, right?
	(PERSON)	Right.
	(ANNOUNCER)	So what do you do?
Looks at watch	(PERSON)	I usually grab a
		hamburger. Can I
		go now?
Off-camera announcer hands	(ANNOUNCER)	Not yet. Have you
person a Denny's sandwich		tried this?
	(PERSON)	No, I haven't.
	(ANNOUNCER)	Take a bite.
Takes a bite	(PERSON)	This is *great!*
		Where can I get
		one of these?
	(ANNOUNCER)	Ever hear of Denny's?
	(PERSON)	Denny's? Sure!
		This is delicious.
	(ANNOUNCER)	We thought you'd
		like it.
	(PERSON)	Can I go now?
	(ANNOUNCER)	Sure.
Takes another bite	(PERSON)	Can I take this with me?
and walks off		This is terrific.

Prepare for this as you would an audition. By the way, you are playing the Person and the casting assistant is the Announcer. (In a class situation the teacher or another student can play the Announcer.) Make sure you slate before each take. When you tape it, shoot the person from the waist up and make sure the camera can pan from side to side.

After everyone has been taped, play it back and discuss it. In your analysis of the commercial, here are a number of things to look for:

- Did you create the situation? The situation is someone on a busy street (the Announcer) stopping someone who is going someplace (the Person) to ask him where he usually goes to eat lunch. OK so far. But how many of you just stood there in front of the camera? If the Person doesn't make a choice about where he's going, given that his first line is "I'm in kind of a hurry," it doesn't look very believable if he isn't going somewhere. Since he is supposedly going somewhere, obviously the best choice is to start out of frame and walk *through* the frame. That way you can be stopped by the announcer and "caught" in frame.

- Looking at your watch on your first line might also be a good choice. Remember that it is very important that you do not become negative. While you are in a hurry, you must not appear too irritated about being stopped. If you give off an attitude that says, "The hell with you, buddy, I'm in a hurry," there is no way you will be cast.

- The Announcer then hands you the hamburger and says, "Try this." This is a key moment in the commercial. This is your opportunity to be tactile in selling the product. It is not out of the realm of possibility to make it appear as though eating this hamburger is almost a sexual experience. Certainly it must be a very pleasurable sensory experience — let us say sensual. If you take a quick bite and dismiss the experience with a cursory reaction, you will have lost a golden opportunity. Don't forget the idea that in all eating commercials the objective is to make the viewer hungry for the product. Therefore you really need to vocalize and physicalize the pleasurable experience of taking a bite.

- "Mmmm." Remember to keep the eyes open as you eat. We want to see your eyes. Saying, "Mmmm" with the eyes open allows you to connect with the lens.

- Many actors hold their scripts too low when they audition, which causes the same problem to occur (see figure 3a). The proper position for holding a script is illustrated in figure 3b. If necessary, fold the script into quarters so that it can be easily manipulated and you can easily see over it into the lens (see figure 4). At the same time, don't hold the script too low or all the lens will see is the top of your head. Find the happy median. You can demonstrate the proper script positioning by videotaping alternatives: Which looks better? The head up where we can see your face? Or the head lowered reading the copy that is down by your stomach? The actual difference in positioning and in the eye line the camera sees is minuscule. Depending on how far the camera is away from you, it is possible to hold the script quite high without it appearing unnatural.
- The script can become a useful prop for you. It can become your burger, for instance. It can become anything you want it to be.

Inevitably, we will all make these typical mistakes. Try it again with these ideas in mind. Find other commercial copy, or better yet, write your own. But keep working, and keep watching commercials.

One of the best things you can do is to read out loud every day. In our culture, we don't read out loud enough. Do it every day! Get used to the sound of your own voice. For commercial auditions (as well as all TV and film auditions), this is a very important skill — to be able to read aloud with a script in hand. A commercial actor, in

Fig. 3a.

Fig. 3b.

Fig. 4. Script-folding diagram.

particular, needs to be able to pick up any piece of copy and read it aloud with confidence and clarity. Get into the habit. It doesn't matter what it is: the morning newspaper, the back of your cereal box, junk mail, a magazine article—*anything* that will sharpen that necessary skill.

The most effective way to develop the skills necessary to successfully audition and perform in commercials is to keep doing it. Rehearse the principles to perfect and expand on them. What's most important is to refine them according to what works for you. Not all the principles are going to work as well for everyone. Through practice you will discover which ones work best for you. If you find any that aren't as effective, don't use them. You may even discover new ones.

SUMMARY

Commercials are lucrative and because of residuals can subsidize an acting career. The first things you need before you start auditioning for commercials are an agent and good headshots. Just don't forget that when it comes to agents and headshots, caveat emptor — let the buyer beware. Be prepared before you go on an audition and once you're there, don't forget what it took to get you there. Being prepared means being on time, wearing the appropriate clothes, avoiding distractions, and presenting yourself as a professional. At the callback, make sure you wear what you wore to the original audition and that you follow directions.

For auditions and acting in commercials, bear in mind the following principles:

1. *Commercials require energy because they are the most theatrical of all television and film genres.*
2. *Be yourself in commercials.* Know and play your type.
3. *The slate in auditions is as important as the audition.* Often it's more important.
4. *Always be aware of selling the product.* With food and beverages, remember: sensory association works.
5. *Always make positive choices.* Don't be negative.
6. *Commercials present a problem and a solution.* The only way to sell something is to create a need for it.
7. *Spontaneity is vital in commercials.* Don't be rigid.
8. *Learn to play the obvious with unique choices.* Be quirky not kinky.
9. *Be open to changes in auditions and on the set.* Be prepared to improvise.
10. *Sex sells.* Be alert to the element of seduction in all commercials.
11. *Always be aware of and look for the tag.* Create something special with the catch at the end.

CHAPTER 3

INDUSTRIALS AND CD-ROMs

Industrial films have been produced as training vehicles for corporate America's employees for years. They are also used as sales tools that inform potential buyers about the qualities of products. I'm sure you've seen these kinds of industrial films in grocery stores, department stores, and even hardware stores. Better known as industrials, they are also used extensively in schools. (Everybody who has a driver's license has probably seen industrials on how to drive a car.) Think of them as short training films (forty-five minutes or less) that are shot on film or videotape and usually shown on a VCR. Originally, they were exclusively shot on film and shown on a screen via a projector. In the last twenty years, however, they have mostly been taped. They are basically made for educational purposes — not entertainment purposes.

CD-ROMs (compact disk, read only memory) are usually used for interactive games and for storing information efficiently, such as encyclopedias or photographs. CD-ROMS are digitally formatted and viewed via a computer or a DVD player. CD-ROMS are also used for educational industrials. The industrial is filmed or videotaped and then transferred to a CD-ROM. The industrial can also be videotaped digitally so that no transfer is necessary. For movies and television, CD-ROMs are mainly a storage medium, however, and not a production medium. Although motion pictures and television programs are being *translated* onto DVD and CD-ROM, at this time it's still too expensive to *produce* most film and television digitally.

However, it makes economic sense for industrials to be produced on CD-ROMS because CDs are better suited for the short format of most industrial films. Corporations are governed by the bottom line. This is probably the main difference between commerce and art in the entertainment industry. Although there is a lot of debate over the artistic quality of producing other genres digitally on CD-ROM, the reason corporations use this format for industrials is purely economic.

It is not my purpose to debate the merits of CD-ROMs or the new digital technology versus film or videotape. When I refer to CD-ROMs, I am discussing their use for interactive games and training purposes only. My goal is to examine what industrial films and CD-ROMs have in common as employment options for actors and to provide some necessary tools for auditioning for and acting in them. Those tools are organized within the five principles and exercises.

WHAT ARE THE VARIOUS EMPLOYMENT OPPORTUNITIES IN INDUSTRIAL FILMS?

For many years actors have been able to supplement their income by acting in industrial films. Although not nearly as lucrative as commercials, they are still a viable source of income. And though the work being done directly for CD-ROMs (which is different from industrials) does not yet represent a huge financial windfall for actors, it certainly has the potential to do so in the future. In 2001, the latest year we have statistics, SAG actors earned $14 million working under both industrials and interactive contracts ("interactive contracts" is how SAG recognizes work done on CD-ROM). AFTRA, which also covers industrial and interactive contracts, doesn't release those statistics.

Let's take a look at the compensation categories for industrials. They happen to be identical for both SAG and AFTRA. Both unions have two categories of industrial film compensation, Category I and Category II. For SAG, Category I represents only training, informational, or promotional programs for places where there is no charge for admission (for example, libraries, schools, museums, and so on). In addition, Category I incorporates sales programs promoting products or services that are only shown on a restricted basis. An example of this would be an educational program designed to teach salespeople the highlights of a new clothing line in their store. Teleconferences and closed circuit transmissions also fall under Category I. For AFTRA, Category I applies to all in-house videos: anything shown strictly for instructional purposes that contains no sales pitch and where there is no cost to the viewer. An example would be a video extolling the safety virtues of car seats for infants — as long as the video is trying to teach you something and not trying to get you to buy the car seat.

SAG's Category II includes industrial films intended for unrestricted viewing by the general public. The biggest difference between both categories is that films in Category II, much like commercials, are meant to sell products or services. Examples would be an industrial film promoting a new clothing line to its customers at a specific department store or a video of someone making a sales pitch at a mall (or any public place meant for business transactions). SAG also places a five-year limitation on the time Category II industrials can be shown. AFTRA's definition of Category II is similar to SAG's, but it is simpler. Basically, a Category II is any video shown at a trade show or anything that contains a sales pitch. The videos in the grocery store showing you how to cook with certain kinds of pots and pans with the intention of selling them to you would qualify as a Category II. Further examples of SAG's Category II are from the contract itself and include "A program outlining the selling features of an automobile, which is available to all consumers entering automobile showrooms. A program promoting fire prevention which sells the benefits of a particular company's fire insurance policies and is exhibited in a shopping mall. A videocassette explaining how to build a recreation room, provided free of charge to anyone who buys a power drill. A videocassette on how to cook with a Chinese wok, provided free of charge to buyers of a home videocassette recorder."

HOW MUCH CAN YOU MAKE ACTING IN AN INDUSTRIAL?

The minimum pay scale for principal performers in both unions (which does not include appearing as an extra) for Category I is $423 for one day's work. If a principal is working three days, the minimum is $1064. The minimum for five days is $1485. The rate is higher for an actor who appears exclusively as a spokesperson or narrator on camera. In that case, for a Category I industrial, the minimum is $769 for the first day and $423 for each additional day. In industrials, spokespeople (or narrators) usually bear most of the burden when it comes to how much work is involved. Both unions also make the distinction of working for one week on location. If you are working six days on location (one day would be for travel), you would earn $1634. For Category I spokespeople and narrators, the rate is $769 for the first day and $423 for each additional day.

The minimum compensation rate in both unions for principals performing in a Category II industrial is $526 for one day's work; $1312 for three days' work; and $1839 for one week's work. If you are on an overnight location for six days, you'll make $2023. For being strictly a spokesperson or a narrator, the minimum is $911 for the first day and $526 for each additional day.

Wouldn't you make more by taking the day rate for three or five days?

It would make sense that agents would want to do that but, alas, it's not possible. Think of it as buying in bulk: The union gives producers a break when they hire an actor for a longer period of time. Obviously, the longer an actor works, the more she is paid, and frankly, I imagine that both SAG and AFTRA want to induce producers to hire actors for as long as they can. Producers, who do nothing but watch the bottom line, would never hire actors for days or weeks if they had to pay the higher day rate for each day's work.

How much can you make if you're an extra?

If you're an extra (also called a background actor), there is no distinction between Category I and II. If you are what the unions call a "general background actor," you would make $110 per day. A general background actor is someone who is just walking by or standing in the background. A "special ability background actor" (a photo double or stand-in who literally stands in for a principal) makes $121 per day. If you happen to be a "silent bit background actor," you make $206 per day. Silent bit background actors have special skills; if you were eating fire in the background, for instance, that is what you'd make. (These actors are called "silent" because under union rules the moment an actor has a line of dialogue, he becomes a principal.) Because there are no three-day or weekly rates for extras, if you worked more than one day, you'd make the same rate for each day's work.

Do actors make residuals for industrials?

Unfortunately, they don't. If you remember in chapter 2, over half SAG actors' compensation in commercials came in residuals. Industrials and CD-ROMs are the only genres in this book that don't pay residuals. This is certainly a major reason why actors don't make as much in this genre.

What are the pay rates for CD-ROMs?

Both SAG and AFTRA have contracts and minimum rates that deal exclusively with CD-ROMs; they are called interactive contracts. Like the contracts for industrials, both SAG and AFTRA have the same minimums. The rates are $556 for one day's work; $1408 if you work three days; and if you are working one full week, the rate is $1932. Again, like industrials, they have a six-day overnight location rate; the minimum for that contract is $2125.90.

Incidentally, for actors who are employed for anything directly made for the Internet, both SAG and AFTRA have policies that are in embryonic states. This is one of the major issues behind their desire to consolidate. SAG is currently claiming jurisdiction for anything produced on the Internet, but AFTRA also has a minimum rate for actors who work on the Internet. Obviously, this is an area that is still undefined; both unions need to establish clearer guidelines for actors working in this genre. SAG acknowledges that its contract for the Internet is experimental and right now the rates are what they call "freely bargained," which I assume means that producers must bargain in good faith. AFTRA's minimum rate for material directly made for the Internet is $526 for the day. (The same as the minimum rate for an interactive contract.)

What else might I need to know about industrials and CD-ROMs?

Before we get into a discussion of auditions, you should know about the TelePrompTer. A TelePrompTer (that's the trademark way of spelling it) is a widely accepted device used in many industrial films. Its use is de rigueur on newscasts and soap operas.

This machine, put on a camera just below, to the side, or over the lens, magnifies and scrolls the script so that the actor (or newscaster) can read it. TelePrompTers enable the actor to read their script while looking directly into the camera. (If you look closely enough during news broadcasts, you can sometimes see the newscaster's eyes traversing the prompter.) It's the technological evolution of the cue card. (If you watch "The Late Show with David Letterman," you'll notice that he still uses cue cards.)

Becoming adept at reading a TelePrompTer is an art unto itself. Unless you have access to one and can practice, it's difficult to give a clear picture of what it's like working with one. The basic idea, of course, is to read aloud effectively without appearing to do so. You'll be better prepared to read a TelePrompTer if you have a good idea what you're supposed to be saying. However, what is key about using one is the speed at which it's scrolling. Before you start to shoot anything that entails reading from a TelePrompTer, make sure you rehearse with it. (The director will always allow you to do that.) The most important thing you can do is to be comfortable with how fast the dialogue is moving. There's nothing worse than speeding up the pace at which you are speaking to catch up to the TelePrompTer, or conversely, losing the essence of an idea while you wait for the TelePrompTer to catch up to you.

WHAT'S THE AUDITION PROCESS FOR INDUSTRIALS AND CD-ROMS?

The process for getting and going out on auditions for industrials and CD-ROMs is quite similar to commercials. In a nutshell, agents submit your picture to a casting director who selects the types that are right for the audition; the actors are then called in to audition.

Unlike commercials, however, casting directors for industrial films and CD-ROMs are not like independent casting directors who cast for a living. Many times the person doing the casting is employed by the corporation that is producing the industrial. For instance, many corporations have their own in-house marketing department, which is responsible not only for advertising and promotion, but also works in tandem with other departments to train new employees and conducts sales seminars and various motivational meetings. To do this effectively, marketing produces training, informational, or promotional films — also known as industrial films.

As you would for commercials, you should know what type of character you are auditioning for; make sure that you dress accordingly. Bring a picture and a résumé with you to the audition. Unlike commercials, you may receive copy (the sides) before you go to the audition. If you do, make sure that you familiarize yourself with it beforehand (see Principle 1).

What is the most important consideration regarding my audition?

You'll find that all the following principles address necessary issues concerning auditioning for industrials and CD-ROMs. Each one contains an important element that should be investigated as you see fit. However, if there is one overriding assumption that you should make about your audition, it is this: Never forget that industrials and CD-ROMs are corporate enterprises.

In this respect industrials and CD-ROMs are akin to commercials. However, because of the entertainment aspect of commercials, industrials and CD-ROMs are even more business oriented. While a commercial ultimately concerns a corporation trying to get the public to buy something, the corporations want to disguise that intent and hope that the viewers will associate the product with pleasure and entertainment. For the most part, industrials and CD-ROMs are not so subtle. If you always keep in mind that you are representing the corporation producing the industrial, you'll have no problem. This idea is dealt with in Principle 2.

When you audition for this genre, you will need far fewer acting skills than you would need for a character like Hamlet. All great acting requires skill in communication. In industrials and CD-ROMs, the primary message to be communicated is *information* rather than an intense emotion or psychological state. However, the rules of communication don't change from one genre to another: You must still care that what you have to say hits home with another person.

PRINCIPLES OF INDUSTRIALS AND CD-ROMS

As you investigate each of the following five principles, bear in mind that the essence of every industrial and CD-ROM is information. Also remember that you are the conduit for that information. These principles are designed to help you audition for CD-ROMs and industrials as well as to guide you when you get the job. Each principle should motivate you to think of other ways to help you audition and perform in industrials and CD-ROMs. Each principle is accompanied by exercises. They provide a practical applications for the principles. Don't feel that you need to attempt every exercise. Incorporate the ones that appeal to you and, by all means, have fun!

1. Keep the copy conversational.

This principle is particularly valid for copy that tends to be wordy and technical in nature. Especially for industrial films, you could be asked to represent anything from an engineering salesperson to a medical company rep. Often you'll be reading scripts talking about things you know nothing about and using words you've never heard. Don't worry: the client understands that you're not necessarily literate in the field, but the client also expects you to successfully convince people that you are. Assume that if a company is hiring an actor, they've already tried to use someone in the company and didn't have much luck. (If you've ever seen an industrial or CD-ROM with an employee, you'll understand why companies often decide to hire actors.)

When preparing difficult or technical copy, you first need to keep it as conversational as possible. First, find out everything you can about the topic you are discussing. This may be difficult because you'll be given copy only a couple of days before you have to film (or audition for) the industrial or CD-ROM. Sometimes the production company offers some helpful background information and a pronunciation guide. If they do, great; however, it's up to you to do some detective work to understand what the words themselves mean. It's imperative to learn how to pronounce the words and to comprehend their meaning.

Once you understand what you are talking about and how to articulate it, you should break the copy down. This entails separating the various ideas of the text and establishing transitions between these ideas. Dividing up the text will help you memorize it; even if you are reading from a TelePrompTer, breaking it down will help you anticipate and organize the text and make it sound conversational. (If it sounds conversational to you, it will to others as well.) Breaking it down also helps you to better understand and, therefore, communicate the copy. (Think of eating a sandwich: You don't eat the entire thing at once. You cut it in half and then take bites.) You need to find your own method of dividing the text, but it usually includes devising a kind of shorthand for yourself that essentially adds punctuation that will help you make it sound realistic. Whether you use brackets, parentheses, slashes, periods, or commas, you should take small enough bites so that you can effectively make sense of the entire thing.

While you're breaking it down, look for overly technical key words and phrases. In highly specialized sectors, such as medicine, the sciences, engineering, and computers, you'll find many words and terms that are unique to that particular field. As I mentioned earlier, I call difficult words and phrases "speed bumps." You need to look for these speed bumps and prepare for them by somehow indicating their presence in the script. Don't assume that you can glibly skip over them. Because they are unfamiliar, you need to physically prepare your mouth to enunciate them. This can only be done if you take your time in your preparation and in performance.

Slowing the delivery down is one of the ways you can achieve a conversational quality. The tendency, when confronted with difficult material, is to speed up, as if hoping to get it over as soon as possible. Speeding up usually works against you, since most pronunciation and articulation mistakes happen when you speak fast. Since there is usually a lot of material to convey, it's imperative that the target audience listens and understands you. You will make more sense to the viewers if you talk with them rather than to them. Bear in mind that the audience members not only understand the technical jargon but also talks it.

The best thing you can do for yourself to prepare to act in industrials and CD-ROMs is get into the habit of reading out loud. As I mentioned in the last chapter, you need to develop the ability to take any copy and read it aloud. The ability to read convincingly aloud is necessary to help you perform in this genre and it will aid you tremendously when you audition for this kind of job. This is true for difficult copy as well as working with a TelePrompTer.

At auditions you will be asked to read technical material full of unfamiliar terms specific to that specialty. Getting the copy beforehand and defining the terminology will help you immeasurably. Keep repeating the text until it sounds natural. Remember — you don't need to convince them that you're an expert in this field; you just need to appear to know what you're talking about. Keeping it conversational will do half of that work for you.

EXERCISES

- Spend thirty minutes a day reading out loud. Find a technical journal or legal document to read from (insurance policies are good). Look up any words that you don't understand, and if possible, break the text down by adding your own punctuation. If you need to, make copies so that you can write on the text itself. Read the text repeatedly and try to make it sound as conversational as possible.

- In a classroom situation, bring in a monologue that is technical in nature (keep it short). Exchange your monologue with another actor and prepare the copy as if for an audition. No one should use the monologue he or she brought in. Your objective is to make your copy sound as conversational as possible. Tape the monologue with each actor in a single shot addressing the camera. Play each tape back to see how conversational the audience believes the actor is being.

2. Find the appropriate aspect of your personality for the industrial/CD-ROM.

The gist of this principle is adaptation. Adaptation is the ability to conform to any situation. How many times have you been at an Italian restaurant, for instance, and found yourself unconsciously imitating the waiter's Italian accent? (Well, maybe that's just me.) The point is that human beings can, at various times, be silly, serious, infantile, mature, crazy, level-headed, or Italian — among many other things. Most people reveal only a small percentage of their complexity to the world at any given moment. In fact, we are taught that the best way to assimilate into society is to allow others to see only a few facets of who we really are. However, all of us have many sides to our personalities, and because actors are supposed to represent all humanity, it is especially important for actors to develop the different aspects of their personalities. Therefore, part of actor training is the process of overcoming some of the obstacles society imposes on us and learning to develop all our characteristics, whether they be brilliant or foolish. Think of a toolbox. An actor uses the facets of his personality like tools; in any given audition or performance situation, he can sift through his toolbox to find the right tool for that situation. Whether it's an industrial film for training purposes or an interactive game on CD-ROM, you need to find the appropriate tool(s) and bring that part of your personality to the industrial or CD-ROM.

One way to help you do this is to consider the interests of the producer or corporation that's making the industrial or CD-ROM. This is much like Principle 4 in the last chapter where you figure out the sponsor's objective in producing the commercial. To fulfill the sponsor's needs, you've got to have a good idea of what the sponsor wants. You also have to figure out how your character fits into the sponsor's objective. (There are two ways in which you can find out the objective for the industrial — either a representative of the company or your agent can tell you before you go to the audition, or you can ascertain it through reading the copy.)

Because characters in industrials and CD-ROMs are generally equivalent to corporate spokespeople, you need to bear in mind that you are representing the company that is producing it. It's like discovering the corporate side of your personality: the "corporate you." You need to find the tools in the toolbox that represent the corporate sides of your personality. At the audition behave as if you own the company that is sponsoring the industrial. If you have done your homework with the copy and are successful in making it conversational, then you should be able to walk into the audition and act as if you own the place. In the business of acting, being confident is 90 percent of a successful audition.

Let's say you are auditioning for an industrial film that is highlighting a corporation's recent year. You know it's going to be shown to the sales force as a year-end wrap-up and motivational pitch for the upcoming year. Suppose the company makes some kind of medical pulsation device and the copy consists of a spokesperson doing a twenty-minute monologue full of medical and financial references. (You can also usually tell from the copy if the character serves as a spokesperson for the corporation.) Besides looking up the words, you're going to want to use the tool that gets you in touch with the corporate side of your own personality. Pretend that you own the company; imagine how you might conduct yourself if you did. In your self-examination you should explore what it's like to have that kind of responsibility and determine what traits you possess that would help you bear that kind of responsibility. If done thoroughly, this process will result in the discovery of that side of your personality suitable to this situation.

On the other hand, if you were auditioning for an interactive game on a CD-ROM, you would have a different set of challenges and would need to use different sides of your personality. Imagine that you are trying out for the role of the leader of a worldwide espionage conglomerate, where the purpose of the game is for the players to receive instructions from you as they go about trying to solve mysteries. The audition copy might consist of different phrases the character might say in response to the player's actions. The references in the copy could include obscure international cities and cultures that you would need to know how to pronounce. Certainly, the tools that you would use in an audition for the CEO of a medical corporation would not be appropriate for this audition. You would need to choose the parts of your personality that would best fit this type of character. You would need to find the right tools to help you be the boss of a worldwide espionage conglomerate. You would also need to imagine what it would be like to play the game and, in so doing, discover the things about this character that would make the game more enjoyable.

EXERCISES

- In a group situation, try this adaptation improvisation. There should be two teams: One team is on camera and the other team is off camera. The team off camera comes up with at least a dozen characters that one might find in an industrial or a CD-ROM. In rapid-fire sequence, they shout out these characters to individual members of the team on camera. Each team member on camera has to quickly come up with a one- or two-word response to the character each has been given. The response, however, must be an assessment of a trait that they honestly feel they possess and one that would fit the character. For example: someone off camera says "architect" to a player on camera; the response might be "structured." Or an off-camera player might say "kiddy game-show host," and the response might be "gentle outrageousness." The point is that the response from the person on camera must be as honest and as rapid as she can possibly make it. It should be the first thing that comes into the player's head — it defeats the purpose to think about it too much. During playback, the off-camera group members must tell individuals from the on-camera team if they thought they were truly being honest. Make sure you switch groups so that both teams get a chance to be on camera.

- In a group, the actors should think up possible scenarios for industrials and CD-ROMs. (Use the ones I've given you above as examples.) Once everyone has come up with a number of them, actors conduct a mock casting session. Three or four members of the group act as the client(s) and casting director(s). Together they should determine what qualities each role should possess in each of the given scenarios. They can hold auditions with the remaining group or cast people in the group based on matching the physical qualities of both the characters and the actors. Tape the casting sessions and discuss why people were cast the way they were. The importance of this exercise it to let people see how other people perceive them based on their qualities.

3. Talk to the camera as if it were your best friend.

Now that you've broken the copy down, made it conversational, and have adapted your personality to it, you next need to personify the camera: You want to imagine the camera is a person. Personifying the camera will help you be more comfortable on camera. What better person to visualize than a good friend?

In industrials and CD-ROMs, much of the time you're required to be alone on camera looking directly into the lens. You've not only got a mouthful to say, but you're also being asked to portray a part of your personality that may not be natural. This is daunting, and it doesn't help if you come across stilted and uncomfortable. If you've done the hard work necessary to get the job, you now deserve to do it well. Imagining that you're delivering the copy to someone you know well should ease the burden of having to talk to a group of people that you might not feel comfortable addressing. Go ahead and pretend that your best friend is directly in the lens or on the other side of the camera.

For instance, if you were filming a CD-ROM where you were portraying a doctor leading a group of interns through a difficult procedure, you might be justified in thinking, "Hey, this isn't really me. What if they don't believe that I'm a doctor?" Sure, you look the part, you sound good, and you obviously convinced them at the audition, but you may still feel insecure about what you are doing or saying. If you visualize your best friend within the lens of the camera, you may feel more comfortable on camera. Because you're comfortable, you'll end up appearing more relaxed to your audience.

This tactic may also help keep you from taking the copy too seriously. The danger of overseriousness is especially important for auditions. One of the pitfalls of doing highly technical copy is assuming that people who talk this way are overly solemn. Corporations hire actors to do industrials because they want charming, animated people who can bring lightness to highly technical subject matter. Generally, this is true; actors can do this. Don't be the one to disappoint them. Make sure that, as you talk to your best friend about the "highs and lows of this year's widget sales," you keep a twinkle in your eye.

Try using this principle at your auditions. Imagine that your best friend is with you and that you are talking to him or her. If the copy is highly technical and you are supposed to be educating your audience, really try to deliver the material as if you were teaching your best friend something about the subject. If it's an interactive game or something more informal and fun, then imagine that you are having a good time playing with your best friend. Chances are that if you treat your audience as your best friend, some of that warmth and personality will translate across the lens and captivate your audience. When the effect becomes less of a lecture or instructional guide and more like a conversation between friends, then you know you've succeeded.

EXERCISES

- Using the same monologues that were used in the exercise for Principle 1, tape the actor addressing the camera. Shoot the actor in a single shot. For the first take have the actor literally place a good friend directly off to one side of the camera so that the actor is talking to that person. Immediately following the take, have the friend leave, then retape the actor repeating the same monologue. Before the playback, survey the other actors and ask if they saw any difference between the two shots. During the playback, notice the difference between the two. Discuss if there seemed to be a greater level of comfort between the first and the second take. Also, try to determine if during the second one, the actor was able to retain any of the informality that she achieved during the initial taping.

- Have a group of actors obtain some highly technical material. This can be legal documents, or as I said, insurance policies work well. The actors should prepare them as monologues and treat the whole exercise as if they were going to an audition. This time, not only should they imagine their best friends on the other side of the camera, they should also deliver the copy as if they were sharing a private joke or story with this person. It's important to avoid any sense of ridicule, however. The actor must walk a fine line; while the urge may exist to make fun of the copy with an imaginary friend, he has to avoid doing that. The actor has to genuinely appear as if he's enjoying himself while sharing something important with someone else. During the playback, have the audience try to determine if the actor was successful at it.

4. Take into account your body language.

In Principle 3, I noted that all your hard work will be meaningless if you come across awkward and uneasy. Just because you are being conversational, adapting to the situation, and imagining your best friend on the other side of the camera doesn't mean that you are taking care of the physical aspect of your job. Sometimes doing all those things will result in an effortless grace (and I hope that will happen), but it's still important to be aware of the message your body is sending to your audience. Never forget that everything you're feeling will manifest itself physically. This is especially true when you're on camera. So no matter how you are feeling, you've got to "check in" with how you are physically presenting yourself.

Let's face it, one reason actors are hired to do industrials and CD-ROMS is because they are often perceived as being more composed than other people under stressful conditions. (People tend to forget how much work goes into relaxation!) If this is the case, then you don't want to undermine everything you're saying by physically betraying it. Just as you need to choose the right facets of your personality for the situation, you also need to discover the best way to physically express the part. Let me give you a couple of examples.

Many actors don't know what to do with their hands. When

asked to portray someone who is mature, serious, and powerful — traits often associated with corporate spokesperson types — the actor invariably folds her arms as a gesture of superiority. Therefore, one of the most ubiquitous gestures is the "folded arms" look. In the actor's mind, this often kills two birds with one stone; it automatically takes care of the "hands problem," and it gives an appropriate physicalization for the character. Sure, at times it's OK to fold your arms, but you've got to be careful not to get locked into it. If you maintain any position for too long, the physical gesture draws too much attention, and the audience starts to wonder when the actor will change it. I'm sure you've seen this happen.

Another popular gesticulation is the "head shake." The head shake is a literal shaking of the head, as if saying no, no in slow motion. I'm sure you've seen it — the fervent emphasis of what the actor is saying accompanied by the equally emphatic side-to-side movement of the head. I often see student actors do this to physically underscore what they are verbalizing. The actual effect, however, is that the actor involuntarily negates her message by implying that she is either unsure of what she is saying or subconsciously she doesn't want to be there.

Many gesticulations are crutches. See if you can come up with some of the things you do that you shouldn't, like the head shake. You have to guard against these and other physical crutches. As well intentioned as they are, you should be wary of the mixed messages they send. You must be as vigilant with your character's physical objectives as you are with your character's personal desires. For this to happen, you have to develop physical awareness.

Actors can start to develop physical awareness by watching themselves and honestly assessing their physical language. In many ways this self-involvement feeds into the schizophrenic nature of acting. The brilliant actor George C. Scott once said something like, "What's tough about acting is that you not only have to be on stage completely focused on what you are doing, but you simultaneously also have to be the little old lady in the last row watching it." You can't get so wrapped up in your acting that you lose sight of its effect on your audience; you must always remember the technical responsibilities for how you appear and how you are heard.

The great thing about studying acting on camera is that you have a chance through playback to see the results. This can only be done, however, if you are able to objectively evaluate your work. You can develop self-evaluation skills while studying acting and seeing yourself on camera. If you are in a situation where you are able to experiment in class, use the time to candidly evaluate yourself and your classmates on the physical statements that you and they are making. When you watch the playback of each exercise, try to ascertain every physical choice. Ask yourself if what you are doing is the best physical statement that could be made for that moment.

As you prepare to go on an audition, evaluate your physical choices. Or, better yet, get an impartial observer to look at what you are doing and let you know if everything you present physically is harmonious with what you are saying. Believe me — directors and casting directors look for this kind of congruity during auditions.

EXERCISES

- If you still have the first exercise from Principle 3 on tape, you can use it for this exercise. If not, it's OK; use another exercise that already exists (preferably one from an industrial or CD-ROM). The point is to play back an exercise where the initial objective had nothing to do with the actor's physical choices. As you review the taped exercise, consider each actor's body language and discuss the believability of his or her physical choice in the given circumstances. Assess if the actor is sending a double message with her body and if her gestures are appropriate. If it is a class situation where everyone knows each other well, try and help one another become aware of individual physical choices. Many times a person's unique physicalization will help him get work, so I don't want you to change that. Instead, you need to assist each other to become aware of the messages your body is sending while you are doing this type of work.

- Make sure you have done the previous exercise before you do this one. Find new copy that's suitable for industrials and CD-ROMs. As you prepare your material, focus solely on your physical choices. Ask yourself these questions: Do I tend to be self-conscious about my body? Do I make choices because they're the most comfortable ones to make? Do I make choices based on my physical repertoire (ones that I make repeatedly), or are they character based? Do I tend to become too attached to a specific body position? And, most important, ask yourself if your choices are based on any kind of stereotypical idea of the character you are playing. The actors should be standing and taped in a full-body shot. During playback, discuss the validity of each actor's physical choices. Get into the habit of pointing out to each other when someone is falling back on old habits. Actors sometimes become too self-conscious to critique themselves honestly, especially while watching themselves on videotape. The group must strive to establish trusting relationships. By honestly analyzing the others, each member of the group will help him- or herself because his or her truthfulness will be reciprocated.

5. Always empathize with your audience.

Actors are supposed to represent humanity; to do this, they need to understand their subject material. The challenge when doing industrials and CD-ROMs is that it's not always easy to comprehend the people you are being asked to portray. You may feel that you have nothing in common with your potential audience. What they do for a living may seem remote to you. That's perfectly normal. But despite the fact that we are all different, many of us share the same wants and fears. Those bonds are common between all human beings, and the awareness of those bonds will ultimately enable you to be sympathetic with your audience regardless of what they do for a living. It's the same kind of sensitivity as laughing at a joke that you may think isn't funny, but others do. For example, I'm sure you've heard something like: "Why are wide receivers always depressed?" "Because they're always down and out." Now, you may think that's a stupid joke and not find it funny, but a group of wide receivers at a football convention might think it's hilarious. And if you're playing a wide receiver on an industrial or CD-ROM, you've got to empathize with those audience members and see the humor in the situation from their perspective. Even though you may not fully relate to your audience, you need to empathize with them as human beings.

Also keep in mind the basics — whatever excites you will excite most people, whatever bores you will bore most people, and so on. I think many actors make the mistake of thinking that they're different from other people. As a result, they tend to play up the most mundane characteristics about certain groups when they are auditioning for or acting in industrials and CD-ROMs. Just because you're auditioning for an accountant doesn't mean that you have to live up to some stereotypic idea that accountants are dull and boring. In fact, they might take more notice of you at the audition if you give the accountant a more vibrant personality. In other words, don't presume a stereotype about someone. When you do, you show your own limitations.

Follow your instincts, not the instincts of someone you are trying to be. If the character you are playing is completely foreign to you, you can't possibly try to behave as you might think they do. Keep in mind that your instincts are still viable. This is particularly true for auditions. Actors tend to have built-in reflexive gauges that make them play it too safe in an audition situation. They figure that, because so much is riding on it, they can't afford to make any mistakes. More than anyone, actors need to dispel the notion that playing it safe is good. Courageousness is not found in people who play it safe. It takes extraordinary courage to be an actor, and directors and casting directors are looking for actors who possess an abundance of courage. Bringing freshness to industrials and CD-ROMs calls for courage. Don't err on the side of sobriety. As cautious as you might want to be at the audition, play against that. If anything, try entertaining them at the audition with the material. Don't get me wrong — I'm not suggesting that you joke around with the subject matter (you never want to do that); but just because the material is extremely restrained doesn't mean that you have to be. It's also a good idea to put yourself in the shoes of your auditors.

EXERCISES

- This is an exercise for dispelling stereotypes. You're going to create characters by compiling random pieces of paper; therefore, *it's very important for this exercise that everything is individually written on separate pieces of paper.* In a group, everyone should write down *one* of each of the following *facts* about imaginary people (remember that each thing you write is on a separate piece of paper): occupation, neighborhood/city/state where they live, marital status, number of children (for example, one boy and one girl can be written on the same piece of paper). Everyone should then write down at least *two particulars* (again, on separate pieces of paper) such as: hobbies, likes, dislikes, specific attitudes, TV shows or books they like, or one adjective describing them. After everything has been written out, collect the pieces of paper, being sure to keep them in their individual groups — i.e., occupations together, hobbies together, and so on.

Each person in the group then picks one piece of paper from each of the "facts" category — occupation, and so forth — without looking. He or she then picks two pieces of paper from each of the "particulars" category — hobbies, and so on. After group members have all their pieces of paper, they should go off on their own, start creating this fictional person, and prepare an improvisational monologue.

Let the main points of the character that you have chosen be the main components of your monologue. You can embellish as needed, such as by naming the children. But try to build your story solely around what you know. The monologue itself should be no more than one or two minutes. After each person performs his piece, he will be asked questions by the rest of the group. Of course, during the questions he must remain in character. I recommend that you tape this exercise with one camera. During the playback, try to determine if anyone in the group played an obvious stereotype. By picking random pieces of paper, everyone was able to get a fairly diverse picture of who their character could be.

- Everyone should bring in material from either an industrial film or a CD-ROM. Pass the copy around. Each actor should not use the scripts that he or she brought in. Without breaking the copy down or memorizing it, actors should first formulate an idea about the types of characters they have received. Based on their idea of that character, the actors should then determine who the intended audience is of the industrial or CD-ROM. The actors should then improvise monologues in character about their audience. The copy should serve only as a springboard for the actors. This exercise is about how the actor perceives the intended audience. For example, if the copy calls for an accountant speaking to other accountants, the actor's monologue will be about his or her fellow accountants. If the copy is an interactive game meant for teenagers, the actor's monologue should be about the teenagers the game is meant to entertain. Tape the monologues; during the playback, try to assess how effectively each actor connected with his or her audience.

INDUSTRIAL FILM AND CD-ROM EXERCISES

For these exercises, I'm providing you with examples of two different kinds of copy used for industrial films and CD-ROMs. They are the typical spokesperson type and, to be quite honest, not very inspired. These are likely the least entertaining exercises in this book. However, it's best to start with the kind of material that you are going to find in a real audition. You need to get a feel for the sober corporate style that is often used for industrial films. I also urge you to provide copy for yourself so that you can simulate an interactive game on CD-ROM.

Use this copy to put all five principles into practice: break the copy down to make it conversational; adapt to the situation; personify and talk to the camera as if it were your best friend; pay attention to your body language; and make sure that you define who your audience is and put yourself in their shoes.

You should tape each exercise with one camera, and as a spokesperson, enact them addressing the lens. Also, because of their length, feel free to break the copy up and assign different actors different sections. As always, play the exercises back and discuss each actor's effectiveness in dealing with the principles. Good luck!

Copy 1: An Introduction to Teleconferencing

If the last century was known as the Information Age, then this century marks the immense impact technology makes on the way business is conducted. For example, the swift electronic storage, retrieval, and dissemination of information is already upon us.

Today's managers have learned to rely on the results of that technology, from word processing to sophisticated computer analysis. The proven technological breakthroughs of the Information Age make the job of managing easier, more competent, and more productive.

That's the big picture. Now, let's focus on a resourceful way to use technology — communications technology — to help preserve our valuable time, curtail unnecessary travel, speed up the decision-making process, and intensify your organization's productivity. What single tool can accomplish this and more? Teleconferencing.

Teleconferencing enables people at different locations — using specially equipped conference rooms — to conduct business meetings. Basically, a teleconference is an electronic hullabaloo; an Information Age meeting where the participants are no longer confined to one meeting room. It's simple. Teleconferencing makes doing business easier by moving *ideas* rather than *people*, whether domestically or even internationally with your overseas associates.

Teleconferencing can work for you in your home, office, or even while traveling on the road. It keeps you plugged into your organization's vital communications loop. You can stay in touch . . . wherever you go!

Teleconferencing has the features that benefit you. It brings together a variety of communications tools to allow you the greatest agility to do your job. It lets you conduct business meetings as usual, while offering three special benefits:

- More timely decisions

- More informed decisions

- Better use of time

Teleconferencing allows you to do your job more effectively. It gives you fast, expanded access to key people and data in your base organization at home and around the world. A teleconferenced meeting is easy to assemble. This puts every meeting within your reach *and* within your budget.

Decisions and actions don't have to be delayed until everyone can be actualized at one location; all the necessary information, trends, and analysis can be used since they are readily available.

Copy 2: Somewhere Vocational School

Somewhere Vocational School holds your opportunity to meet tomorrow's employment challenges. With a variety of two-year job preparatory course offerings, Somewhere is one of the largest vocational centers in Wisconsin, serving students from local area high schools.

Since 1966 when the Somewhere Vocational School was established, our motto has been "The Very Best." Over the years, the students, instructors, and staff members have given their very best in every endeavor. As a result, our instructors, equipment, students, and placement rate are among the very best in the state.

You can become one of "The Very Best" and meet tomorrow's employment challenges by selecting one of our job preparatory programs. We will show you each program and give you the opportunity to choose the one that best suits your interests and career goals.

Many of you will be interested in one of the two automobile related programs: Collision Repair and Auto Mechanics.

Collision Repair will teach you to repair and replace parts of an automobile that are damaged. This repair and replacement involves not only metal repair, but also refinishing, structural repair, fiberglass, plastics, and welding. Certification is made available during the second year by A.S.E., a volunteer national association endorsed by most major automobile manufacturers. You may also continue training after graduation at Somewhere Vocational School or Somewhere Auto School.

The Auto Mechanics program is designed for those seeking a rewarding career in the automotive field. Automotive services have changed dramatically in recent years. The auto mechanic must possess skills in servicing four-wheel alignment, fuel injection, digital instrument panels, computers, and automotive electronics. At Somewhere's Auto Mechanic's Program, you will receive both theory and practical experience that will prepare you for entry-level employment or further training at a postsecondary institution. The auto mechanic is a well-trained craftsman, and as such, receives excellent pay.

The Cosmetology program involves both classroom and hands-on training. You will learn to style hair, perform facials, manicures, special conditioning treatment, perm waving, chemical relaxing, hair color and bleach, plus chemistry. This experience will enable you to take the examinations given by the Wisconsin State Board of Cosmetic Art Examiners in the spring of your senior year to become a licensed cosmetologist.

In addition to skill-training activities, you will participate in field trips to local companies, club activities, student organizations, and skill contests. You may join organizations such as the Vocational Service Club of America, Future Business Leaders of America, and the Health and Organization Students Club of America to develop leadership skills. Many of you will also participate in district, state, and national skills competitions.

During your second year of training, you will be offered the opportunity to participate in the cooperative method of education. If you qualify, you will spend class time in local businesses and industries to receive on-the-job training. Valuable experience is gained through this method of education on a limited basis.

Upon completion of programs at Somewhere Vocational School, you are ready to pursue your career goals. You may choose to continue your education by enrolling in a two- or four-year college or university, or you may apply your vocational skills immediately by enlisting in the military.

Tomorrow holds many employment challenges. Let Somewhere Vocational School help you to meet those challenges today!

SUMMARY

Although you cannot categorize both industrials and CD-ROMs as one genre, they are similar. It's best to think of industrial films as short training, informational, and promotional corporate films; anything that is filmed or taped (either industrial films or anything else) can also be digitally translated to CD-ROM. For the purposes of this book, we cover the use of CD-ROMs only for interactive games or training films.

Both unions, SAG and AFTRA, have contracts that provide minimum pay rates for industrial films, interactive media, and any work done on the Internet. For both unions, the minimums are the same for both principals and background performers.

Auditions for industrials and CD-ROMs are almost identical to commercials. For the audition, however, the most important thing the actor should remember is the corporate nature of the genre. The actor must always take into account that her primary responsibility is to communicate information.

There are five principles to consider when auditioning and performing for industrials and CD-ROMs.

1. *Keep the copy conversational.* The best way to do this is to learn the pronunciation as well as the meaning of what you're saying. Breaking the copy down will also help.

2. *Find the appropriate aspect of your personality.* As you adapt to the situation that's called for, pretend that you are the owner of the company making the industrial or CD-ROM.

3. *Treat the camera as your best friend.* Imaginatively personify your best friend in the lens of the camera. Even with highly technical dialogue, try educating a close friend about your subject matter.

4. *Be conscious of your body language.* Learn to become aware of the physical message you are sending. It is as important as the verbal message.

5. *Always empathize with your audience.* Make sure that you put yourself in your audience's place.

CHAPTER 4
SITUATION COMEDY

Situation comedies are a distinctively American phenomenon, unique to our culture. Commonly known as *sitcoms*, they are thirty-minute television comedies that are videotaped or filmed in front of a live audience. Although contemporary, their roots go as far back as Aristophanes, commedia dell'arte, the English music hall, burlesque, and vaudeville. They also partake of other comedic genres: slapstick comedy, satiric comedy, black comedy, absurdist comedy, comedy of manners, sentimental comedy, and tragicomedy.

Being American by nature, they're synonymous with that most American pastime — television. Television gave birth to the sitcom, and that's where sitcoms still make their home. In fact, situation comedies have been a cultural force in this country for over fifty years! Some of the icons of modern American culture are sitcom characters. In fact, they just might be our most influential ambassadors to the rest of the world. (Probably a close second to our fast food.) It might be a frightening thought to some, but other cultures often study our sitcoms to learn about the way we do things here. In many ways, situation comedies have helped raise recent generations of Americans. Not only have they reared us, they have given us our styles of dress, mores, vocabulary, and much of our humor.

Up to this point, we have been focusing on commercials and industrials, both of which use a single camera. To begin the discussion on sitcoms, we have to look at the challenges of working with three or more cameras, which is the typical setup for a sitcom. In fact, sitcoms and soap operas are both taped or filmed with three or more cameras, and it's important to deal with those challenges. In this chapter, I discuss how to work with three cameras, as well as employment options and audition procedures.

For our discussion of television and film, I distinguish between what's filmed and what's videotaped. Some sitcoms and soap operas are taped, while episodic television and films are filmed. *Taped,* of course, refers to videotape, whereas *filmed* refers to film. For the most part, sitcoms are videotaped using three cameras. Some programs — "Ally McBeal," for example — are situation comedies but are filmed using one camera. There's even a new term today called *dramedy:* productions that are a cross between drama and situation comedy. These are filmed with one camera much like an episodic television program. In this chapter, I discuss only sitcoms that are taped with three cameras in a studio in front of a live audience. "Friends," "Frasier," and "Seinfeld" are some examples.

WHAT ARE THE DIFFERENT EMPLOYMENT CATEGORIES IN SITCOMS?

Sitcoms that are taped are covered by AFTRA and those that are filmed are covered by SAG. In this chapter, I will use the contracts covered by AFTRA as examples. AFTRA has two basic employment categories for sitcoms: principals and extras. Having lines of dialogue is the only criteria that separate these two categories: Principals have lines, extras don't. For principals, the employment options are synonymous with the categories of an actor's billing (billing is literally how someone is listed in the credits). From the smallest to the largest roles, an actor's employment scale (and billing) range from *featured* (a very small part with usually five lines or less) to *co-star* (still small but with over five lines of dialogue) to *guest star* (an important role in the episode that gets important billing), and *regular*. A regular on a sitcom is an actor under contract and considered a lead or a recurring character. (All the friends on "Friends," for example.) For obvious reasons, regulars have the most important billing. While the unions don't regulate the billing, it just so happens that billing and salaries are usually related.

Like all the other genres, agents or managers negotiate all billing and salaries. Since the union prohibits actors from receiving less than the minimum after paying an agent's commission, agents will always negotiate at least 10 percent above the minimum for their clients. The current AFTRA minimum for principal work on a thirty-minute sitcom is between $861 to $992 per week if you have more than five lines of dialogue. If the actor has under five lines, the minimum is $270 to $452 per week. AFTRA's minimum for doing extra work on a thirty-minute sitcom is $85 per day. Extras are normally hired for the day of taping, while principals are hired for the duration of the shoot (generally one week). This isn't a bad income. However, the *real* money is made when you have a contract as a regular on a series.

Because of these contracts, the regulars are in another ballpark altogether. They are usually guaranteed a salary per show based on a certain number of episodes per year. It can range from $10,000 to $250,000 or more per episode. One of the highest reported amounts ever negotiated was Kelsey Grammer's $1,000,000 per episode for "Frasier" — not bad for a week's work!

And, yes, like commercials, actors receive residuals for appearing on a sitcom — but only as principals. For a first prime-time network rerun, a principal can make up to 100 percent of their original salary. Residuals decrease over time depending on when it's on, where it's syndicated, and how many times it's shown.

HOW DO I AUDITION FOR A SITCOM?

Depending on whether an actor is being considered for a regular role, a guest star, co-star, or featured part, there are basically two different ways to audition for a situation comedy. The regulars or main characters are normally cast when the show is created (or as a replacement after the show has been running for a while). All the others are cast on a show-by-show basis during the season.

Being Cast as a Regular. First a sitcom is sold to a network: The producer and/or writer pitches the idea for a sitcom and the network buys it. Next, the network invests in a pilot. A pilot is a probationary episode. If the network likes the pilot, they pick it up and add it to the season. (Currently, the networks sometimes bypass the pilot and invest in what is essentially a ten- to fifteen-minute video presentation. This is not aired, but it is used as an audition. It ends up saving them a lot of money.)

When the network agrees to tape (or film) a pilot, the producers hire a casting director, who, in turn, sends out a breakdown of the roles to all the agents in town. As in commercials, all the agents in Los Angeles or New York (frequently both) submit pictures and résumés of the clients they feel are appropriate for the pilot. The casting process for the pilot is arduous. First, the casting director and the director must like the actor. Then the executive producer (the person responsible for the pilot and most likely the person who initially pitched it) makes the penultimate decision, but it is the network that always has the ultimate decision.

This is how it works. You first audition for the casting director. If the casting director knows and likes you, you can go straight to the callback. At the callback you generally read for the executive producer, the director, and the casting director. Sometimes other producers and writers attend the audition. Upwards of a dozen people can be at your audition. Because a regular character is so important, they can call you back as much as they want. They might also want to see you read with some of the other people they're considering to determine what kind of connection there might be between you and to see how well people match up physically, and so on. Unless they have already cast a star, they then choose two or three actors they like for every role and whom they would be happy casting in the pilot. Those actors then *go to network*.

Going to network is literally going to the corporate offices of the network and auditioning for all the brass. Because the network is basically paying all the bills, network executives have the final say. If they choose you, you're in. The interesting thing about going to network is that you have to sign a contract *before* you go — as if you'd already been cast. Everyone involved must understand the conditions that are binding in the contract before the final audition. The conditions may include your agreement to accept the role if you are cast, the duration of the contract, and, of course, how much money you are going to make. Going to network for a pilot (it works the same for both sitcoms and episodic television programs) might be the only time in your life where you have signed a contract and aren't guaranteed the job! Because so much is riding on these decisions (especially financially), this process can take weeks or months.

Being Cast as a Guest Star, Co-Star, or Featured Character. Being cast as a guest star, co-star, or featured character is somewhat simpler and less time-consuming. Once the show is being produced on a weekly basis, roles will be cast a few weeks before each episode is to start taping. Casting usually takes a week. Generally the same casting director who cast the pilot will be hired to cast the show on a permanent basis. The same process exists whereby the casting director sends out a breakdown to all the agents in town, and the agents, in turn, submit pictures and résumés of their clients. The first step, again, is to audition for the casting director (if he's not familiar with you), and if he likes you, to be called back. They will call back approximately five actors for each role, and they will see all five actors one at a time at the same audition. Like the casting for regulars, the casting director, the director of the episode, the executive producer(s) and, sometimes, the writing staff will all be in attendance. I have been called back for some sitcoms where there seemed to be a small army at the audition. (I sometimes felt that the writing staff was at callbacks to get a free tryout of their material.) This is the final audition for the weekly characters. The only difference between casting for the regulars and the other principals is that you don't have to go to the network for approval to cast guest stars, co-stars, and featured characters.

Different casting directors cast the extras. In fact, there are casting directors who are hired by producers and do nothing but cast extras (for all the genres). There are also agencies (like Central Casting in Los Angeles) that do nothing but cast extras for television and film companies. The difference between sitcoms and soaps is that soaps tend to have their own in-house casting directors.

A word of advice about auditioning for sitcoms (and for all of television). If you are called back, try to re-create the same audition that you did for the casting director (like commercials). I have a friend, a very funny and excellent actor, who auditioned for a casting director and was called back. Over the few days between his initial audition and the callback, he kept working on his audition and came to the callback with what he thought was a better audition. After coming out of the audition, the casting director followed him and vehemently proceeded to reprimand him for his audition. She said something like, "How dare you! What happened to the audition you did for me two days ago? I will *never* call you in again, and I will definitely talk to your agent about this." As you can imagine, my friend was devastated. He had only tried to do his best and improve on his original audition. The lesson here is that you will be called back based on what you did for your initial audition, so try to maintain that same performance at the callback. If the casting director gives you direction at your first audition, do it and continue it at the callback. At the callback, if the director or executive director wants to give you direction to help improve your audition or to see how well you handle direction, by all means do it.

Remember that auditions are about getting the job, not necessarily about being right. It's hard sometimes to go against your instincts in how a character should be played, but it's a business, and in business the people who pay the salaries have the final say. This business is not often kind. It is sometimes difficult to please people when you instinctively feel that a character might be better played another way. But you need to play the game their way, especially when you're new in the business. If you don't get a job (which will happen frequently), you need to prove that you are viable and should be given many chances in the future. Casting directors especially love it when actors make them look good, even if the actor doesn't get the job. So even when you don't get the job, it's still important to have the casting director think well of you and want to call you in again for future auditions. When you become indispensable, then you are able to call the shots. In this business, indispensability means becoming a financial force to reckon with. Until you become indispensable, keep proving how brilliant you are by making them look brilliant.

WHAT ARE THE DIFFERENCES BETWEEN FILM AND VIDEOTAPE?

Now that you have a basic idea of the audition process, let's deal with some of the technical things that you should be aware of after you get the job. Although not necessarily relevant to acting only for sitcoms, it is important for anyone interested in acting for the camera to understand some of the distinctions that are endemic to the different genres. What better place to start than the contrast between film and videotape?

To help you remember the dissimilarity between the two, here are some unique and interesting differences between film and video (and, most recently, digital). The chemical makeup of each is different: film is literally made with silver and videotape with rust. Film is shot with one camera, and video is shot using multiple cameras; film must be developed (just like your 35mm print film), while video has immediate playback (just like a home movie shot on a camcorder or a digital camera). These contrasts are important because — more than anything else — they reflect the financial difference between the two.

Film is more expensive than videotape, not even considering the costs incurred for developing and editing. Television that is shot with one camera and films have longer shooting days because of the innumerable setups required. (I talk more about this in chapter 6.) Videotaping requires expensive equipment in a booth, but this setup basically gives the director instantaneous editing capabilities by switching shots. *Switching* is the ability to immediately cut or dissolve from one camera shot to another.

However, many feel that the expense of film is justified because film images are much richer looking than videotape or digital pictures. In many ways film is more three-dimensional, while videotape (and digital) tends to be more two-dimensional. (In a conference I attended where the controversy between film and digital was discussed, an apt description of the difference between the two was that film is like taffy while digital is like cotton candy.) The implication of this, of course, is that film is more textured and refined than videotape or digital. I personally agree, but we are certainly moving to digital.

Another distinguishing characteristic worth noting between film (movies) and television (either film or video) is that film is intended for viewing on a big screen (in a movie theater) and productions filmed for television are meant to be watched on a small screen (your TV set). Because of this, films are made for public viewing and television is made for private viewing; films are made to be viewed in the dark and television is generally viewed in the light; and film is a story that is told in pictures while TV programs are stories that are told in words. Where the stage might be said to be the actor's medium, television is the writer's medium and film the director's and editor's medium. Whatever the differences, it is crucial that the actor understand the conditions of working within the medium.

AS AN ACTOR, WHAT DO I NEED TO KNOW ABOUT WORKING ON VIDEO WITH THREE CAMERAS?

Let's start with the prerequisites of working in the three-camera video-tape world of sitcoms. (This discussion also applies to soap operas.) The challenge for an actor is mostly knowing what shots the cameras are getting (what the cameras see) and where she needs to be so that she is in the shot. These cameras capture different shots. *Wide* or *long shots* get the broadest picture possible. If you think about it in terms of an actor's body, the wide shot usually contains the entire body. (See figure 1.) A *three-quarters* is intended as a wide shot that is slightly closer. Three-quarters refers to the body from the head to the knees (see figure 2). A *medium shot* is slightly closer than a three-quarters; it's a shot from the waist up (see figure 3). *Medium close-up* comprises the chest, shoulders, and head (see figure 4). A *close-up* usually refers to a shot of an actor's head (see figure 5), and an *extreme close-up* usually signifies a shot where less than the full face is shown. (see figure 6). Some of these are shot over the shoulder, which means that the shot is seen from over the shoulder of another character (see figure 7).

In a three-camera setup, the cameras are usually numbered 1, 2, and 3, moving from left to right as you look at the set. Camera 2, the center camera, is usually responsible for getting the *master shot*. A master shot is generally a wide shot intended as an establishing shot. It establishes where the scene is taking place by showing as much of the set as possible and as many of the characters as feasible. For example, if a scene calls for a husband and wife in a kitchen, the

Fig. 1 (left) The wide or long shot.

Fig. 2 (right) The three-quarters shot .

master shot will shoot as much of the kitchen as possible and the two people in it (see figure 8).

Camera 1 is responsible for shooting diagonally across the set to its right, or stage left (the actor's left). Camera 1 might be enlisted to shoot a three-quarters, medium close-up, close-up, or an extreme close-up shot of any character on the stage-left side of the set. Let's use the husband and wife as an example; as long as the wife is somewhere stage left, camera 1 would shoot her. Depending on the director's choice, it could be any of the shots listed above (see figure 8).

Camera 3 is responsible for shooting diagonally across the set to its left, or stage right (the actor's right). Camera 3 has the same shot options that camera 1 has. As long as the husband is on the right side of the set, camera 3 would shoot him (see figure 8).

Of course, these are only the typical shots used. There's no law prohibiting camera 1 from shooting a master shot or camera 2 getting a close-up of a character. For the most part where the characters are and what they're doing dictate how the director is going to shoot the scene. Ultimately, it is the director who is responsible for

Fig. 3 (far left) The medium shot

Fig. 4 (left) the medium close-up shot

Fig. 5 (below left) The close-up shot

Fig. 6 (below center) The extreme close-up shot

Fig. 7 (below right) Over the shoulder

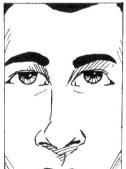

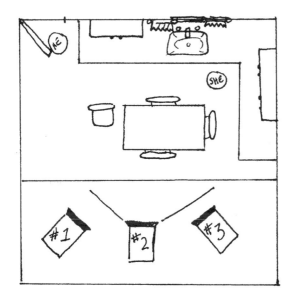

Fig. 8   A three-camera setup.

choosing what shots are to be used and when. They can certainly choose (and often do) to shoot things in an unconventional way.

Let's look at how a scene might be shot. Our scene takes place in the kitchen between a husband and wife. At the beginning of the scene the wife is on the phone. Here is the script:

Wife: *(On phone.)* I can't believe he said that. Marge, I'm so sorry. Wait till I tell his father.

Husband: *(Entering.)* Honey, I'm home.

Wife: *(To him.)* Hi, sweetie. *(Back on phone.)* I've gotta to go, I'll call you back. *(Hangs up.)*

Husband: *(Kisses her.)* Who was that?

Wife: Marge.

Husband: *(Putting down his briefcase and his coat on the back of the chair.)* How's Margie?

Wife: Not too good . . . She's really angry.

Husband: Why?

Wife: *(Pause.)* Well, her sister Janet is visiting, and Bobby was over there earlier today . . .

Husband: *Our* Bobby?

Wife: Yes, our son . . .

Husband: Uh, oh. What'd he do *this* time?

Wife: It's not what he did, it's what he said.

Husband: Uh oh. What'd he *say* this time?

Wife: Well, Janet is rather large . . . and Bobby asked Marge — *in front of Janet* — "Does she have to wear a 'caution, wide load' sign on her back?"

Take a look at figures 8, 9, and 10, which illustrate the set and camera positions for this scene. Follow along with the illustration of the storyboard of this scene as I take you through it. Although this example probably contains too much camera movement, it's fairly typical of the types of shots you'll see and it's certainly a good representation of what the director's script might look like. "Cut to" or "Dissolve to" indicates a switch of cameras that the director orders to be carried out, all of which takes place in the booth where the director has at least five monitors. She has one monitor per camera showing everything that each camera sees, a preview monitor that shows her the next scheduled image, and a monitor displaying the shot actually being taped. The director is in communication with each of the camera operators so that she can talk them through their list of shots and give them cues to prepare for their next ones. The cameramen line up their next picture when they know another camera's shot is the one being taped.

Fig. 9   Shot from camera 1.

Fig. 10   Shot from camera 3.

DO I NEED TO KNOW ABOUT
ALL THESE CAMERA SHOTS?

Yes. When I get to the discussion of a typical schedule and what to expect on the set, you'll notice that there's a lot of time spent on blocking (blocking is plotting out the movement patterns). There is blocking for actors and blocking for cameras; the actor working on camera needs to be aware of both his own blocking and the camera's blocking. The actor's movement is of utmost importance because the cameras' blocking cannot be done until the action of the actors has been set. But the actors also need to be conscious of blocking for two reasons: to hit their marks (the spot they need to be in) and accurate framing (their position within the shot). Kathleen Turner once said, "If you can hit your mark, bring every gesture within frame and give your voice emphasis when the shot needs it — if you can do all that without fail, then you get to act."

WHAT DO I NEED TO KNOW ABOUT
HITTING MARKS AND FRAMING?

It's imperative that an actor understands the technical nature of working on camera. Having this knowledge indicates an actor's professionalism and appreciation of what is required to work in the various media. Part of this knowledge is an awareness of the shot. If you know what the cameraman is seeing with his camera, you can better cooperate with the director and the cameraman by hitting your mark and staying in frame.

Spike marks are frequently used in theater and in film. A spike mark is a mark (usually a piece of colored tape) that indicates where things need to be. Furniture is spiked, props are spiked, and when working with a camera, actors are spiked. "Hitting your mark" is another way of saying "hitting your spike mark." It's important that actors are adept at hitting their marks because the director is often waiting for you to move in to a particular shot. Let me explain. Let's say that camera 2 is getting a master shot of a scene. An actor must cross over to a phone that's ringing. Well, the director will have either camera 1 or 3 in place waiting for the actor to answer it. Therefore, because the camera is already focused on the exact spot, the actor

Shot 1   *Camera 1 starts out on Wife in a medium shot.*

Wife: *(On phone.)* I can't believe he said that. Marge, I'm so sorry. Wait till I tell his father.

Shot 2   *Cut to camera 3 as it picks up Husband entering the door in a wide shot.*

Husband: *(Entering.)* Honey, I'm home.

Shot 3   *Cut to camera 1 on Wife in a close-up.*

Wife: *(To him.)* Hi, sweetie. *(Back on phone.)*

Shot 4   *Dissolve to camera 2 in a long master shot of Husband crossing to counter as Wife hangs up the phone.*

Wife: *(Continued.)* I've gotta go, I'll call you back. *(Hangs up.)*
Husband: *(Kisses her.)* Who was that?

Shot 5 *Cut to camera 1 of Wife in a close-up.*

Wife: Marge.

Shot 6 *Dissolve to camera 2 in a three-quarters master shot of both Husband and Wife.*

Husband: *(Putting down his briefcase and his coat on the back of the chair.)* How's Margie?

Shot 7 *Cut to camera 1 of Wife in a medium close-up over the shoulder of Husband.*

Wife: Not too good . . . She's really angry.

Shot 8 *Cut to camera 3 of Husband in a medium close-up over the shoulder of Wife.*

Husband: Why?

Shot 9 *Cut to camera 1 of Wife during pause in a close-up.*

Shot 10 *Cut to camera 3 of Husband's reaction during pause waiting for his wife to answer in a close-up.*

Shot 11 *Cut to camera 2 of Wife and Husband in a medium master shot.*

Wife: *(Pause.)* Well, her sister Janet is visiting, and Bobby was over there earlier today . . .

Shot 12 *Cut to camera 3 of Husband in a medium shot over the shoulder of Wife.*

Husband: *Our* Bobby?

Shot 13 *Cut to camera 1 of Wife in a medium shot over the shoulder of Husband.*

Wife: Yes, our son . . .

Shot 14 *Cut to camera 3 of Husband in a close-up.*

Husband: Uh, oh. What'd he do *this* time?

Shot 15 *Cut to camera 1 of Wife in a close-up.*

Wife: It's not what he did, it's what he said.

Shot 16 *Cut to camera 2 of Husband and Wife in a medium master shot.*

Husband: Uh, oh. What'd he *say* this time?

Shot 17 *camera 2 starts to zoom in slowly from medium master shot.*

Wife: Well, Janet is rather large . . . and Bobby asked Marge — *in front of Janet —*

Shot 18 *Cut to camera 1 of Wife in a close-up.*

Wife: *(Continued.)* "Does she have to wear a 'caution, wide load' sign on her back?"

Shot 19 *Cut to camera 3 of Husband's reaction in a close-up.*

Shot 20 *Dissolve to camera 2 of Husband and Wife in a medium shot and fade to a commercial.*

must make sure she hits the exact spike mark so that she's in focus when she crosses into the shot. Spike marks can vary depending on the genre, but right now I'll concentrate on how to work with spike marks when dealing with three cameras — as in sitcoms and soaps.

Let's use the same scene with the wife and the husband from before. In the very first shot, the wife needs to be in a specific spot for her phone conversation. The actress can take as her mark a spot on the counter where she is standing; this is pretty easy. It starts to get complicated when the husband arrives. Since camera 3 is picking him up as he enters, the husband needs to arrive at a precise spot in the doorway. This spot would be spiked with a piece of tape (usually a *T*, which indicates that you place the feet on either side of the vertical line, or else an *X*). If there's a lot of movement that needs to be spiked, each character will have his or her own color tape. (For example, the husband might be red, the wife blue, and so on.) The actor playing the husband cannot look at the tape mark on the floor when he enters, yet he needs to be aware of its exact location. This actor also needs to worry about hitting his mark when he crosses to the counter and puts down his briefcase and coat. He must end up in an exact spot at the counter. There could be a piece of tape there, or the actor could feel his mark by having his leg brush up against part of the stool on the stage-right side of the counter. It takes a lot of time getting used to hitting marks. In this case, both actors playing these roles would need to spend a lot of time on the set rehearsing with their marks.

Actors deal with hitting their marks in different ways; it is actually something of a science. One thing is certain: Actors are expected to be proficient at it when they are on a set. Some actors mentally count out the steps needed before they reach the mark. Others line up sight-line objects with their mark. For instance, the actor playing the husband may reach his mark by aligning his line of vision with a fixed piece of lighting equipment that's off camera. At that point, he knows he has reached the tape or spike mark on the floor. Some actors rehearse walking forward and backward between marks so that they can program it into their bodies. Others will find a justification for looking down when they know they're near the mark. You want to be careful of this, however. If you watch sitcoms closely, sometimes you'll notice actors looking for their mark on the floor.

Everyone adopts his or her own unique strategy for mastering this science. But whatever you choose, it has to be done. If you are working on camera in class, treat it as an exercise. Find scenes or write your own brief scene. Block the movement of the actors, as well as the shots for the cameras. If you're lucky enough to be dealing with a three-camera setup, block the shots as I have done for the hypothetical kitchen scene. (If you're only working with one camera, treat the entire scene as if it were a master shot.) Make sure to tape out spike marks that the actors have to get to during the course of the scene. I recommend that you experiment with all these different ways until you feel comfortable with finding your spike mark. Don't expect it to come easy. You need to work hard at it and practice, practice, practice until it becomes second nature. Repetition is the surest method of mastering finding your mark.

Now that you're an expert in hitting your mark, let's make sure you're in frame. *Framing* is a technical term for compositionally centering the shot. Much like taking a photograph with a camera, you don't want to cut someone's head off. Cameramen pride themselves on getting a well-framed shot. This usually means perfectly centering the focal point of the shot (usually the actor) in the frame. The best example I can think of is "The Late Show with David Letterman." If you watch carefully, whenever Dave is alone at his desk he is perfectly centered in the shot. When he makes a full arm gesture, the camera almost imperceptibly widens to keep his entire body centered in the shot. Watch it; it's wonderful how perfectly he's framed. What's even more impressive is that the camera operator is spontaneously doing it. Dave doesn't need to concern himself with staying in frame. But he always knows what camera he's on. He also knows he can't make too drastic a move otherwise the cameraman might not be able to widen fast enough to keep him in the frame.

An actor needs to know when she is on camera and what kind of shot it is. In a three-camera setup, each camera has a red light; when the red light is on, that camera is the one doing the taping. Actors must peripherally watch these lights. It would be inappropriate to start talking if the camera hasn't switched to you yet.

It would also be inappropriate to act as if the person you were talking to were far away if you're in a close-up. During camera blocking, the actor should know when the shots are scheduled and what kinds of shots are being used. An actor onstage instinctively knows he must face in the general direction of audience members or they won't see him. The actor has to be aware of the same thing on camera; brilliant acting is not going to mean anything if the audience doesn't see it, or if it doesn't fit the scale of the shot. The actor also needs to keep in mind that an abrupt movement can ruin a shot. Unless the cameramen or the director is prepared for it, a quick move will probably go out of frame.

Let's use our wife/husband scene again as an example. The wife in the first shot should know that she's on camera 1 and that it's a medium shot. She should also know that in a medium shot she is visible from the waist up. She knows she has some leeway in her movement. (A rule of thumb is the wider the shot the freer you are to move; the closer the shot, the less room you have to move.) Obviously, she can't turn her head suddenly to her left because she would then be turning her back on camera 1. When the husband enters, he should know that he's in a wide shot, and as long as he's on his mark, he doesn't need to overly concern himself with his framing. The wife, meanwhile, has to understand that her line to her husband ("Hi, sweetie") is a close-up. All she needs to do to is turn and look at her husband; camera 1 should be able to catch her as she turns. I won't take you through every shot, but I suggest that you examine the scene and talk yourself through the framing. Keep in mind that the closer the shot, the more specific you have to be in your movement.

Finally, the actor must always respect the *angle* of the shot. It's not enough to know what camera *you're* on; you must also appreciate the camera your partner is on. On the wife's line, "Not too good . . . She's really angry," the shot is *Cut to camera 1 of Wife in a medium close-up over the shoulder of Husband*. The husband must be aware that the shot is coming from behind him on camera 1 and that it's over his right shoulder; therefore, he cannot scratch his right ear because then he would interfere with camera 1's shot. He also can't be busy with his coat and briefcase. He should know when the shot changes so that he can stay out of its way. Think of it as upstaging. You don't want to do anything that's going to upstage someone else who is supposed to be the focal point.

Picture an imaginary lane from the camera to what the camera is shooting. This is the camera's eye line. You must not interfere with that eye line unless directed to do so. This is why it's important to heed the blocking. As you incorporate the earlier exercises on hitting your marks, also investigate framing. Experiment with what movement works and what doesn't work within different types of shots.

Practice shooting over-the-shoulder shots and close-ups with two people. Observe the limitations imposed by the camera's eye line and how much room you have to maneuver in those situations.

You never want to "strike the lens." Striking the lens is accidentally looking into the lens of the camera. Unless you are directed to look directly into the lens (which of course you want to do in commercials), *never* make eye contact with the camera lens. This may sound simple, but even the most seasoned professional will sometimes make that mistake. The most tempting moment is when you are looking from one side of the shot to another. There's always the threat of making the briefest contact with the camera that is in your eye line as you sweep across. Try not to do it. When you review videotaped scenes or exercises from this book, it will always be obvious when you see yourself or someone else, even fleetingly, strike the lens. If you see yourself do it often enough, you'll stop.

WHAT IS A TYPICAL SITCOM SCHEDULE LIKE, AND WHAT CAN I EXPECT ON THE SET?

Now that you've got a basic foundation of some of the technical considerations when working in a three-camera setup, let's get back to dealing specifically with situation comedies.

The majority of situation comedies are taped in Los Angeles on a soundstage in front of a live audience. Lined up on one side of the stage are the various sets for the episode. On the other side of the stage are bleachers for the audience (see figure 11). Normally the episodes take place in the same locations (a character's apartment, place of business, etc.) week after week, so the sets live (stay there permanently) on the soundstage. Like soaps, sitcoms are similar to plays, that is, they are first rehearsed and then performed. (Not always the norm in television and film.) Whereas soaps are daily minitheatrical events, sitcoms are scheduled very much like summer stock productions. Every week there's a new show.

The typical sitcom tapes an entire episode over a five-day period. The schedule is comparable to a five-day work week, Monday through Friday, nine to five. There are variations, but for our purposes let's use Monday through Friday.

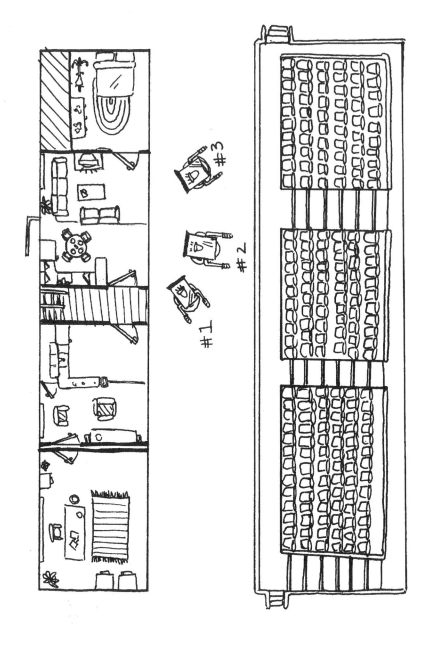

Fig. 11. Overhead view of sitcom soundstage in front of a live audience.

The first thing that happens on Monday morning is a "table reading." Much like the first rehearsal for a play, the sitcom starts out with a read-through of the script. Everyone is called in on Monday at 9:00 AM for the first rehearsal. The director and the cast sit around a large table (usually on the set), and perhaps after some introductory remarks by the director or the executive producer, everyone reads that week's script for the first time. At this rehearsal, it's common for the entire staff of the series to be present, including the writers, designers, and even some network representatives. Generally, the only people *not* there are the crew, the cameramen, and the various technical support staff. (They'll be there soon enough.)

The read-through gives everyone a chance to hear the script for the first time, read by the actors who will be playing the roles. Based on the reactions to the reading by everyone present, the writing staff leaves and possibly makes some changes. It's worth remembering that the actors can receive changes to the script throughout the entire week. The read-through itself can last until the lunch break.

After lunch, there might be another read-through, or the director will start blocking. Because sitcoms are taped on the same soundstage during the entire season, blocking rehearsals take place on the sets. At this early blocking stage, the director will give the actors explicit blocking for each scene. He generally blocks the show in order, from the first scene to the last. Many times the director is amenable to ideas from the actors about movement, business (actors' activity), and so on. During this early blocking rehearsal, nothing is written in stone, but at some point the director and the actors will have to set the blocking before the camera crews arrive. These rehearsals can take one and a half to two days of work. They're not merely about blocking; they can become more advanced rehearsals, analyzing relationships and working on characters — not to mention trying to incorporate changes to the script that are happening daily.

On Wednesday, the tone of the rehearsal changes. It's at this point that the technical crew arrives. Like technical rehearsals in the theater, the actors who have had their own rehearsals in private must now give way to the technicians: It's their turn to rehearse. After talking the cameramen through the various shots, the director conducts a camera-blocking rehearsal. Much like the blocking rehearsal for the actors, the cameramen get to set their shots knowing when the actors are moving and where they are going. The lighting and sound crews will also be adding their elements at this point. By this time the director leaves the stage floor and manages the show from the booth.

Thursday's rehearsals are the equivalent to technical run-throughs and dress rehearsals. All the elements have been added by this point — the camera shots, the lights, the sound, and the costumes. The production starts to look like a television show. The director will give the actors notes after each run-through. It's important to note that throughout the week, actors' rehearsal calls may be flexible (much like a play's rehearsal schedule). After the table reading, actors may only be called for rehearsal when they are needed. Of course, every sitcom is different and not all of them adhere to the same policies; the producers have every right to call the principals to every rehearsal if they want because they are paying them. By Thursday, however, the entire cast will probably be needed for the entire day.

Friday is tape day. It's usually a long day. This is when the extras are commonly brought in to work, so there may be a rehearsal in the morning to block in the extras, and then more technical run-throughs. This may last until late in the afternoon. Because of the long day, the actors and the crew are fed dinner. Early in the evening (5:00 or 6:00 PM) an audience is brought in to the soundstage to watch a taping. The process can be slow — more than one take may be taped, there may be technical errors, the actors may forget their lines, and so on. Therefore, stand-up comedians entertain the audience before and between shots. Before each taping the regulars are also introduced to the audience. The show is then taped in order of the script. The audience is guided when to laugh and to applaud by the stand-up comic and signs that hang above the audience. (On some shows the director augments the laughter by adding a laugh-track sound cue.) For a thirty-minute episode, the taping can last an hour or longer. After the taping, the audience leaves, and the actors and crew take a break.

During the break, another audience is brought in, and the process is repeated almost verbatim. It's after this taping that the actors and the crew are finished and the week is over. What the television audience ends up seeing at home on television is, more or less, the best takes of each performance. It is very likely that a scene worked better in one taping than in another: the audience found a joke funnier and the actors were more relaxed or confident. Whatever the reason, because of the cost and the importance to the network (in network television, if a show fails, it's cancellation), there's a lot riding on making sure that the final product is good.

Your behavior as a professional actor will help make that happen. Unless the show is a megahit, there is a lot at stake. You don't want to be the one that keeps anyone waiting, or be the one not doing his or her job. (Of course, people don't behave less professionally when the show is a megahit; in fact, they act more professionally and there's usually more confidence on the set.) You are hired to do a job. This means that you have to be punctual and prepared for each day's work. I recommend that you get to know the assistant director (in sitcoms this person is equivalent to a stage manager in the theater). If you have a schedule problem (an audition, for instance), go to the assistant director with your concerns — *not* the director.

PRINCIPLES OF SITUATION COMEDIES

Let's turn to some principles for you to contemplate. Now that you have some idea about the genre, think about and use these six principles as a way to explore your process for auditioning and acting in sitcoms. Experiment with the exercises that appear at the end of each principle, and by all means, devise your own!

1. Always look for and play the comedy and poignancy through the situation.

The term *situation comedy* not only inextricably links these two words together, but it also conjures up images of a specific type of comedy. We take for granted what we think situation comedy means. You'd think that it should be obvious for an actor to look for the comedy in the situation. This principle may be obvious, but you'd be surprised how often people look for comedy in all the wrong places. The mistake many actors make when cast in a comedy is to be, what I call, self-involved; they try too hard to be funny. It's as if they think humor for its own sake is entertaining. How often have you found someone boring who was trying too hard to be amusing? The result of this is a performance that is imprecise because the actor invariably makes random choices trying to do anything that will get them a laugh. For an actor, it might be best to begin by studying and defining the words *situation* and *comedy*.

A *situation* is many things. It is certainly a place, but it's also a job, status, a circumstance, a moment, or a state of affairs. In a sitcom, it can be any or all these definitions. The first thing you need to do when approaching the comic possibility of a sitcom is to *define* the situation. The situation is where you'll ultimately find the comedy. One of the greatest moments in the history of sitcoms was in the classic episode of "I Love Lucy" when Lucy and Ethyl got jobs on the chocolate candy–wrapping assembly line. I won't summarize it in depth because my description would never be able to do it justice; hopefully, you've all seen it. (If you haven't, go out and rent it ASAP, or watch reruns.) What Lucy and Ethyl thought was going to be an effortless job turned into an absolutely outrageous fiasco when the conveyer belt that brought them the chocolates went out of control. What was hilarious was the *situation* they were in. Being funny was the last thing on their minds; they were trying to get out of there alive. It's funny because they played the situation — the comedy was the result.

Comedy can elicit smiles and laughter. It implies ludicrousness, farce, and happy endings. But it can do more. To me it also intimates a certain degree of seriousness. There can be a very fine line between comedy and tragedy; often they are intermingled. In the above example of Lucy and Ethyl on the assembly line, it could have ended tragically (depending yet again on that beguiling word *situation*). Part of the reason it didn't was the circumstance of the moment. If we thought that Lucy and Ethyl were in real jeopardy, it wouldn't have been funny. A good way to define comedy might be to say that it's the light side of tragedy. What true comedy is *not,* however, is self-involved and imprecise.

Poignancy in comedy is certainly a by-product of flirting with tragedy and coming away from it unharmed. Sitcoms not only make us laugh but they also touch us and move us. Some of the best sitcoms celebrate the imperfections of life by letting us laugh at moments that we might otherwise find sad. But as an actor, your goal cannot merely be to move an audience or to make them laugh or cry. The comedy and poignancy is a result of the actor thoroughly playing the situation. In "The Honeymooners," the outward circumstances were fairly depressing — in a tiny New York apartment a bus driver, a sewer man, and their wives try to make ends meet. If it weren't for the genius of Jackie Gleason and a brilliant cast always finding the comedy and poignancy of the situation, the show might've been a tragedy.

When auditioning for a sitcom, read the script (or the sides) and focus on the situation — *not* the jokes. Remember that the situation is not just where the characters are. It can also be the state of affairs between the characters, including what has happened before this moment; it can be the juxtaposition of the characters to a place; or it can be the status of the characters. Think of it as cause and effect. The situation is the cause and the comedy and poignancy are the effects. If you pay attention to the cause, the effect will come naturally; never play the jokes. If you honestly play the situation, the laughs will come.

EXERCISES

- As you watch sitcoms, see if you can summarize the situations of each one. In a group, discuss what you thought was funny and how much of it had to do with the actors playing their situation.

- In a class, have everyone write down situations for two people. (Experiment with different ideas of what constitutes a situation.) You should include a relationship for the two people, but let the situation be the governing factor. For example, a son and father unexpectedly meet in the porno section of their local newsstand; two archrival beauty queens meet waiting in line for the ladies' room. Create an improvisation based on the *situation* and see where it goes. Remember not to make it humorous for its own sake. Tape it, play it back, and discuss it.

2. Pay attention to the inherent rhythm in every situation comedy.

Rhythm can be defined as the characteristic flow, pace, or even *feel* of the sitcom. Rhythm is the individual fingerprint of the production. Perhaps it's best to describe it as the individual tempo of the show. Whether it's "Friends," "Seinfeld," or "The Beverly Hillbillies," every situation comedy has its own personal, distinct rhythm. Many times you have to watch the show repeatedly to learn what that rhythm is, but they all have one. Many factors go into this — the cast, the writer (or group of writers), the director, the production values, and so forth. Each one is different. You need to detect what the rhythm is for each sitcom that you audition for and act in.

You can be sure that all comedy has its own definite rhythm. In many ways comedy is a science. If scientific tenets are founded on experimentation, then so are the tenets of comedy. Comedians perfect their craft by studying and experimenting with their material; they work very hard on writing funny jokes, but they work just as hard or harder on their delivery. Often, it's more important *how* something is being said than what is being said.

Ask any comic and he'll tell you that comedy is timing. Certainly timing is involved in telling a joke and delivering a punch line. Some sitcoms employ this joke/punch-line style. Others, however, couldn't be more different. Some sitcoms are funny because they try very hard not to be funny; many are funny because the situations and characters are so unlike what any of us are used to seeing; some are loose and some are glib. What most of them generally have in common, though, is that they are fast-paced.

Comedy is not slow. Certainly, one of the differences between sitcoms and soap operas is speed. You can take your time on soaps, but not on sitcoms. You can't drag out comedy; it doesn't work well when it's slow or when there are long pauses between lines. Most sitcoms share the quality of being active. Activity breeds speed, and most sitcoms are rapid in their unique ways. I should clarify that *speed* is not necessarily the only way to describe situation comedies. *Specific* might be another word. Like an arrow being shot, it doesn't matter how fast the arrow is traveling — as long as it has a specific trajectory, it will hit its mark. Sitcoms tend to be specific in their dialogue, timing, and characterizations. Certainly, some sitcoms are quick, and others aren't. If they're not fast, you can be assured that they are very specific.

When analyzing rhythm, look for places where the tempo changes in the dialogue. Look for ways the show or the script incorporates these kinds of changes. An oft-used device for comic effect is the abrupt stop: Someone races along with her dialogue then comes to an abrupt stop and makes a sudden change. I'll illustrate with a character who is panicking because she thinks she has misplaced her glasses and is screaming, "Ohmygodwherecouldlhaveleftthem? What amIgoingtodo? I'mjustthebiggest . . . *(Pause.)* They're on top of my head . . . I could die." The moment she discovers her glasses on top of her head and skids to a halt is obviously the tempo change, but it's important to know that the tempo change is a transition. You generally get a laugh in transitions. (This example also illustrates comedy arising out of the situation.) Of course, the script is not going to be written like that; the actress must make that choice for herself. My point is that transitions are a way to determine rhythm.

So learn to detect the specific comic rhythm of the sitcom that you're auditioning for. Obviously, if it's a sitcom that's running, make sure you watch it. When you're studying the audition material, make sure you take out all unnecessary pauses. Keep the dialogue fast (and/or specific) and pay attention to transitions. One thing you don't want to show overtly at the audition, though, is your technical agility in playing transitions. Actors are supposed to represent humankind, and they have to be transparent about it. None of us think consciously about the glorious transitions we're making; we just do them naturally and realistically. Only Robin Williams can make the kind of lightning-fast transitions that has become part of his inimitable style. You don't have to be like him; find your own way of making transitions. Don't try to wow the casting director by showing off your incredible talent at making transitions; just make sure they are realistic. Remember that comedy is best when it's not self-involved.

EXERCISES

- Two people start improvising a scene. The scene contains twenty-six lines. Each line must begin with the next sequential line of the alphabet. (There is no need necessarily to start with the letter A; you could start with V.) Tape the scene, keeping in mind the need to maintain speed. Try not to let there be any pauses between the lines. Play it back and discuss it. Did the partners create a distinct rhythm for the scene?

- This improvisation is called TV Remote Control. Decide on a real sitcom that everyone is familiar with. Begin an improvisation trying to recreate and emulate the rhythm of the sitcom. As the scene is played, an offstage (or off-camera) voice "changes the channel." The improvisers momentarily freeze and then start a fictionalized sitcom with a new rhythm based on their physical positions. This scene is played for a while before the offstage (or off camera) voice "changes the channel." Again, the improvisers freeze and then start yet a new fictional sitcom with a new rhythm based on their physical positions. After this scene develops, the offstage (or off-camera) voice indiscriminately "changes the channel" at will. At this point, the improvisers must rotate between each of the three sitcoms. The purpose of the improvisation is to develop three defined rhythms and be able to switch from one to the other. Tape it and feel free to let other members of the class jump in and out of the improv at will. Play it back and discuss it.

3. Don't be afraid to make bold choices.

Not only is rhythm important in comedy, but so is boldness and energy. You can get away with outrageousness on a sitcom in a way that you can't with almost any other genre on television or in film. Not only that, comedy demands energy. Comedy hails from a larger-than-life physical ancestry: Jesters, lazzi (slapstick antics), and pratfalls are not subtle. Commedia dell'arte was aggressive in its stylistic approach, and so are sitcoms.

Let this principle liberate you. When it comes to acting on camera, actors often play it too safe. They have been told, rightfully, to keep their choices small. I will be the first to tell you to keep your choices precise when it comes to acting for the camera. In sitcoms, however, *if the situation warrants it,* go for it. But you shouldn't make bold choices just for the sake of making bold choices. The choices must be justified by the circumstance of the situation or the character.

In chapter 2, I urged you to make positive choices. In sitcoms I urge you to make bold choices. In acting for the camera, commercials and sitcoms may be the only genres in which you can make big choices in an audition. In a sitcom audition, it is better to overdo it than underdo it. The director or producers may request that you adjust your choices downward to be less bold. They may ask you to "Do less" or "Bring it down," but they're sometimes more forgiving toward the overly large choice. In auditions for film, episodic television, or soap operas, they will be less inclined to be so. They will usually say "Thank you," and send you on your way.

EXERCISES

- Tape the following improvisation, focusing on being as outrageous and bold as you can. It's called Alien Honeymoon. A hotel manager shows a newlywed couple into their bridal suite and then leaves. After looking around, the couple grab imaginary knives and "cut" their bodies open. Two other creatures emerge, moving around the room and interacting with each other. When they hear a knock on the door, the creatures panic and climb back into their old bodies — in a hurry, they put them on wrong, or put on each other's bodies, and so on. The hotel manager enters, says, "I know what you've been doing." He then proceeds to cut himself open in the same manner, and so forth. Play it back and discuss it. Were you self-conscious about your choices? How did it look on tape?

- This improvisation is called The Blank Family. A group of four people are a typical sitcom family (father, mother, son, and daughter). An audience member gives them an adjective that might best describe the family. The family then has to enact an improvisation using its interpretation of the given adjective. For example, if the adjective is *stingy,* then the four actors must improv a scene where they are all stingy. Tape the improv and try to make the choices as bold as possible. Try not to make all the characters carbon copies of each other. Play it back and discuss it.

4. Use your charming personality, but remember that you are playing a character.

This principle differentiates commercials and industrials from sitcoms. In commercials and industrials you are basically yourself. In situation comedies, you draw on elements of your personality, but now you're playing a character.

But what exactly is a character? Is the character merely an extension of the actor's self, or does an actor *become* a character? It is my belief that all great acting has to evolve from the self. Actors cannot "become" someone else; if they did, acting would then be a form of mental illness. Actors become different parts of themselves. They explore different parts of their personalities to tap into the necessary traits of the characters they are asked to play. And we all have many different parts to our personalities.

The challenge in actor training, of course, is to get people to explore themselves completely so that they can realize the full potential of their personalities. We all have the capability to do this. Children are natural actors. They are allowed (and expected) to play make-believe. However, most of us lose this capacity when we become adults. Once we reach adolescence, parents, teachers, older siblings, religious figures, and anyone else who has influence over us inform us how we are supposed to behave. We accept what these people say because we want to belong. We're afraid that if we don't conform to what's expected, we'll be ostracized; we become afraid of rejection. We stop exploring different parts of our personalities and instead opt to fill a traditional role in society. So learning to act is, in many ways, a journey back to childhood.

Sitcoms are a good place to begin to combine self and character. Your character must contain the charming and eccentric parts of your own personality. Leave the dark mysterious parts of your personality at home (where they can rehearse for soap operas). The makers of sitcoms and the audience are not interested in your depressed state unless it's funny. Concentrate on what makes you charming. What do other people find charming about you? Or, better yet, discover the charming qualities in other people and discover if you share any of those qualities.

Eccentric people live in a world of their own, with their own methods and priorities. They're fascinating *because* of this. If you opt for eccentricity (which is abundant in sitcoms) make sure it's not the kind of eccentricity that scares people. The eccentric character has to be likeable and, above all, well intentioned.

Most important, characters on sitcoms are people we as an audience want to spend time with. Whether it's acerbic military doctors on "M.A.S.H." or a self-involved waitress on "Cheers," on some level we like these people and want to spend time with them. Quite simply, audiences tune in to these shows because they value the time they spend with these characters. We tend to laugh when we feel comfortable with and enjoy the company we're around. Keep this in mind when you are thinking about a character for a sitcom.

When you're auditioning for a sitcom, don't take the character too seriously. Look for ways to be agreeably eccentric and enjoyable.

One of the best ways to do this in an audition situation is to be honestly interested in the person (or people) who are auditioning you. Actors tend to be very self-involved. There is good reason for this, but imagine being a casting director seeing dozens of actors who all end up talking about themselves! Now imagine an actor who comes in and seems genuinely interested in the casting director. This is certainly a way to be attractive. But don't confuse this with going into the audition and wanting to do nothing but talk about the casting director. (He might think you're strange if your response to the question, "How are you?" is "Let's not go there; what's really important at this moment is how are *you*?") But if you genuinely engage the casting director, you just might score points.

Don't forget that, while you want to be charming, you are, in fact, playing a character. If you've thought about the character and made choices about how you're going to play the character, it will show at the audition. The bottom line is the character's objectives. Those objectives and the way you play them need to be so appealing that the people at the audition will want to spend time with you.

EXERCISES

- Watch your favorite sitcoms and determine what makes the characters likeable. Make a list of the characters' specific traits that make you laugh. Try to determine what makes them appealing, or eccentric, and why you like spending time with them.

- In a group of people you know well, have everyone identify the charming and eccentric characteristics of each person in that group. It may open your eyes to how you are perceived and what people determine to be the engaging parts of your personality.

- Along the same lines of the previous exercise, play the game "If this person were a _____, what would they be?" A group of people well known to each other send one person out of the group. When that person is out of earshot, the group chooses someone within the group to be "it." The person who was sent out comes back into the group and starts asking questions about the person who is it. Obviously the person's intention is to find out the identity of it. One question can be asked of each person in the group. The questions, however, must be abstract. For example, a question might be, "If this person were an item on a restaurant menu, what item would this person be?" The person asked must give the most appropriate answer to that specific question. What's interesting about this game is hearing what people's responses are about the person who is it. For the person who is it, it's interesting to hear how other people perceive him or her. Make sure everyone has a chance to be the person guessing and to be it. After everyone has taken a turn, discuss your reactions.

5. Think of physical choices to add to the character.

Physical choices can be anything from a twitch, to a laugh, to a grimace, to a limp. Explore ways to incorporate something physical into your character. Classic sitcom characters have physical embellishments that create memorable and lasting impressions on audiences. Kramer on "Seinfeld" is a walking physical exaggeration. All he needs to do is enter, and the audience goes wild with delight. Michael Richards, the actor who played Kramer, is obviously a talented physical actor and is personally responsible for Kramer's brilliant physicality. However, Kramer is an exception and not the rule. It's nice when an exceptional physical actor plays a character who needs a strong physical characterization. Most of the time, however, characters won't have that much physicality. Your physical choices don't need to be eccentric to be successful.

Subtle choices for physicalizations can be effective. Lucy's crying when she was upset, Mary Tyler Moore's stutter when she was nervous, and the Fonz's thumbs up accompanied by "Heeey" are examples of this principle. (I'm sure you can think of many more.) These are physical character choices that audiences immediately identify with and find funny. Physical choices in comedy are sometimes called "bits" — as in "a small comic bit of business." These bits become classic when they are inextricably tied to the character. The character need only start the bit and the audience laughs in anticipation. Lucy only needs to make her "I'm going to cry" face and we know what's coming. Besides creating identification with the audience, a physical bit, once it's established, does half the work for the actor. When the audience can read the character's mind, then you know the character is successful.

A word of caution, though. You don't want to overuse these bits. You also don't want to use them randomly. These choices must be used at the exact right moment. Otherwise, if they are used arbitrarily, the audience will easily tire of them (and you). If you think the situation governs the use of these bits, right you are! Lucy would usually cry to get something from Ricky; Mary would stutter when she was trying to overcome her nervousness about doing something (usually dealing with Lou); the Fonz did his "Heeey" to impress and prove how cool he was. These physical bits are best done when there is a specific purpose behind them. Usually the character is trying to get something from somebody. So for an audition, make sure that when you use a bit that there is motivation behind it (governed by the situation) and that it is done with an objective in mind.

EXERCISES

- As you watch sitcoms, see if you can define physical character choices. Notice how integral they are to the character. See if you can discern a reason for their use. Are they motivated for the purpose of getting something from someone else? Discuss your findings in a group.

- Videotape this improvisation called Twitch Jump. Person A starts a scene sitting in a reception area of an office waiting to be called in for a job interview (pick the job). Another actor enters also waiting for an interview for the same job. The second actor (let's call him Person B) has a physical twitch (make sure to keep it simple and subtle; you'll see why momentarily). As they start a conversation, Person A "catches" the twitch before being called in for his interview (by someone off camera). Person C enters with both the first twitch and one he adds, continuing the improvisation. Person B, maintaining his twitch, catches C's twitch before being called in for his interview. Person D enters with both the initial two twitches adding one of his own. Person C, maintaining B's twitch as well as his own, catches D's twitch before being called in for the interview. The cycle continues. Each actor waiting for his interview has to maintain all the previous twitches as well as pick up the additional twitch before being called in for his interview. By the time you get through everyone, the last actor is a twitching *mess*. (By now I'm sure you understand why it's important to keep the twitches simple and subtle). All the actors should maintain an appropriate conversation for a job interview while all this is happening. It's very funny to do — and to watch during playback.

6. In sitcoms, a take is worth a thousand words.

A take is synonymous with comedy. It is a wordless reaction or expression indicating an implied thought shared with an audience. Think of it as a mental aside that is meant to be funny. I don't know the specific origin of the word *take*, but I'm sure it's been around since Plautus, the Roman comic playwright, had his plays produced. It's certainly a technique employed by clowns and mimes. It was popularized in vaudeville and the silent movies and is incorporated today in stand-up comedy and, of course, situation comedies. Whenever you see comedy, you'll see takes.

There are many kinds of takes. The eye roll used to imply droll indifference or a reaction to someone's stupidity. The blank stare, made popular by Buster Keaton in the silent movies, is funny because precisely at the moment when there should be strong reaction, there is none. Then there's the slow burn. This is a take used when a character has seen or heard something that really makes him upset; he'll use the slow burn as a reaction before he explodes. The audience enjoys it because they know the character is furious, and they love reading the thoughts of the character before he explodes. One of the most popular is the double take — the character looks again to make certain that what she thought she saw, she did indeed see. It's funny because of the timing and because the audience knows the character wants to see what she's initially missed.

Takes are ubiquitous in comedy because they say a lot without saying anything at all. Sometimes the best comedy is the most economical, when it's grasped easily and without too much thought. Generally, this kind of comedy is not too complicated, and it's funniest when a general audience understands and identifies with it. In many ways comedy is the world's great common denominator. Takes evolved from physical comedy and transcend language. (Specifically they were introduced and incorporated by actors wearing masks. When wearing a mask, an actor has no choice but to rely on his physicalization.) To a worldwide audience, what's funnier: a take where we all recognize what the actor is thinking even if we don't understand the language, or a complex joke that only people who speak the same language are going to understand? Situation comedies are meant to appeal to a mass audience. A take can help you do that whether the audience understands the language or not.

However, do not confuse a take with mugging. Mugging is derived from the word *mug*, which means face. In acting, mugging is overacting — making faces, or trying to get attention. Call it what you will, it's not a take. A take is like a fine wine; mugging is like cheap rotgut. A take is art, while mugging is artificial. Don't do it.

As in everything else in sitcoms, a take should be grounded in character and situation. As funny as a take might be, if done at the wrong time, it becomes deadly. If it's supported in reality and is motivated by a worthy situation, by all means do it. Don't overdo it, though. There's nothing worse than an actor who gets a laugh doing a take and then keeps doing them every chance he gets. Takes should be judiciously handled and sparingly done. It should also always be accompanied by an internal monologue. The audience has to be able to read your mind more or less, so be sure to internalize your thought process.

In an audition, try to find one place in the sides (the audition scene) where you can do a take. Only do it, though, if the situation justifies it. Some takes work best where they are least expected. For example, if you're reading for a character who you think would never do a take but the situation is begging for it, give it a shot. You may surprise the casting director and producers and unveil a new facet about the character. If it doesn't work, at least you've made a bold choice.

EXERCISES

• Watch sitcoms and be cognizant of the characters' takes. Notice when they're done, why they're done, and their effect. Could you read the character's internal monologue? Are takes being done honestly and in appropriate situations? Can you tell the difference between takes and mugging?

• With material from sitcoms (sitcom scripts are now available in book form at your local bookstore and I would recommend their use), find scenes that you can do on camera in a class environment. Look for ways to incorporate takes into the scene. Most important, play them back and discuss their effectiveness. Did a suitable internal monologue accompany the take? Were the takes justified? Were they overused? Did they help further the story?

SITUATION COMEDY EXERCISES

As in all exercises for the camera, what's most important is that you get on camera as much as possible. Incorporate the following exercises that most appeal to you or best fit the objectives you're working on in class. In that respect, it almost doesn't matter what exercises you do as long as you are getting more and more comfortable being on camera and watching yourself during playback. Just keep in mind that whatever exercises are being done, they're accompanied by an objective; in other words, always make sure that you can articulate why you are doing the particular exercise.

If you're working in an environment where you have access to a three-camera setup, use the cameras as described earlier with the husband/wife scenario — i.e., use camera 2 for wide master shots; camera 1 to shoot the stage-left area; and camera 3 to shoot the stage-right area. Experiment with different shots and switching effects. Also be sure to deal with issues of hitting marks, framing, and respecting the camera angles. If you only have access to one camera, don't despair; you can achieve excellent results. Use the camera as one long continuous master shot. If someone running the camera is adept at it, he or she might be able to zoom in for different close-ups at various times.

Possibly the most valid part of the exercise is the playback and discussion, which should always follow. If you happen to be the subject of the playback, try to get over the self-consciousness that is natural in watching yourself on tape. The sooner you can get over what I call the "I look so fat on camera" phase, the sooner you'll be able to objectively see your work and start learning from watching it.

EXERCISE 1

This is an improvisation where the character or the situation is the primary consideration. Tape the exercise as you would a scene from a sitcom.

Two people do this exercise. One stays in the room. The other leaves. The class picks a situation for both people and tells Actor 1, who stays in the room, what the situation is. That person then leaves the room and Actor 2 comes in. The class then tells that person what the relationship is between the two people. So, one of the people in the exercise knows the situation and one knows the relationship. For example, the class gives Actor 1 a situation of a flight deck during battle on an aircraft carrier, and Actor 2 the relationship of Santa and an elf. *The purpose of the exercise is for each partner to figure out the information that he or she does not know by playing what it is he or she does know.* In other words, Actor 1 must find out what the relationship is, and Actor 2 must find out what the situation is. Each person must "play" what he, in fact, does know; but he is not allowed to deliberately give away what he knows to his partner. (For instance, Actor 1 can't say, "It's hell out here on the flight deck of an aircraft carrier during battle," and Actor 2 can't say, "You know, Santa, you promised me a raise last Christmas and I haven't received it.") They are each to play what they do know in a subtle fashion. When, during the course of the improvisation, one actor figures out what he needs to know, he must incorporate it into the dialogue. When both partners have figured out what each needs to know, the exercise is over. This is a great exercise for situation comedies because the actors have to focus on situation and character.

While doing this exercise you might find it necessary to provide some side coaching as a way of reminding the actors to find out what they need to know. Be sure to play it back and discuss it. Did the actors effectively play what it is they did know? Notice how much of the comedy came from the juxtaposition of the situation and the character.

EXERCISE 2

An improvisation called Hitchhiker (similar to Twitch Jump in Principle 5). This is an improvisation in which bold character and physical choices are vital. It's also a great improvisation to force actors to deal quickly with changing styles and rhythms. This exercise is easy to tape with one camera. (If you're using three cameras, use one for a master and the other two to get various close-ups during it.) Place four chairs (two in the front, two in the rear) facing the camera as if the camera were looking into a car.

A group of four actors inhabits the "car" and decides on a destination. They also choose a characterization for the entire group. (It can be anything: a group of surfers, Holy Rollers, slobs, investment bankers, etc.) The key is that *everyone* in the car becomes the character (everyone is a surfer, Holy Roller, etc.). These characterizations should be distinguished by some kind of strange affliction — a physical characterization or verbal oddity.

As they travel, they come across a hitchhiker. They pick up the hitchhiker and rotate in the car. (To accommodate the hitchhiker, someone in the car always has to leave.) The hitchhiker must bring into the car a totally novel yet discernible characterization. The hitchhiker should only reveal the character through her physical and vocal choices. (A Holy Roller could refer to a Bible, but the point is to act it, not merely talk about it.) As soon as the hitchhiker gets into the car, everyone in the car must immediately abandon his or her previous character and adapt to the new one. Another hitchhiker is picked up and the improvisation continues until everyone has played a hitchhiker. To justify the situation, the car can become another form of transportation if necessary — if an alien hitchhiker arrives, the car can become a spaceship; if a cowboy hitchhiker arrives, the car can become a stagecoach, and so on.

Play it back and discuss it. How nimbly did everyone accomplish the changes of character? How adroitly was everyone able to deal with the change of rhythm every time a new hitchhiker came into the car?

EXERCISE 3

Next try the caricature improvisation. In this exercise, actors identify eccentric traits in someone and create a character based on those traits. No one, however, should be mocked or criticized. The spirit of impersonation should be one of affection. Tape this improvisation as you would a scene.

In a group where everyone knows each other well (in a school, as part of a department, members of a class, etc.), each person impersonates someone well known to everyone else. You can't share whom you have chosen with anyone. Using the charming and eccentric traits of that person, impersonate him or her in an improvisation. For the given circumstance within the scene use a common location also well known by the class — for instance, the departmental office or the student union. Remember, the objective is not to ridicule the person, but to try and capture something essential about his or her behavior, character, or demeanor.

For example, if you are doing this exercise as part of a class, you might put it in the school (or departmental office). Everyone in class will probably impersonate a teacher or another student since the impersonation has to be someone everyone knows. Therefore, the improvisation is going to concentrate on the relationships between these people within the common location of the situation.

Play it back and discuss it. Was the class able to guess the identity of the impersonations? Were the impersonators able to successfully capture charming, eccentric qualities about the person? How well did the impersonators handle the relationships and the situation?

EXERCISE 4

Now let's try caricature improvisation, part 2. This is a continuation of the earlier exercise, essentially adding text to the impersonation. Everyone in class should write out situations (relationship and location) for two people for the following contentless dialogue.

Person A: Have you seen it?
Person B: I'm not sure.
Person A: Well, you couldn't have missed it.
Person B: Mmm . . . Maybe I did.
Person A: What did it look like?
Person B: It looked square.
Person A: Are you sure you saw it?
Person B: No.
Person A: Where have you been?
Person B: Right here.
Person A: No, I mean before.
Person B: I was there.
Person A: That's what I thought.
Person B: That's where I was.
Person A: So you didn't see it?
Person B: I don't think so.
Person A: Why didn't you tell me?
Person B: I dunno.

The pair should be believable, imaginative, and interesting. For example, the conversation could be between two brothers at a baseball game, two women waiting to get their hair dyed, or a married couple at the beach. However, this time actors don't impersonate individuals that everyone in the class knows well personally. Actors must choose famous people — celebrities, politicians, or sports figures. (The relationships don't have to be famous relationships, however. The "famous" brothers don't have to be real brothers, the "famous" married couple doesn't have to be really married.) Hand out the situations to pairs of actors.

Create a scene with the dialogue playing the situations while letting the impersonations govern the characterizations. Tape these scenes as you would a sitcom scene. Play them back and discuss them. Did you play the situations? Was the audience able to guess the identity of the characters? Were you successful in capturing an essence of the person being impersonated?

SUMMARY

Situation comedies are a distinctly American genre of comedy. They are analogous with television. Most of them are taped with three cameras in a studio in front of a live audience.

The two different employment categories include principals and extras. The principal roles include regulars, guest stars, co-stars, and featured parts. There are basically two types of auditions: one for the regulars when the sitcom is being made into a pilot; and once running, weekly auditions for all the other principal roles. Extras are cast separately.

Actors must be aware of how to work with a three-camera setup. Professional actors must be cognizant of the different kinds of shots used in a sitcom — not only of the shots they are in, but also those of their scene partners. They must also be able to hit their marks and stay in frame.

Sitcoms are taped very much like summer stock productions. An episode is typically rehearsed and taped in a five-day period culminating with two tapings in front of a live audience.

Here are six principles to observe when auditioning and acting in sitcoms. Use them as a guide to help you.

1. *Play the comedy and poignancy through the situation.* The situation is the cause, and comedy is the effect. Never play for laughs; always play the situation.

2. *Pay attention to the inherent rhythm.* Every sitcom has a distinct tempo; it's the actor's job to be sensitive to it. Pay attention to the transitions.

3. *Make bold choices.* Don't be afraid to be outrageous and eccentric in your choices. They can always request that you tone it down.

4. *You must use your charming personality, but always remember that you are playing a character.* Learn to find your personality traits that correspond to the character. Never forget that these characters have to be likeable.

5. *Look for physical choices to add to the character.* They don't have to be big; sometimes comic bits are appropriate.

6. *A take can be worth a thousand words.* Make sure that the take is justified and that it's not mugging.

CHAPTER 5
SOAP OPERAS

Soap operas are colloquially known as soaps, daytime dramas, melodramas, serials, and sometimes just daytime. They are about as popular as any television genre and have been around as long as television itself. Their history is rooted in the old-fashioned melodramas that appeared on stage (which are actually still popular in some places today). The term *soap opera* comes from the original sponsor, Procter & Gamble, which makes, among other things, soap.

In the 1930s, soaps began their broadcast history as radio dramas. When television became prevalent in the 1950s, soaps were embraced even more fully. As proof of their durable success, the earliest daytime drama "Guiding Light" (which began on radio in 1937 and on television in 1952) is still a recognized favorite today. Soap operas didn't change much between the radio and television versions. Then as now they could be distinguished by the melodramatic story lines, music underscoring the action, tempestuous love affairs, and overwrought lives. One of the biggest differences, of course, is that the original soaps were produced live on both radio and television. Today, they are all taped. Although they are still found on daytime television, the ultimate compliment to their popularity is that some nighttime dramas have been patterned on them as well.

Sociological studies have been done on why soaps are so beloved and enduring, but you don't have to be a sociologist to know that soaps are still popular. People are hugely devoted to their favorite soaps. When I teach my camera-acting class, the unit on soap operas is the students' favorite. There are always students in my class who are enormous soap fans and want to study acting just so they can act on daytime someday. When I first became an actor, my wonderful Aunt Virginia would not take me seriously *until* I appeared on a soap opera. After I did, I could do no wrong.

I once was a guest on a afternoon talk show promoting a production of an adaptation of Orwell's *1984* at the Kennedy Center in Washington, D.C., in which I played Winston Smith. The interview wasn't going well (I sensed a certain disinterest) until I mentioned that I had once arrested Erika Kane on "All My Children." All of a sudden the host perked up — *this* is what his audience wanted to know about — and I became an interesting guest.

Currently there are ten soaps on network television. Approximately half are taped in New York City and half in Los Angeles. There are many more on cable and local access stations around the country. Almost every country in the world has its own soap operas running on television. The advertising revenue is immense for daytime dramas and — best of all — soaps employ lots of actors.

In this chapter, I discuss the different types of employment contracts and what to expect in auditions. I provide information on how soaps are produced, as well as what a typical day on a soap opera is like.

WHAT DO I NEED TO KNOW TO BE ON A SOAP OPERA?

We've already discussed the difference between SAG and AFTRA, so you know that soaps, because they are videotaped, fall under the jurisdiction of AFTRA. The information I'm going to give you is based on AFTRA rules regarding all the employment categories on network daytime. There are basically five different employment categories: contract roles, recurring roles, day players, under-fives (someone who has under five lines of dialogue), and extras.

Contract Roles. Contract roles are filled by the actors who play the principal roles on soaps. Also known as contract players or regulars, these actors have signed a contract to appear exclusively on that particular soap; they play the characters that the storylines revolve around. Generally, contracts are for a specific time frame and guarantee a definite salary based on appearing in so many episodes a week. For example, Stephanie, a hypothetical actress, signs a contract for a daytime drama; she is guaranteed $3000 per week for a minimum of three episodes per week, which breaks down to $1000 per episode. The minimum salary for a principal role is currently between $548 to $731 per episode, depending on whether it's a thirty- or a sixty-minute program. However, salaries are negotiated by agents or managers and are always variable. Agents are never going to negotiate for the minimum salary. As you know, the unions prohibit it because actors can never make below minimum *after* paying the agent's 10 percent commission. So let's say Stephanie signs a three-year contract, renewable every twenty-six weeks for a guaranteed three-show minimum at $3000 per week. That means that Stephanie is guaranteed to appear in three episodes a week for $3000. If her character is only written into one or two episodes in a week, she still gets paid $3000. If, however, her character becomes very popular or she is involved in an important storyline and she appears in four episodes, she'll make an additional $1000 in addition to her guaranteed salary. Of course, this is all negotiable, but the union has a definite scale regarding these things.

You may wonder what the "three-year contract, renewable every twenty-six weeks" means. Well, this arrangement protects Stephanie as well as the producers. Let's say Stephanie's character becomes the hottest thing on soaps. At the end of three years (the maximum length of her contract), she can negotiate a much more lucrative contract. But let's say that the producers really don't like her character (or Stephanie) and they want to "kill" her off. This happens all the time. Contractually, she's guaranteed at least six months work before the producers can get rid of her. Therefore, every six months she's guaranteed another twenty-six weeks before they can end her contract. So if she has been on the show for fifty-two weeks and a day, the producers would still have to honor the next twenty-six weeks of the contract before they could fire her. Basically, it's equivalent to Stephanie's contract protecting her six months at a time. Unless they tell her otherwise, her contract is going to last a minimum of six months and a maximum of three years. According to the union rules, she has to be notified four to six weeks before the end of a six-month period if the producers are not going to renew her contract.

Recurring Roles. Recurring roles are merely actors working as day players over an extended period of time. In other words, recurring roles are nonbinding-contract characters who appear sporadically over a duration of time. Generally, an actor starts out as a day player, and because of the story line or because the producers like the actor or the character, the actor is asked to return. Let's say that Pete has been hired to play JT, a bartender at the local pub. He starts out being hired for one day's work. (The minimum salary is the same as the contract player, $548 to $731 per episode as long as he has over five lines of dialogue. If he is playing a recurring role and has under ten lines of dialogue, the scale varies based on how many shows he appears in, from $214 to $762 per episode.) As far as Pete knows, he is only going to work one day. If the producers really like him, they might bring him back; in that case he'll probably make the same amount of money as he did before. In some cases, the producers will know in advance that JT is going to be a recurring role, and they're going to need Pete to play JT at least three times over the next month; then they'll negotiate a daily rate of pay with Pete's agent for each appearance. Because a contract has not been signed, there's no obligation on either side. Pete could end up playing JT for years in this way if he were comfortable with the arrangement. Or the producers may never call him again after three weeks or three months. Occasionally this type of character might become a contract role, but it's not the norm. Recurring roles are usually tied to a specific story line. I had recurring roles on a number of soaps, some of which began as a day player and developed into a recurring role and others I knew would be recurring roles from the beginning. The best way to determine the distinction is to look at the story lines. They tend to specifically revolve around the contract players, while the recurring roles aren't as essential to the plot.

Day Players. Day players are actors who have over five lines of dialogue and only work one day. As I mentioned above, the pay scale is $548 to $731 per episode. An example of a day player might be a cop arresting one of the contract players. A day player is a one-time appearance; the only thing that differentiates a day player and an under-five is the number of lines.

Under-fives. *Under-five* is the term for a character who appears in an episode with five lines or less. (For a recurring role, the cutoff is ten lines or less.) The pay scale for an under-five is $287 to $355 per episode. These are generally very small speaking roles performed by someone who appears only once. An example would be a waitress who asks, "Can I have your order?" Even though the roles are small, taking under-five parts is a good way for actors to learn the ropes on soap sets. Many times I have also seen extras get upgraded (the term used for stepping up in the employment ladder) to an under-five. For instance, the director might ask an actor to bump into a principal character and say, "Excuse me." In this case, that's all it would take to get a significant pay raise.

Extras. Extras, also called background and atmosphere, are actors with no lines. Customers eating in a restaurant, for instance. Many times you'll hear extras murmuring in the background. (Just so you know, murmuring doesn't constitute dialogue.) The scale for extras is $102 to $132 per day, depending on whether the soap is thirty or sixty minutes. I recommend that all actors do extra work in soaps — especially if you're new to town and have never done a soap opera before. Working as an extra is like getting paid to watch up close how soaps are made and to learn by studying the principals' performances day after day.

Most soap operas have two casting directors. One who exclusively handles principals, recurring roles, and day players, and another who only handles the extras and under-five roles. If you are new to Los Angeles or New York, you should send pictures and résumés to both casting directors for all the soaps. However, soaps are always in need of fresh faces to play extras and definitely hire more extras than anything else. My recommendation is that you pursue the extra and under-five casting director of the various soaps. Your chances to secure work from them are much greater than with the principal casting directors. In soaps, extras are not looked down on, and it's a good way to get noticed. In addition, extras aren't susceptible to over exposure and can be used many times in a short period. If, however, you ultimately want to play larger roles on soaps, don't make a habit out of playing extras.

HOW ARE SOAPS PRODUCED?

I think it's important to understand and respect how soaps are written and produced. Soap operas do not have a reputation for being models of artistry. The dialogue can be mundane and bland — some would even say boring. But soap operas are unique; and when you understand how much talent they require, you'll learn to appreciate them.

Soaps are always written by groups of writers; these writers work for the executive producer (many times the executive producer is the person who created the soap and is sometimes also the head writer). They have a formidable task: to create and maintain interesting story lines that will enable the producers to tape over three hundred episodes a year. A film can take over a year to write, produce, shoot, and edit; episodic television can take months to create a single episode; and plays can take weeks to rehearse and produce. Soaps tape five days a week for almost fifty-two weeks a year. It's little wonder why soaps aren't the most sophisticated programs on television.

Considering the output, soaps are miraculously well written, produced, and acted. This genre requires enormous concentration and talent. Many famous actors — Meg Ryan, for one — got their start in soaps and obviously learned a great deal about acting from them. Soaps also instill wonderful discipline.

The writers, producers, and casting directors of soaps have great respect and admiration for trained and talented actors. If you appear in soaps, it might behoove you to get on the writers' good sides. They really do appreciate good actors and can help — or hinder — characters.

HOW DO I AUDITION FOR SOAP OPERAS?

Included in each of the principles are thoughts on what to incorporate into your auditions for soap operas. The same submission system for commercials and sitcoms is relevant for getting an audition in soaps. However, because soaps have two casting directors, there is a slight difference.

As I've mention earlier, soaps have casting directors solely for casting extras and under-fives. Generally, these casting directors do not cast through agent submissions; they look at pictures sent directly from actors. (They are probably the only casting directors in this business who will.) This is why it's a good idea to pursue these casting directors first; sending them your picture and résumé can achieve relatively quick results. I would also suggest that in your cover letter, you express interest in working as an extra as well as an under-five. In most cases, unless you come highly regarded, they'll give you a shot as an extra before they hire you to do an under-five. They are going to want to see if you're dependable. Many times the casting director will call you in for an interview. Don't be disappointed if she tells you that you're being interviewed for work as an extra. Some casting directors even have open calls for actors. (Open calls are auditions or interviews where you don't need an appointment to be seen. Always be prepared to wait when you go to open calls.) Remember how important attitude is — when you're new to a place, everyone you meet is a potential ally. Even if you're being considered for work as an extra, the casting director may want to hear you read something. If this happens, this is your chance to show her why she should be using you as an under-five! If she likes you, she may have you meet the principal casting director. That's usually the process when you get a job as an extra or an under-five. Once you get the job, it's up to you to make sure that you behave professionally on the set. They tend to use extras and under-fives a lot if they like you.

It's a different story when you audition for a principal role. You can be hired as a day player or a recurring role if you've been on the show as an under-five and the principal casting director knows and likes you. You can also be considered for one of these roles through an agent's submission; in this case you'll have to audition. If you audition for a day player or recurring role on a soap that you've never been on, make sure you find out as much as you can about the soap before you audition. I recommend watching a couple of episodes to get a feel for what the soap is like and to familiarize yourself with the current story lines. Like sitcoms, you will be given sides (the scene from the script that you're auditioning from). If the casting director doesn't know your work, you will have to read for the principal casting director first. If the casting director knows your work, sometimes this step is eliminated and you read for both the executive producer and casting director at the same time. After you read for the casting director and he decides that he likes you, you will almost always have to read for the executive producer. The executive producer has the final say. Under some circumstances, the executive producer will respect the principal casting director enough to give him the responsibility to make the casting decision for day players and recurring roles.

Auditioning for a contract role is yet another distinctly unique process and much more strenuous. When a soap needs a new principal, breakdowns are sent out to all the agents in town. Agents and managers submit clients that they think best fit the description of the role. Like day players or recurring roles, the first step is to audition for the principal casting director. You may have to read more than once for the casting director; sometimes she will put you on tape. If you are called back, you will then meet the executive producer. This is the most important meeting and audition. The executive producer will normally choose two or three actors whom he would be happy with and then brings them before the network, either via tape or in person. The network normally has the final say. I should mention that all the networks employ a casting director who is responsible for all the daytime shows on that particular network (for example, the head of daytime casting for ABC). Somewhere in this process the network's casting director gets involved. Make sure you treat him or her as you would the principal casting director.

Contract roles are important on soaps, and the networks along with the soaps painstakingly do everything they can to hire the most appropriate actors. The networks are highly influenced by the sponsors of the individual soaps. There used to be a notion on particular soaps (and it still may exist) that you needed to "look PG" — or Procter & Gamble. Because so many soap stars started to share a distinct look, their appearance become known as PG, as if Procter & Gamble, which makes many household products (including soap), were endorsing them. Procter & Gamble wanted actors to have a certain look for the contract roles on the soaps the company supported, and if an actor fit that mold, then he stood a better chance of being cast. Judge for yourself if this attitude still exists by watching soaps that are sponsored by Procter & Gamble. If you get a sense that there is a definite type for this particular soap, this typing may still be true.

WHAT IS THE SCHEDULE LIKE ON A SOAP OPERA? WHAT CAN I EXPECT IN A TYPICAL DAY?

As an actor, the first thing that you'll get is a script for the day(s) you are working. If you are working more than one day over the course of a couple of weeks, you'll normally receive only a week's worth of scripts at a time. The writers work five days a week and are usually ahead only by two or three weeks. You can also expect script changes at any time. They will send you the new pages if they are available before you shoot, or new pages may be waiting for you when you show up on the day you are working. You'll also have to go in beforehand for a costume fitting. Of course, you or your agent will receive a call time for the day(s) you are working.

Soaps are shot on soundstages. A soundstage is something like an airplane hanger (some are bigger than others). The night before each day's shoot, a crew comes in and assembles the sets needed for the next day's episode. Because the story lines revolve around specific and identifiable locations, most of the sets are pulled out of storage whenever they're needed. The sets are lined up along both sides of the soundstage with a space in the middle for cameras to travel. (See figure 1.) Even if the script calls for a park outside, the interior of an airplane, or even a driving scene where the car is visible, these are usually brought onto the soundstage. Soaps do occasional location shooting (some even go to Europe!), but this is rare and usually done only for a major event in the story line (like a wedding). In such cases, they will travel with only the necessary cast and a limited crew. Normally, however, everything needed is on the soundstage. This is based on the tradition of the earliest days of soaps when they were shot live. Soaps are still shot as if they were live. For instance, if a character is talking to another character on the phone within the same scene, they shoot it in real time. One camera will be in one part of the soundstage shooting one character on the phone, and another camera will in another part of the soundstage shooting the other character. To maintain the "live" sensibility, the phone conversation will be taped as if it were actually happening instead of waiting for postproduction cuts and editing as they do in episodic television and film.

Because individual soap operas are different, each one has unique script changes, scheduling, rehearsing, and shooting. Most soaps start their day very early. Characteristically, soaps start from the beginning of the episode and work their way through to the end. Let's say you've been hired for a sixty-minute soap and you're in one of the early scenes of the episode. Your call time might be 6:00 A.M. First, the entire show is *dry blocked*, scene by scene from beginning to end. (Blocking is plotting out the movements of the actors; dry blocking is blocking without the cameras.) Much like a play, you will work in a rehearsal studio with the sets taped out on the floor. The director will have worked out the actors' movements beforehand. This first rehearsal takes the actors through their movements before they get on

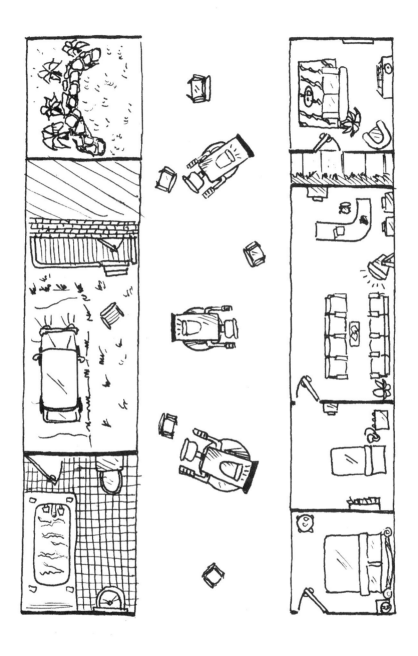

Fig. 1.   Overhead view of a soap-opera soundstage.

the set. They may dry block the entire show from 6:00 to 9:00 A.M. At 9:15 the director will move onto the soundstage and *camera block* the entire show. (Camera blocking means diagramming the movement and shots of the cameras to correspond with the movements of the actors.) At this point, the cameramen and crew members will be on the set. The director will verbally direct the cameramen through each shot. This is a rehearsal for the cameras and the crew as well as the actors, and the first time the scenes are rehearsed on the real sets. The actors, however, are still in their street clothes. This rehearsal might last from 9:15 until 12:00. Lunch will be from 12:00 until 1:00.

A dress rehearsal of the show begins at 1:00, starting with the first scene and going through the complete show. This rehearsal is a run-through of the entire episode, with the actors in full makeup and costume. It's during the dress rehearsal that *show conditions* exist, and the director is in the booth, switching shots and adding sound and music cues. (Show conditions means that the conditions for the final videotaping are in place.) After each scene or at the end of the entire dress rehearsal, the director will give notes to the cast and crew. This process can last from 1:00 to 3:30 or 4:00. At 4:00 or 4:15 the final taping begins. Some soaps tape each scene twice, but generally they pretty much adhere to what the audience sees in the final product. Unless special effects or scenes have been taped at another time, no editing is involved in the final product. All the scenes progress from one to another, and all the music and sound effects are dubbed in at the time of the taping. The presence of children in any of the scenes can affect this schedule. Because of child labor laws, soaps try to incorporate children as quickly as possible. For example, children might not be called until after lunch, when their scene (or scenes) are dress rehearsed and immediately taped. These scenes will be edited into the final version at another time.

OK, so let's say that you've been hired as a day player and your character is a nurse at a hospital. You're in two scenes — one at the beginning of the show and another toward the end. If this particular soap shoots according to the schedule I've just outlined, you might be called at 6:00 A.M. for a blocking rehearsal. You may finish that rehearsal by 6:15. You won't be needed again until probably around 8:30 to block your last scene. You'll be called to the set (the location of the actual shoot) at approximately 9:00 for camera blocking. You may finish at 9:15 and not be needed again until 11:30. After you finish your last scene, you're free to go to lunch. You'll have to be in costume and makeup by 1:00, so that you are ready to be on the set to start your dress rehearsal. If your scene is done by 1:30, you'll be free until approximately 3:30 when you'll have to be back on the set to dress rehearse your last scene. After the dress rehearsal, you may have to be on the set for notes. Your makeup will need to be touched up so that you're ready to start taping at 4:15. Of course, the taping follows the same format. If you're lucky you may finish by 6:00 P.M.

You've probably realized by now that you're going to have some downtime during the day. Basically you're free to do whatever you want, but *always* make sure that you can be found by the stage manager. That means stay in your dressing room or in a common area like the green room (the waiting room just offstage — sitcoms also use this term). If you need to leave the studio for any reason, make sure you check in with the stage manager to let her know where you're going. Also, always be aware of the day's schedule and where you fit into the schedule. If, for example, you are in the first scene and need to be in costume and makeup immediately following lunch, which is scheduled from 12:00 to 1:00, you will not have the same lunch break as everyone else since you'll be needed on the set at 1:00. It is extremely important to be on the set when you're called. I have seen under-fives fired for not being on the set after lunch. (In my case, one person's mistake was my good fortune: The director looked at me and said, "You take his lines," and I was upgraded from an extra to an under-five.)

The other method of scheduling is similar to the last one. Again, the cast and crew work their way through the episode from beginning to end. The exception is that after dry blocking, they get each scene completely out of the way before they move on. For example, the soap dry blocks from 6:00 until 9:00 A.M. At 9:15 they camera block, dress rehearse, and tape each scene in order, one at a time. If you've been hired as a day player and have one scene at the beginning of the episode and one scene at the end, your day might be as follows: At 6:00 A.M. you would be called to dry block your first scene. You would be needed again at 8:30 to dry block your last scene. However, now you'll need to be in costume and makeup by 9:15, so that when you get to the set, you can camera block, dress rehearse, and tape your first scene. Let's say that you're finished by 10:15 A.M. Because you're in one of the last scenes, you may not be called for your last scene until later that afternoon. This is a worst-case scenario, but it can happen. But if you're only in one scene at the beginning of the show, you could be completely finished by 10:15. Conversely, if you're only in one scene late in the show, you might be called at 8:30 A.M. for dry blocking and not be needed again until late afternoon.

The examples I've used apply if you're cast as a day player. The same schedule would apply if you were cast as a contract player, recurring character, or under-five. Notable exceptions are the extras. If you were hired as an extra, you would not be called for the dry blocking. You would need to arrive in costume (extras wear their own clothes) for dress rehearsal, but the rest of the schedule is the same.

As you see, you need to be creative about your use of time. Contract players generally have a routine. I have seen many contract players show up at the dry blocking rehearsals wearing their sweats so that they can jog after they've finished. Depending on the schedule, it is useful to remember that you're going to need to conserve your energy for the final taping. Don't waste all your energy in the early part of the day. The worst thing you can do is to be exhausted by the time of the actual taping. Remember that everything up to the taping is a rehearsal. What the audience is going to see is the actual taping. Generally, your episode will air only about two to three weeks after you tape it.

PRINCIPLES OF SOAP OPERAS

Now you have a sense of the types of employment options that exist, as well as the different schedules and how soaps are produced. Use the following ten principles to augment the information you have learned about auditioning and performing. More important, however, incorporate the exercises that follow each of the principles. When you do them, keep in mind that the purpose for each one revolves around the principle. Soaps are fun, so enjoy the exercises!

1. Know the story line.

A story line in a soap opera is many things. It is literally the *story* of the individual soap opera. It certainly represents the plot, but it's also a time line of the plot and can delineate different themes of the soap opera as well. Perhaps the best way to think of the story line is to imagine it as the story of the history and future of the individual soap. Story lines can also represent a character's story, a family's story, a building's story, a town's story, and so forth. The story lines of "All My Children" revolve around the various narrative plots, but they also tell the history of Pine Valley, and most important, the families of Pine Valley. One of the story lines of "General Hospital" certainly revolves around the hospital where it takes place.

Because soap fans have usually been watching their favorites for a long time, they know the story lines intimately. They feel like they are part of the family. When these fans discuss their favorite soap, they talk about the characters as they would a family member or friend: "I really feel that Nicole married Gabriel to get back at Simon." "You won't believe what Dalla said to David!" "Erika's done a lot of bad things in her life, but this takes the cake." "You'll never believe who is starting to hang around Tuscany's."

Because soap story lines develop slowly, they are fairly easy to pick up. They are like slow-moving streetcars; it's easy to jump on while they're moving. You don't need to have watched a soap forever to understand what's happening. But bear in mind that *all* story lines revolve around big issues such as life, death, sex, jealousy, or revenge. In fact, many countries today are starting to use soap opera story lines as a tool to teach audiences about AIDS, overpopulation, teenage pregnancy, environmental topics, and other major societal issues. You'll be much better off if you start with one of those dominant issues when considering where your character is in the story line.

If you're auditioning for a soap, you'll need to have at least a casual idea of what's happening. It's especially imperative to know the history of the character you are auditioning for, or to create one based on existing story lines. A new character is like a stranger with a past — everyone in town wants to know what it is. When I've had recurring roles on soaps, I've had fans write me letters welcoming me and telling me a little about themselves. A lot of daily newspapers and TV magazines also print a syndicated column once a week called "Soap Opera Flashback," recapping what's happened on every soap that last week. Reading that column will give a sense of what is going on.

EXERCISES

- Bring in a taped soap opera to class. Have everyone in class try to figure out the various story lines based on one episode. Make up detailed histories for the characters and relationships. Continue watching it to see how the story lines develop.

- Based on the synopsis of a soap from "Soap Opera Flashback" or something equivalent, create a detailed timeline involving the plot, characters, locations, and so on.

- Create a fictional soap opera world. Make sure you provide a detailed description of all the given circumstances: where it takes place, the families and people who live there, relationships among the characters, and anything else you can think of. Make certain to incorporate issues involving life, death, sex, jealousy, and revenge into all story lines.

2. The dialogue is always conversational and personal.

Because of the time it takes to develop story lines, nothing ever happens quickly on soaps. If you've ever watched them with regularity, you know that months can go by without much happening except in the most extraordinary circumstances. Even if you stop watching for several weeks, when you return, the characters will still be undergoing the same trauma they were the last time you saw them. This is done on purpose. Producers want the audience to be hooked on the story lines. They do this by making them as accessible as possible.

Soap opera fans are addicted to their favorites soaps: They tape episodes they miss and watch them in their spare time. The various soap opera magazines and "Soap Opera Flashback" are testimony to their addiction. Producers want the average soap addict to remain fixated for as long as the principal characters and the story lines take to establish and unfold. To accomplish this, the dialogue is always very conversational and personal.

The characters' dialogue almost always reflects the speech of the fans; you could say it lacks any kind of artificial theatricality. Call it "soap naturalism" if you will, but this conversational quality helps prolong the story lines. There is also a casualness to the characters' dialogue that is immediately identifiable to the average soap watcher. That quality enables viewers to feel as if they know the characters and that they share the same kinds of problems. Watch soaps and discover how conversational even the big, dramatic moments are.

Soap characters always seem to have extraordinarily private, intense conversations. Even when a discussion is about something innocuous, there has to be the threat that intense drama or conflict may happen at any moment. Watch a soap and notice how even the most trivial situations occur amidst a background of tension.

In auditioning for soap operas, keep the scene conversational. Don't let it get overly dramatic or theatrical. Also, maintain eye contact with your scene partner or whoever is reading opposite you in the audition. Often you will read with the casting director, who will try to be doing two things at once — read with you and watch your audition. Don't let her watching you during your audition rattle you. Maintain eye contact as if she were just another actor playing opposite you in the scene.

EXERCISES

• Tape the following non-gender-specific scene, or find one of your own. (If you do, make sure you choose a tension-filled scene. Although soaps are a good resource for this exercise, the danger of picking a scene from your favorite soap opera is your impulse to want to imitate the scene you transcribed it from. Try not to do that.) Make sure you keep the scene as *conversational* as possible. Try not to let the scene become too theatrical.

Person A: Hi.
Person B: *(Pause.)* Oh, hi.
Person A: How are you?
Person B: *(Pause.)* OK.
Person A: What's the matter?
Person B: I think you know.
Person A: Make it easy for both of us and tell me.
Person B: You're smart enough to know all by yourself.
Person A: Was it the article I wrote in the paper about Jack?
Person B: You shouldn't have done that.
Person A: Maybe not, but that's my job.

Person B: How could you? He's never hurt you in any way.

Person A: I know, but he's hurt you and many others. Maybe it's time that everybody knew about it.

Person B: When are you going to stop trying to play God, deciding what's right for everyone? You've meddled in everyone's lives for too long.

Person A: I had no idea you felt this way. I only want what's right.

Person B: "What's right" might be for you to leave everyone alone and go back to where you belong.

Person A: And where's that?

Person B: To hell, for all I care. *(Exits.)*

Play it back and see if you and your partner were able to keep it conversational. Were you casual? Did you have the impulse to hurry or to raise your voice? How well were you able to maintain eye contact?

- Tape the following non-gender-specific scene. You can also write your own or find a scene from another source. It needs to be an obscure scene that is neither dramatic nor contains conflict of any kind. Make sure to play the scene very personal, with great intensity. Maintain eye contact and take your time. Don't forget that something important could happen at any moment.

Person A: Do you take cream?

Person B: Yes, thanks.

Person A: Are you going to the parade?

Person B: I thought I would. How about you?

Person A: Wouldn't miss it.

Person B: Last year's was amazing I thought.

Person A: I agree. *(Pause.)* Do you remember when Mrs. Ale's dog, Luke, ran off after the balloon exploded on that float?

Person B: Didn't they find him under the old Stephens barn?

Person A: Yeah. It took Mrs. Ale weeks to stop talking about that.

Person B: Hopefully she'll leave Luke home this year.

Play it back and discuss it. What did you notice? Although it may have felt strange doing such an informal scene with so much intensity, I'm sure it created its own tension. After watching it, see if you felt the need to know more. Show it to a third party and get his opinion as to what is going on.

3. Soap opera acting always contain the Three Rs.

This is my favorite principle for soaps. The Three Rs are merely a technical means of building a reaction to any given dramatic situation in a soap opera. It's a three-step sequence to listening and responding in soap operas. The Three Rs stand for *revelation, realization,* and *reaction.* They should be used in every enhanced moment in a soap opera situation.

Revelation is what I call the "Aha!" moment. It's equivalent to hearing news for the first time. For instance, Polly declares to Jim, "Heather is not your child!" The camera zooms in for a close-up, and by his surprised expression, the audience realizes that Jim is shocked at the news. The music swells; at this point, for dramatic effect, then they usually cut to another scene or a commercial. This is Jim's "Aha!" moment, his revelation. (The reason it's not Polly's revelation is because the Three Rs always lead to a reaction to previously unknown information.) Different physical manifestations like a furrowed brow, narrowing eyes, or a slight intake of breath can accompany the revelation. Don't try to falsely manufacture an expression; see what happens naturally. Since soap operas are not very subtle about the big dramatic moments, it's vital that you clearly establish the moment of revelation. I might add that seeing something and not just hearing it can also motivate a revelation. Jim could just as easily have found out this news by reading a letter. (In fact, that can be the primary means in soaps for delivering this kind of information.) What's important is that you make sure that the revelation is identifiable and strong so that the next two steps are just as dramatically powerful.

The revelation is immediately followed by the *realization.* You cannot have a realization without the revelation — the realization is the character's *interpretation* of the revelation. If the revelation is the shock of hearing something for the first time, the realization is registering the implications of that revelation. In Jim's case, it delineates what he feels about the news he has just received. Textually or tacitly his reaction might be something like, "Oh my God, this can't be possible. My world is over." At this moment we might see Jim's shock turn into anger or hurt. It's generally during the realization that they cut back to the scene from another scene or from a commercial. The realization is usually accompanied by a physical manifestation of the emotion being felt: the jaw clench (more about that later), an exhalation of breath, or a concerned look away from the source of the information. You don't want to contrive any kind of physicalization; discover what happens naturally. But the realization has to be significant and specific, because it's almost indistinguishable from the reaction.

The *reaction* is the payoff moment. It is the culmination of the Three Rs; it's what the audience has been waiting for. We want to see how Jim is going to react to this news. (Chances are Polly wants to see how Jim is going to react too.) This is always the moment of truth for a character; there has to be an almost seamless transition between the realization and the reaction. The more distinctive the realization, the more successful the reaction. It is on the reaction that Jim speaks a line if there is one.

The reaction is the most dominant of the Three Rs and always concerns one of three things: *the self*, *the other*, or *the circumstances*. Using our example of Jim, his reaction will be centered on one or more of the following: how it affects him; how it affects other characters, whether that is Polly or Heather or some other character; or how it affects the circumstances, which may include the relationship among Jim, Polly, and Heather. Reactions can incorporate one or more of these, but they must relate to at least one.

If Jim's response line is, "Oh my God, this can't be possible. My world is over," his reaction is obviously about himself. He's concerned probably with how *he* is going to go on. But let's say Jim's response line is, "You bitch! How could you?" we know that his reaction is focused on Polly. He is angry with *her*. But if his response line is something like, "We can never be a family again," his reaction concerns the circumstances of the family and that relationship. In that case, his reaction concerns *all* of them. There are many variations on these reactions, and you should look for ways they can intersect. If there is a response line, that will obviously dictate the focus of the reaction.

But what if a line of dialogue does not follow the realization? Then it's even more imperative that the actor chooses a reaction. This happens frequently on soap operas. Supposing the actor playing Jim decides his reaction is focused on himself. The actor could decide that this news gives Jim a perfect reason for divorcing Polly; his reaction then is to smile. This reaction will intrigue the viewers. They will to try to guess the meaning of his smile and will want to know why he reacted this way. But his reaction is only going to attract us if an interesting revelation and realization have preceded it. Remember: the success of the reaction is only as strong as the lure of the revelation and realization.

In auditions, always study the scene you're given for opportunities to play the Three Rs. Make a notation where a reactive sequence is and make sure you make a choice about where the focus is for the reaction. When you come across a reactive sequence in a script, you should break it down, study it, and rehearse it. However, under no circumstances should your technique be apparent when you are playing the Three Rs. Like all technique, you should refine it and incorporate it; but it should never be conspicuous when you perform it.

EXERCISES

- If you are in a class situation, have everyone write out a simple relationship between two people. (husband/wife; employer/ employee, etc.). Write out two lines of dialogue. Make sure one of the lines is a momentous piece of news that one person in the relationship is delivering to the other person. Then give the actor receiving the news a reactive line of dialogue. For example, Person A says, "I'm leaving you!" and Person B says, "Oh no, you can't." Tape the scene, making sure that you get a close-up of Person B (the actor receiving the news). That actor has to incorporate the Three Rs. Play it back and discuss the effectiveness of the actor's interpretation of the Three Rs. Could you see the distinct differences between revelation, realization, and the reaction? Were there seamless transitions between them? Were they precise and specific? Could you tell where the reactive actor had focused his reaction?

- Have everyone write out another simple relationship between two people. However, this time the reactive actor doesn't have a reactive line of dialogue. Write out a line for only one of the characters. Make sure it's a momentous piece of news. For example, Person A says, "I saw you kill Capodici!" Tape the scene making sure that you get a close-up of the actor receiving the news.

The actor must incorporate the Three Rs. Play the tape back and discuss the effectiveness of the actor's interpretation of the Three Rs. How interesting was the reaction as compared to the revelation and realization? Did the actor's reaction motivate you to want to know more? Could you tell where the reactive actor had focused her reaction?

4. Soap characters always have a problem.

Soap characters are so earnest because they all have problems. One reason soaps are so successful is that the audience empathizes with the soap characters and the problems they face. Compared to the predicaments of their favorite characters, the viewers' problems are small, which likely adds to the appeal of soap operas.

Much of the time the characters' difficulties are elemental parts of the story. These problems can encompass everything from suspension from school for purchasing a term paper to finding out that a baby is really someone else's. They can be as minor as finding out your boyfriend lied to something as serious as a kidnapping. The important thing to remember is that for each of the characters, these events — lying and kidnapping alike — are of the utmost importance, which is why audiences find these problems so fascinating. On some level, soaps are very similar to real life. We all find our problems, large or small, to be highly important. It's no wonder that even the most mundane conversations on soap operas are fraught with angst.

Sometimes, however, it's not obvious what the problem is. When that happens, it's up to you to create one. You always have to make sure that the character is undergoing some kind of difficulty. If it's not in the script, you have to provide a dilemma for your character. This creates conflict, which is the fuel that all soaps run on. The story lines revolve around soap characters trying to overcome the obstacles. Obstacles can be external, created by outside stimuli; or they can be internal, created by internal stimuli. Soap characters are always dealing with one of these two. In fact, dramatic characters in all genres are dealing with either internal or external obstacles.

So when auditioning for soaps, make sure that you acknowledge problems the character faces; or if none exists, create problems for yourself. Remember, though, that it's not enough to simply acknowledge the problem. Your acting task is to try to *overcome* the problem. This will give you an automatic objective.

EXERCISES

- Tape the first non-gender-specific scene from Principle 2, creating a problem for your character. Make sure that the problem revolves around your partner and is something that you're trying to deal with or change about that person. For example, he might be having an affair with your spouse, or she could have just received a promotion over you. Don't share the problem with anyone — especially your partner. Play it back and see if the audience can guess what problems exist between the two of you.

- Tape the same scene again; this time select a problem that is internal, a problem that you're dealing with that doesn't affect your partner. Choose a means of trying to overcome that problem in the scene. Let the scene dictate the method you elect as the means of dealing with it. For example, you've just found out that you have cancer; in your inability to deal with the news, you end up taking your anger out on your scene partner. Again, don't share your choice with anyone. Play it back and discuss the results. Is the audience able to guess the problem each of you has picked for yourselves?

5. Characters always have mysteries and secrets.

Some of the early soap operas began as mystery series; popular serials included "The Shadow" on radio and "The Secret Storm" on television. More than melodramatic, these shows were eerie and mysterious. Today, radio soap operas are very rare, and television soaps have certainly evolved in different directions. But many of the soaps on television still retain some of the mystery that helped make them so popular in the beginning.

The mystery genre in novels and films is beloved because audiences like the excitement of a good whodunit. Soaps incorporate mysterious features into their production values just as they did when they first began: dramatic music to punctuate climactic moments, cliffhanger endings where you have to wait to find out what happens next, people reincarnated from the dead, ghosts, voices from the beyond, people appearing out of nowhere, odd discoveries, and so on. These are all instruments of good mystery and are meant to gain and hold the audience's attention.

I once appeared in a soap opera that used mistaken identity to incorporate an element of mystery. I played Nick Barnes on "General Hospital," a master of disguise and the head of security for an evil conglomerate that wanted to take over the world. (No joke.) In this particular story line, Nick infiltrated the police department impersonating another character, one of the heroes of the show. Nick's intention was to make it look like the hero had committed a series of crimes. The hero actually played me posing as him until he took off the mask, revealing his true identity as Nick. The viewers did not know it was Nick until the moment of truth when Nick, disguised as the hero, goes in to the restroom of a club and peels off his mask. At that moment in the videotaping, I stepped in and was taped peeling off a mask of the hero. With some clever camera shots no one ever suspected a thing.

Everyone on soap operas also has a secret. Show me a character on a soap opera without a secret past, and I'll show you a character not worthy of being on daytime television. Characters are always hiding something from someone (or everyone) else. Everyone, that is, except the audience. Dramatic irony — when the audience knows what is going on and one or more of the characters doesn't — plays a big role in this principle. Most of the time the audience is aware of each character's secrets while the other characters are not: "Oh no, don't marry him! He's no good. I know where he's been." A friend of mine who became a contract player on a particular soap received a letter from a fan who seemed to know even more about his character than he did, and who warned him of other characters. "I know you're going to be involved with Summer; she has waited a long time for someone like you. But make sure you stay away from Stan and Betty!" the fan warned him.

The consequence of everyone having a secret is that everyone is somewhat mysterious and enigmatic. Very few soap characters are totally open and willing to be vulnerable (if they are, they are usually in trouble); there's too much at stake. When you're auditioning for a soap opera, appreciate this characteristic of soap characters. Like a good poker player, don't let anyone know your hand; always keep something in reserve. Create a secret if there isn't an obvious one. Act as if you know something that no one else knows — even if you have to pretend to hear your own private scary music accompanying you as you say your lines.

EXERCISES

- As a warm-up in a group setting, try this game: Have the group members sit on the floor with their eyes closed. With a tap on the head, the group leader randomly chooses one person to be the "murderer." On cue everyone opens their eyes and wordlessly starts moving around the room. The only way to communicate in this group is to make eye contact. The murderer kills by blinking twice at his victims. When killed, the victims have to fall to the floor and are out of the game. If possible, tape this exercise. Play it back and pay close attention to the behavior of everyone. How did the murderer behave knowing his secret? Was there a mysterious air in the crowd created by not knowing who the murderer was?

- With the first non-gender-specific scene from Principle 2, choose a secret that might fit with what you know about the scene. Do not share your secret with anyone else, especially your partner. Tape the scene, letting the secret influence your performance. Play it back and discuss it. Did having a secret result in the scene being mysterious?

6. Subtext is always present.

Subtext literally means "under the text." It may be better described as the implication of what is being said, or what you really mean to say, but don't. Most of us employ subtext every day whether we are aware of it or not. How often have you said one thing only to mean something else? We'll say, "I'm hungry," and really mean "Where do you want to go eat?" or "Why aren't you in the kitchen cooking dinner?" or "I'm bored." How often have you heard someone say, "I wish you'd just say what you mean."

Because the dialogue in soap operas can be rather pedestrian, subtext abounds, and because of Principles 2, 4, and 5 (the need for the dialogue to be conversational and the problems and secrets that every soap character has), an undercurrent always has to be played beneath the dialogue. It's as if soap characters never really say what they mean.

There's also an element of dramatic irony going on in soaps regarding the subtext. Let's take a hypothetical scene with two doctors, one of whom is sleeping with the other's wife, going over a patient's file. The audience and the adulterous doctor know what is going on, but the unsuspecting doctor doesn't. The audience gets a vicarious thrill seeing how the adulterous doctor deals with the unsuspecting one and will certainly read into his subtext. Another example would be when the unsuspecting doctor finds out (after playing the Three Rs!) that the adulterous doctor is sleeping with his wife; the audience knows this, but the adulterous doctor doesn't yet. That scene would definitely contain a lot of subtext.

The given circumstances combined with the relationship of the characters always determine the subtext. Everyone always has a dramatic agenda; genuine small talk is rare in soap operas. Even in a seemingly relaxed moment, something important is always going on. The actor's job is to discover the appropriate subtext and incorporate it into acting the scene.

When auditioning for soaps, make sure you are aware of the given circumstances and the relationship between the characters. If you are reading a casual scene for the audition, select a subtext. Uncover what the character is really saying. I recommend *writing out the subtext* alongside the audition sides or on a separate piece of paper. As you read the scene, try thinking the subtext.

EXERCISES

- Watch your favorite soap opera. If you don't have one, randomly choose a soap to watch. As you are watching it, vocalize what you think the character's subtext is. It would be fun to do this with someone else and to have each of you, in a two-person scene, verbalize a character's subtext; pretend you are an interpreter and you have to interpret what the characters really mean.

- Create an improvisation with two actors "performing" a soap scene while two other actors offstage are vocalizing the subtext of the soap characters. Tape the scene and try it two different ways: Have the onstage soap actors aware of their subtext, then have them unaware of their subtext. Play it back and discuss it.

- Have everyone in class write down a given circumstance and relationship for two people on one piece of paper. All the scenes should take place in a coffee shop. Make sure that they are "soap worthy" in the spirit of the earlier example of the two doctors; (two doctors on a break in the hospital cafeteria, one of whom just found out that the other one is having an affair with his wife). Pass them around so that each pair of actors receives a given circumstance and a relationship. Memorize the text from the second non-gender-specific scene from Principle 2. Using the text from that scene, each actor should write down a corresponding subtext. If possible, tape the scene without the rest of the class present. Play it back and see how much the audience can describe about the scene. See if they can guess the relationship, the given circumstances, and the subtext.

7. All soap characters undergo suffering, which leads to tension.

The natural consequence of characters having problems and enduring mysterious secrets is that they're going to suffer. Suffering is a principle of soap opera acting because you want to expose it rather than hint at it. The consequence of all this suffering is tension.

These people are under a lot of stress; the audience knows this and wants to see it. The progression goes like this: problems = secrets = subtext = suffering = tension = conflict. Conflict is something soap operas have in abundance. In films, an interesting acting choice would be to play against the suffering, not to acknowledge it. (I deal with this in the chapter on film acting.) But this nuance does not exist in soap operas. The soap opera genre simply doesn't allow for that kind of finesse.

In a way, this lack of subtlety is fun to act. Soap characters are not afraid of showing their suffering and the resultant tension — they seem to revel in their torment. The more you as an actor can communicate that torment, the better off you will be. I know fine actors who cannot do soap operas because of their instinctive reluctance to play the obviousness called for in soaps. They shy away from the perceptible suffering that these characters endure. Excellent soap actors have the ability to incorporate all these qualities yet still appear honest and real.

When auditioning for soaps, don't be afraid to reveal the suffering and tension that is the consequence of the character's problems and secrets and the subtext. Do not be timid about letting the casting director see your wonderful capability of suffering and withstanding tension. Since auditions are naturally tense anyway, I suggest incorporating that tension into the character. Auditioning for a soap opera may be the only time in your career where you might want to let them see you sweat.

EXERCISES

- Review both exercises in Principle 4, the second exercise in Principle 5, and the third exercise in Principle 6. Repeat them, making sure that you bring suffering and tension to them.

8. Every soap opera character has a job.

An actor's homework is to uncover everything she can about the given circumstances. This includes discovering what a character does for a living. Like the real people who make up the audience, characters always have jobs. The irony is that viewers seldom see characters actually doing their jobs, and yet many story lines center on characters' place of employment. You always have doctors, nurses, and administrators running around hospitals, but you rarely see them treating anybody. In fact, you know them by how they look, how they dress. The same is true for police. Activity is always going on at the police station, but frequently it's not police business. Soap characters are always involved doing something — but it's rarely doing their job.

A notable exception might be in courtrooms. Court scenes are legendary in soap operas because, like weddings, they are highly anticipated by the audience. They also tend to revolve around climactic moments in plot or character story lines. Because of the length of time it can take for courtroom story lines to evolve, actors who are day players or under-fives are eager to work on them. Actors are also enthusiastic about doing extra work as jurors because it will mean a lot of employment.

When you're auditioning, it's imperative that you are aware of how characters in the same profession dress. In a way that's more critical than knowing what your character does for a living. The best advice I can give regarding this is to watch soaps and see what the different characters are wearing by profession. This is especially true if you get a call to audition for a specific soap opera. What the lawyers wear on "General Hospital"might be different than what the lawyers wear on "All My Children." For soaps this kind of research is more important than knowing anything about the job or profession. Each soap opera has its own unique look and style. This is evidenced primarily in the economic and social status of the characters, and this status is directly linked to the jobs of the characters and what they wear to work.

EXERCISES

- Watch different soap operas and create a chart based on the jobs prevalent on each of the particular soaps. Categorize each job by what the individual characters wear. For instance, do the doctors all wear shirts and ties under their white coats? Do all the lawyers wear suits?

- As part of this chart, categorize the characters by their status and social standing. Discover if there is any correlation between this and the jobs prevalent on each soap opera. Try to determine the difference of status and social standing between soaps. Which ones are more upscale? Which ones better represent lower classes? Try to discern the relationship between class and the kinds of jobs common on that particular soap.

- Have everyone in class write down a job in pairs (for example, two carpenters, two social workers, two waitresses) and pass them out to pairs of actors. Each group should memorize the second nongender-specific scene in Principle 2. Tape the scene, playing your idea of that particular job. Play it back and discuss it.

9. Always bring the intense part of your personality to the character.

Soap characters are uniquely intense. By now, you should understand the reasons behind this. Call it the "knitted brow" look or whatever you like, soap characters always have a highly concentrated demeanor. Whether it's a lusty affair, a nasty confrontation, a sorrowful confession, an intriguing scheme, or a dream come true, it's all done with intensity in soaps. This quality is, of course, the opposite of the charming quality that you need for sitcoms.

A physical characteristic designating intensity shared by male and female characters in soaps might be the squinty-eyed glance, which is going to automatically produce a knitted brow. A particularly feminine characteristic during these moments would be the pursed-lip pout along with the squinty-eyed glance. For men, it will be the jaw clench. The jaw clench results from the teeth being clenched so tightly that the jaw visibly undulates. Both these physical characteristics are common on soaps. They are usually evident as a reaction (a customary summation of the Three Rs) and coincide with an internal monologue. An internal monologue is a discernable thought process that can also be defined as the subtext of the silence.

An example of an intense physical characteristic used by a woman might be when she has found out that her rival has just set her up for a downfall. Angered, she might look away and externalize her thoughts of "I'll get her" with the pursed-lip pout and a narrowing of the eyes. An example for a man might be when he sees his best friend escort his girlfriend outside at a party. Jealous, he could choose the jaw clench as an indication of "I knew it."

Don't feel as if you have to adhere to these prescribed physical characteristics, however. There is no formula. What's important is that it's obvious to the audience that you are *thinking*, which tends to be more fervent during a passionate situation. If you are being honest in your thought process, something physically dramatic will automatically happen. Discover the physical characteristics that are endemically yours when undergoing intense periods.

Do not overlook the need for intensity in your audition. Be aware that casting directors choose emotionally charged scenes to have actors audition from — and bring the necessary intensity to those moments. Also, don't make the mistake so many actors do by assuming the audition is over when the dialogue stops. Rarely in soap operas do they immediately cut to a commercial (or another scene) at the end of a highly dramatic scene. The camera usually lingers on the character who is affected by the situation to let the character have his or her moment. In your audition make sure you seize the time independent of the dialogue to give yourself an internal monologue.

EXERCISES

- Have everyone in class write down strong emotions (rage, love, jealousy, happiness, and so on). Pass out the slips of paper so that everyone gets one. Using the first non-gender-specific scene from Principle 2, everyone should play the scene with as much intensity as possible. Try not to let the emotion force you into overacting. Tape them. Play them back and discuss the effectiveness of the intensity.

- Like the exercise for subtext in Principle 6, tape two actors improvising a soap scene. However, the two actors are not allowed to speak. Off camera actors are to articulate the inner monologues of the two actors. The challenge for the on-camera actors is to justify the inner monologues provided for them. Play it back and discuss it.

10. Energy.

Last but not least, this principle is important for soap acting because it takes an enormous amount of energy to act effectively in soap operas. Again, I suggest that you do as much extra work on soaps as possible so that you become familiar with the process. When you are in the soap environment for any length of time, you develop a keen appreciation of the skill required to do this material two, three, or four days a week. To take dialogue that is written for soaps and make it effective is a process that demands talent and energy. Everyone who works on a soap is a consummate professional who brings enormous vitality to his or her work.

If you thoroughly observe and habitually exercise the principles of soap acting, you are going to need a lot of energy; the concentration alone needed for acting in soaps requires a great deal of energy.

Like any work done on camera, the key is gauging your energy so that you will have it when you need it. When your important scene is being taped at 7:00 P.M. and you've been at the studio since 7:00 A.M., you're going to need to summon the necessary amount of energy to perform with intensity, mystery, and subtext. To be able to do this day after day requires amazing stamina. Don't trust me; ask any of the regulars on soaps who have been doing this for many years.

EXERCISES

- Exercise to get in shape and exercise to stay in excellent physical condition. This is a principle that really applies to all acting. Acting is like a sport; it requires tremendous physical and mental strength and endurance. For anything you do on camera — whether it's commercials or soaps or films — you're going to need to be in excellent shape.

SOAP OPERA EXERCISES

At this point it might be a good idea to apply these principles to your work. These exercises will work best if you are working in a class situation and, ideally, have access to a studio containing three cameras and switching capabilities. Switching is what the director does in the booth; it's the process whereby the director either cuts or dissolves from one camera shot to the next. Don't worry if you don't have access to highly sophisticated equipment. If you're in a class situation and only have one camera, that will be sufficient. The technical prowess isn't what's important — the emphasis should be on the acting values.

If you do have access to a three-camera setup with switching capabilities, tape the following exercises as a simulation of a real soap opera. As a refresher, let's review the camera angles and what happens technically during taping. (Of course, this applies only if you have rather sophisticated equipment.)

The center camera is for the master shot that is meant to establish the whereabouts of the scene, as well as to shoot wide shots containing more than one character. The camera to the left of the center camera is meant to shoot diagonally to its right, or camera left from the actors' point of view (POV). The camera to the right of the center camera is meant to shoot diagonally to its left, or camera right from the actors' point of view. The main purpose of the left and right cameras is to get individual shots of actors in a two-person scene.

On a soap opera, the director is in the booth wearing a headset so that she can communicate with the camera operators. The director also has monitors that show her the pictures of what all three cameras are shooting. For example, if the master shot is the shot the director is currently using — she can tell camera 1 (the left camera) to get a close-up of the actress in the scene. When the director switches to that shot (camera 1), she can then set up the next shot, and so on. These are all pretty much rehearsed during the camera blocking and dress rehearsals. During the following exercises, experiment with switching between camera shots. Notice the different results you achieve between cutting to another shot versus dissolving to another shot.

On a simpler note, if you are only using one camera, try to maintain a master shot of the scene but be prepared to zoom in on a close-up during an intense or significant moment. With one camera you can also shoot a two-person scene three times, once as a master and once as a single shot of each character.

EXERCISE 1

Everyone is to create an individual brief scenario to be filmed without sound (also known as MOS). The situation must incorporate a simple activity combined with an inner monologue. Make sure each character has a specific job, problem or secret and is suffering because of it. The activity you choose must motivate the character into playing the Three Rs: revelation, realization, and reaction. Make sure the reaction is strong and specific. Do not share any of this with your fellow classmates.

Don't worry if this sounds a little complicated. I'll give you an example: The setting is my kitchen table; my activity is coming in for breakfast and reading the paper. I do this every morning. *Job*: I'm a lawyer. *Problem*: I am breaking the law, therefore I could be in trouble. *Secret*: My partner and I are embezzling money from our firm. *Suffering*: I am feeling extreme guilt about it. As I enact the scenario, I maintain an inner monologue the entire time. The activity of reading the paper is going to help motivate me into playing the Three Rs: revelation, realization, and reaction. Now it sounds simple, doesn't it?

As I do every morning, I come downstairs to have my coffee and read my newspaper. I take up the paper and see the headline that says my partner has been arrested for embezzling funds from the firm. As I read the headlines my inner monologue becomes my revelation: "Oh my God. My partner has been arrested." My realization becomes, "He's going to implicate me." My reaction (focused on myself) as I put down the paper is, "I'm screwed. My career is over."

That seems rather soaplike doesn't it? Now create your own scenario and make sure you don't share it with anyone. Everyone should tape his or her scenario. After the entire group is finished, play back the tape for everybody and have them guess what is going on with the character and what his inner monologue seems to be. See how many of the specifics they can guess about each scene.

EXERCISE 2

Everyone pairs up. Determine which partner is A and which B. The entire group should memorize the following contentless scene.

> A: If I ask you one more time to do what I've asked, you'll regret it for the rest of your life.
> B: I can't understand why you want me to do that. But if it's part of my job description, then fine.

Each pair writes down a scenario that might fit this dialogue. Try not to make it gender-dependent, but make sure you include the *situation*, a *profession for each person*, and a *secret problem for each character*. For example, you might invent the following — *situation*: strip club where A is teaching B the ropes; *profession*: strippers (A is the veteran and B is the novice); *secret problem*: B is actually an undercover cop and doesn't want to get caught; and A realizes that B is actually her long-lost daughter.

After each pair has written a scenario, these scenarios are collected and randomly passed them out; pairs should not perform the scenario they wrote. Each pair rehearses the scene as an rehearsed improvisation that revolves around the situation. Try not to let the lines completely dominate the scene. Also, make an effort to incorporate as many of the other principles as possible into your improvisation. For instance, keep the lines conversational, play the intensity of the moment, and try at some point to include the Three Rs.

Tape the scenes. Play them back and talk about them. Let the issues for discussion consist of the clarity of the relationships, situation, soaplike qualities, and evidence of principles. See how much of the story line the audience can guess.

EXERCISE 3

Choose the juiciest scenarios from "Soap Opera Flashback" or *Soap Opera Digest*, from one of the following, or write your own. Keep the scenarios limited to those suitable for two or three people.

Pass them out in a class situation and cast them. Each group should prepare an improvisation based on the situation. Emphasis in this exercise should be on the subtext, intensity, and tension while maintaining the integrity of the given story line. Feel free to add other principles as well.

Tape them, play them back, and discuss them.

Possible scenarios:

For Two People

Blythe's actions make Fritz suspicious. She ends up telling him that she is leaving him for another man.

Mourning over Kurt's frozen body, Lindsee is overjoyed to discover that Kurt's heart is actually beating.

Jake confronts his brother Douglas about Douglas's affair with Jake's wife.

Julie served her friend Olga cocktails spiked with a truth serum in order to get Olga to confess that she killed Scott.

Dana threatens Florence that he'll go to court if Florence doesn't let him see his son Steve.

Chief and Maura make sure that the people eavesdropping in the next room get an earful.

After Jo confesses her love for Billy, she is shocked to learn that he wasn't who she thought he was.

For three people

Peter startles Alexis and Brad as they are getting ready to go for a late-night swim.

Rosaline stuns Charlie and Celia by declaring that she killed Penny.

Loretta intervenes just as Kim is getting ready to kiss Annie.

Allan enters the bathroom just in time to prevent Josh from drowning Munch.

Max tries to make Lee jealous by flirting with Sara.

Hunter is furious when he hears his daughter, Delanie, refer to Clyde as her father.

SUMMARY

Soap operas are a highly enduring form of entertainment and extremely popular with audiences. They are favorites with actors as well because a lot of them are employed in soaps and many actors get their start on soaps. The different employment opportunities on soaps are contract players, recurring roles, day players, under-fives and extras.

Most soaps have two casting directors. The casting process for the contract, recurring, and day-player roles is quite strenuous, but a newly arrived actor has a pretty good chance to get under-five and extra work. While it's advisable to send pictures and résumés to both casting directors, you will probably stand a better chance of being seen if you pursue the under-five and extra casting director.

No matter what kind of rehearsal schedule a particular soap uses, make sure you know your place in the schedule.

Keep in mind these principles when auditioning and acting in soap operas:

1. *Know the story line.* There are different types of story lines, but almost all revolve around big issues like life, death, sex, jealousy, and revenge.

2. *Dialogue is always conversational and personal.* This helps keep the story lines drawn out and helps create a bond with the audience.

3. *Soap acting always contains the Three Rs.* It is a listening and responding technique that stands for *revelation* (the Aha! moment), the *realization* (the implication of the revelation), and the *reaction* (which is the payoff of the previous two). The reaction can be focused on the self, the other, or the circumstances.

4. *Soap characters always have a problem.* If it's not apparent, create one. What's important is that you try to overcome the difficulty.

5. *Characters are* endowed with *mysteries* and *secrets.* Find the enigma, but make sure you don't show too much.

6. *Subtext is constantly present.* Find the underlying meaning and write it out.

7. *Characters undergo suffering, which leads to tension.* Don't be afraid of revealing both.

8. *Every character has a job.* Make sure you know what he or she wears doing it.

9. Always bring the *intense* part of your personality to the role. To physically manifest the intensity, remember to have an inner monologue going.

10. *Energy.* You can't perform in soaps without it.

CHAPTER 6
EPISODIC TELEVISION

Considering the ubiquity of television today, it is truly remarkable how far programming has come since its inception in the late 1930s. Early TV sets had seven-inch screens, and if you received any picture at all, it was mostly snow. Televisions were expensive, and few people owned one or took the medium seriously. Radio was still the most popular home entertainment, and what was being produced were mostly serials (the soaps), news, sports, and variety shows.

The 1950s revolutionized television, ushering in the "Golden Age of Television." Television became as popular as radio had been before it. People started to watch in staggering numbers. The increasing popularity meant a growing demand for more programming and for more TV sets. On December 31, 1949, for instance, there were 3 million television sets in the country; at the end of 1950 there were 10 million, and by the end of 1955 there were 35 million. The number of TV sets has continued to grow exponentially.

"Philco-Goodyear Playhouse" (on NBC) and "Studio One" (on CBS) were early examples of nighttime series, what we call episodic television today. Playwrights wrote them, and they were shot live. (In fact, playwright Paddy Chayefsky's "Marty" was one of the first live dramas to appear on television; it was subsequently made into a movie.) Television writers didn't exist at the time, and screenwriters wrote only for films. (Because of television's fledgling existence, screen writers would likely have been insulted if confused with playwrights writing for television.) Not only did these productions give many playwrights a chance to get their scripts produced, but they also gave directors and many underemployed New York actors options for work apart from Broadway and other live theater. These shows were all shot in New York, which at that time was the epicenter of this new media.

Although some episodic programs are still shot in New York, the vast majority are now filmed in Los Angeles. As proof of television's current dominance, its production has now supplanted film production in Los Angeles by a wide margin. Successful television writers today are well respected, work full time for television, and make wonderful livings writing exclusively for episodic television. Directors strive to work in this genre, and actors who are regulars on episodic television become big stars. These nighttime dramas are no longer shot live, but filmed with one camera much like a movie, with the exception that they usually face intense time and economic constraints. Current examples of episodic television include "E.R.," "N.Y.P.D. Blue," "Law and Order," "Alias," "CSI: Crime Scene Investigation," and "The Guardian."

In this chapter we move away from the multicamera world of situation comedies and soap operas and back to the one-camera filmmaking used in making commercials. Acting for episodic television presents unique challenges for the actor, which include the different types of shots, concerns of coverage, and, most important, continuity. Just as the discussion of techniques needed for multicamera shooting included situation comedies and soap operas, the discussion of one-camera techniques incorporates both episodic television and film. However, before we get into a discussion of these challenges, let's look at the employment options of episodic television and what you might expect when you audition for them.

WHAT IS THE PAY SCALE FOR EPISODIC TELEVISION?

The money you can make in episodic television falls under the jurisdiction of SAG. The amount of money is comparable to acting in motion pictures as well as movies of the week and miniseries.

Similar to all the other genres, there are two categories of employment: principal and extra. (SAG also has categories for stunt performers, dancers, singers, special ability extras, stand-ins, and so forth. I'm only going to deal with principals and extras.) Principals have lines; extras don't. The current day rate for a principal performer is $655. For an extra, it's $110. The weekly rate for a principal performer is $2,272. Extras don't have weekly rates; they only have day rates. The amounts that I cite here are *minimums*. Agents and managers always negotiate for more than the minimum rate.

SAG also stipulates that principals and extras receive overtime if they work more than eight hours a day (not including meal breaks). Overtime can be quite lucrative. Rules vary concerning how much you can make, but, generally, after eight hours you receive time and a half or double time depending on how long you work. There have been instances when I have doubled my day's salary just because of overtime! As a penalty, you can also receive overtime if the production company doesn't feed you at a certain time or if you don't get a break at the correct time. There are rules about how long you must have off between the end of one day's work and the call time for the next day's shoot. It's the second assistant director's job to keep track of breaks and hours. At the end of each day's shooting, this person will ask you to sign a time sheet accounting for the hours you spent working, taking breaks, and eating meals. It is the actor's responsibility to know when breaks are due and when it's time for meals. You need to make sure that the hours and breaks are recorded correctly or you may not get paid appropriately. Because of union rules, you should always get compensated for overtime.

Best of all, there are residuals when television programs and films are rerun. Obviously, you don't make residuals the first time the program is aired; the network has already paid you for the filming. All subsequent reruns, however, are subject to residuals. The amount of money depends on your original contract and where and how often the show is rerun. You receive the full amount of your original fee for a network rerun up to $3162 for a one-hour show and up to $2189 for a half-hour show. If the episide was filmed after July 1, 2003, the rates have increased to $3225 for a one-hour show and $2266 for a half-hour show. Not bad, huh? (This is based on a typical contract. Of course, everything is negotiable.) Unfortunately, this doesn't last forever: the residual decreases for each subsequent showing. And, if the show is rerun on cable, the royalties are less.

For work done on film (motion pictures) the residual structure is similar. You've already been paid for the work done on the movie and don't get anything extra when it is shown in movie theaters. Like episodic television, miniseries, and movies of the week, the residuals for film also decrease during subsequent showings on network and cable television.

When a TV program is released on video or DVD, actors make residuals on its sale and rental. Residuals are also paid for pay TV and supplemental markets, such as TV programs and movies shown on airplanes. (I still receive dwindling residual checks for episodic programs, movies of the week, and films that I did years ago. Sometimes the checks are ridiculously small. There's nothing stranger about receiving and cashing a check for sixty-eight cents!)

Like situation comedies, billing — where the actor is listed in the credits — is subject to negotiation by agents. Basically, the same billing categories apply to episodic television and sitcoms: series regulars, guest stars, co-stars, and featured actors. Guest stars, co-stars, and featured actors are usually only hired for specific episodes. Series regulars are the stars of the series and are under contract. They receive the highest billing. Guest stars are exactly what they sound like — they are equivalent to the series regulars, but generally only work on one episode and are normally not under contract. They receive important billing usually displayed at the beginning of an episode. Co-stars and featured actors usually only receive billing in the cast list at the end of an episode. Extras never receive billing.

HOW DO I AUDITION
FOR EPISODIC TELEVISION?

The audition process for episodic television is similar to situation comedies. When a pilot is sold to a network, the producers (who sometimes already have a star as part of the package) start looking for the needed cast. They send a breakdown to all agents and managers and request submissions. Agents and managers then submit pictures and résumés of the clients who they feel are best suited to play those roles. After an extensive audition process, the producers will send their top choices to the network, and the network decides on who gets the lead roles for the specific pilot. (See the discussion of this in chapter 4.)

Once a pilot gets picked up (the term for the network buying the show and scheduling it), the producers will then cast each of the episodes individually. Again, this process is similar to that of sitcoms. As the producers (and staff) prepare to go into production for each episode, the first thing they do is hire a director (if it's not the one who directed the initial pilot or a series regular director). Usually the original casting director has been part of the show since the pilot, and he or she is, in a sense, part of the production team.

HOW DO THE INDIVIDUAL SHOWS CAST THE GUEST STARS, CO-STARS, AND FEATURED ROLES?

On the basis of cast requirements for each of the episodes, the casting director sends out a breakdown to all the agents in town. Let's say that your agent has submitted you for a role, and you are perfect for it. If the casting director is not familiar with your work, she will have you do a cold reading of the script at an audition. This is done regardless of the size of the role. (If the casting director is familiar with your work and thinks that you're right for the role, you may skip this part of the audition process.) If the casting director likes your audition, you will be called back to read for the director and the producers. Generally, whether it's a guest star, co-star, or featured character, approximately five to six people are called back for each role to audition for the director and the producers.

The two biggest differences between auditioning for situation comedies and episodic television are the time it takes to cast them and how many people involved in the production attend the audition. It generally takes much longer to cast episodic television for several reasons. Nighttime dramas require much more production time and expense than sitcoms. Sitcoms are usually thirty minutes long, are videotaped not filmed, and are taped during a five-day period. Episodic programs, on the other hand, are sixty minutes long, are filmed, not taped, and are shot on a ten-day schedule. Therefore, the length of the casting can be longer for episodic television, and a longer period occurs between getting cast and starting work.

You will also find that fewer people attend auditions for episodic television than for sitcoms. Sitcoms are usually written by a staff who often attend the final callbacks. Most episodic shows are written by one person who may or may not attend the callbacks. Whoever is at your audition, it's important to remember that the producers always have the final say about casting. As influential as the director is, he or she usually has to answer to the producer(s).

The cost of producing a weekly drama is exorbitant. There is absolutely no time to waste either at the audition or on the set. You are more likely to get cast for episodic television if you can walk in and immediately fulfill the producers' idea of who the character is. Many actors are trained or have the habit of *developing* a character at an audition; they come with an idea of what they think the character is and then hope that they are given direction. There is little time to develop anything at the audition. The most successful actors in this genre come into the audition as the character and make the producers' choice easy. One of the best things you can do when you audition for episodic television is to literally *be* the character when you walk into the audition. Don't try to work your way into the character; forget about any kind of process where you hope they will discover the character in you. (If you are given direction, great — go for it, but it's rare.) Just *do* it and *be* it (*do* the audition and *be* the character). If this doesn't make complete sense yet, don't worry. Almost all the principles revolve around this issue in one way or another. Just remember you should always strive to be efficient when working in episodic television.

WHAT'S THE DIFFERENCE BETWEEN ACTING WITH THREE CAMERAS AND ONE CAMERA?

Obviously, the biggest difference between the two is the medium used. I've discussed the contrast between tape and film in chapter 4. One of the most important aspects of working in a one-camera format versus a three-camera format is postproduction. *Postproduction* means everything that happens after filming: editing, sound effects and mixing, adding a musical score, digital special effects, and so on. When you tape with three cameras, the director has instantaneous editing capabilities. When filming with one camera, even though the director may have storyboarded the entire piece and have a fairly good idea of what the final result is going to look like, the entire process is dependent on the editing done in postproduction. For the most part, when taping with three cameras you have a finished product by the end of the taping. Think of it this way: Using three cameras in sitcoms and soaps is like *revealing* a picture a section at a time; using one camera in film or episodic television is like *creating* a picture puzzle one piece at a time. The three-camera format exists to capture existing action, whereas in the one-camera format, action is created and exists for the sole benefit of the camera. Therefore, in the one-camera world of episodic television and film, an actor is totally at the mercy of the director and, most especially, the editor. So, as an actor, you may have some control of your performance in a three-camera situation, but you certainly don't when you work with one camera. You have to hope that your performance is lovingly edited.

AS AN ACTOR, WHAT DO I NEED TO KNOW ABOUT EDITING?

As you now know, editors wield tremendous clout. They assemble the final product by cutting and splicing the film from all the footage, usually shot from a single camera. (A cut and splice is a cut from one film source spliced to what will be the final version; every time you see a change in camera angle, that's a cut and splice.) Actors don't really need to involve themselves in the technical concerns of editing. However, the actor does need to appreciate the editor's influence on his performance. The editor can make the actor look good or bad depending on which shot the editor chooses to use (or not use) in the final product. For this reason alone, actors should understand and respect the editor's job. Beyond that, as an actor you need to consider the technical demands of the one-camera format. The actor should have a fundamental knowledge of the different kinds of shots. Most important, the actor is obligated to provide the editor with an interesting performance so that when the film gets to the editor, she has have something to choose from in postproduction.

For most cuts, editors use movement to cut in and out of frames. Editors try to make cuts seamless; cutting from a static picture can be jarring, while movement makes the job of cutting from one frame to another easier for the audience to view. Watch nighttime drama, miniseries, movies of the week, or films. The movement can be as subtle as the blink of an eye or as obvious as a car careening off a cliff. Actors need to be aware that editors are going to use their movement to cut in and out of frames. Now I don't want to open a Pandora's box and have all of you start moving frantically and arbitrarily because you think you're doing the editor a favor. You shouldn't do that. You should know by now that you always want to keep movement precise and measured. However, you'll help the editor (and possibly get her respect) if you include slight movements during transitional moments within the scene, and especially at the end of a scene. What's most important is that the movements fit the character and are justified. The movement has to make sense or no one is going to believe it, especially the editor. By all means, trust the director. Often the director is involved in the editing process, and he will consider the editing while shooting. If the director asks you for movement, accommodate him. Conversely, if the director asks you not to move, don't.

WHAT SHOTS ARE USED IN A ONE-CAMERA FORMAT?

Two basic shots are used in filming: the *master* shot and the *coverage* shot. The master shot is the primary shot. It's sometimes called the cover shot because it covers the length of the action. It's usually a wide angle shot that establishes the situation, characters, or elements of the story. In essence, it's the shot that tells the story, the "big picture." Most of the time the director shoots a master of the entire scene first. The master is the most important shot because it serves as a template for all the other shots (hence the name *master*). For editing purposes, the master is the shot that all the coverage shots come from. In other words, the editor uses the master as the main shot in which to tell the story, and all the coverage shots are cut from that master.

The coverage shots are called setups and are usually filmed after the master. In a way, the coverage shots are extensions of the master shot. For instance, all the point-of-view shots of characters, reaction shots, close-ups, and extreme close-ups are considered coverage shots. It would be safe to say that the master shot is the entire picture, and the coverage shots are smaller detailed sections of that bigger picture.

WHAT OTHER KINDS OF SHOTS ARE THERE?

Actors don't need to be technically expert, but it helps to be familiar with these technical terms — especially since you'll see them used in scripts.

Essentially, there are four types of shots; the differences among them are based on scale, angle, camera moves, and the camera's point of view. (Some of these terms are also used in videotaping.)

Scale refers to the position of the lens in relation to the subject. Listed below are the terms with their abbreviations and definitions.

Close-up (CU) A shot composed of the head and shoulders of a character.

Extreme close-up (ECU) A shot that is tighter than a close-up. For instance, a section of a face.

Medium shot (MS / MED. SHOT) A shot where the camera views the actor from the waist up.

American shot (Also called a Hollywood, cowboy, or knee shot) A shot framed to include figures from the knees up.

Long shot (LS) Shots composed to see far into the distance.

Wide shot (WS) Shots composed to see a wide vista.

Single A shot containing only one person.

Two shot A shot where the camera frames two characters in a scene. (You could have a medium two shot or a long two shot, etc.)

Full figure A shot composed around the scale of a full human figure.

Two T shot (not a politically correct term) A shot framed from the chest up.

Angle refers to the position of the camera itself. Listed below are the different angles and a description of each.

High angle A shot taken from an angle above the object.

Low angle A shot taken from the angle below the object.

Aerial shot A very high angle shot from the sky (often accomplished with a helicopter or airplane).

High hat shot A shot positioned very low as if it were a hat's height off the floor. (It's named after a piece of equipment called a high hat, which is designed to hold the camera close to the floor.)

Three-quarters shot A shot positioned halfway between a frontal angle and a profile. (Much like a three-quarter position on stage.) It can be either a three-quarter front or back shot.

Profile A shot taken from a side angle.

Straight on or frontal A shot looking directly at the object.

Over the shoulder (OTS) A shot of a character over the shoulder of another character with whom they are having the conversation.

Canted frame (Also called Dutch or Chinese angles) A shot where the camera is tilted sideways and sets the objects on an irregular angle. (Remember the old "Batman" TV series?)

Reverse angle A shot that is 180 degrees opposite the preceding shot. (A good example of this are the reverse angles used on "Monday Night Football.")

Camera moves refer to motion shots, done while the camera is in motion. Listed are the different moves and descriptions.

Dolly shot (Also called a tracking or trucking shot) The camera travels on a dolly track; it is usually used to describe shots moving on the z-axis. (The z-axis means the camera is pushing in or pulling out).

Pan A stationary camera swivels from its base on the horizontal x-axis; a pan is often used to follow the action. (The x-axis is a side-to-side movement.)

Swish pan A very swift pan that blurs the scene between the camera's starting and ending point, done on the x-axis.

Tilt A stationary camera pivots up and down from its base, which does not move.

Follow shot The camera follows an actor. (This is very often also a dolly shot; the only difference between it and a pan is that a pan is always a stationary shot that's swiveling from a base.)

Traveling shot Any shot that uses a moving camera body. (A dolly shot is a traveling shot; a pan isn't.)

Car mount Camera positions that are mounted directly on a car.

Static shot Any shot in which the camera does not move.

Handheld The camera operator braces the camera on the shoulder or at hip height. The resulting footage is often used as a point-of-view or documentary-style shot.

Steadicam shot A camera is attached to a harness that is worn and operated by the camera operator in handheld situations. The steadicam shot produces footage with the smoothness of a tracking shot but with the mobility of a handheld shot.

(Both handheld and steadicam shots are currently widely used on episodic television.)

Zoom Normally used in video. Refers to the movement of a zoom lens.

Zolly The camera dollies in and zooms out at the same time. Hitchcock, Spielberg, and Scorsese love to use this shot.

Point-of-view terms refer mostly to the film-editing process.

Point-of-view shot (POV shot) The camera takes the point of view of a character in the scene; the shot sees what the character sees. To establish a POV shot, usually a shot of the character immediately precedes it.

Objective shot (OBJ shot) The camera sees the scene from an angle not seen by any character in the scene.

Establishing shot Like a master shot telling an audience the location of the action, this is often a wide shot of the outside of a building or structure where the scene is taking place.

Setup This refers to the position of a camera and the lighting of a shot or shots. *New setup* refers to the camera moving to a new position. Every time the camera moves constitutes a new setup.

Offscreen (OS) or **off camera** (OC) A description of what is heard but not seen on the screen.

Cutaway A quick cut to another scene before the camera returns to the master or previous shot.

Jump cut Successive shots cut on the same axis (z or x). This term also describes successive cuts that disrupt the flow of time or space. For instance, think of a series of shots moving closer to the subject without using a zoom.

Match cut or **match dissolve** A cut or dissolve from one similar composition to another (such as a close shot of a wheel cut or dissolved to a close shot of a globe that fills the same size and position in the frame). A classic example is Janet Leigh's eye and the shower drain after her murder in *Psycho*.

CAN YOU GIVE AN EXAMPLE OF A MASTER SHOT AND DIFFERENT COVERAGE SHOTS?

Let's look at a hypothetical scene that takes place in a diner. It's a simple scene between a waitress and a customer.

Joel is sitting at the counter waiting to order. He is keeping his eye on Emily while she is busy bringing food to other customers, taking away dirty dishes, and so forth. Emily has also noticed Joel and is letting him know that she'll be there as soon as she can. She finally approaches him.

Emily: Hi, Joel. How are you?

Joel: Good, Em. How you doing?

Emily: OK . . . Hate being stuck in here.

Joel: I know what you mean. It's beautiful outside.

Emily: Don't rub it in.

Joel: Sorry . . .

Emily: That's OK. Did you want to order something?

Joel: Ummm, sure.

Emily: What can I get you?

Joel: How about a club sandwich. Could I have that on wheat toast?

Emily: Anything you want. You want the works?

Joel: Sure, but tell them to go light with the mayo.

Emily: No problem. Something to drink?

Joel: I'll have an ice tea.

Emily: Coming right up . . . *(Starts to leave.)*

Joel: Hey, Em . . .

Emily: *(Returning.)* Is there something else you wanted?

Joel: Ummm, any chance you'll go out with me Friday night?

Emily: Wow. That came out of nowhere. Are you kidding?

Joel: I've been meaning to work up the courage to ask for a while.

Emily: You're not kidding me . . .

Joel: No. Would you?

Emily: *(Pause.)* Absolutely . . . I never thought you'd ask . . . *(Starts to leave, comes back.)* . . . You said to go light on the mayo?

We'll start off with a master shot of the scene (see figures 1 and 2). The master shot tells the entire story of the scene; to do this we must establish situation and character. Once you establish where you are and who is in the scene, the characters' relationship is a natural by-product. If this were a new scene in a dramatic episodic series, the editor would probably add an establishing shot of the exterior of the diner to let the audience know where the scene is taking place.

Let's identify the types of shots that might be considered in composing a master shot for this scene. For scale, you have your choice of a long, wide, medium, or full figure shot. Because a master is usually a long shot, you wouldn't want a close-up shot. You could choose an angle for your master shot, but I wouldn't recommend it. However, you will need to get angle shots on both the coverage shots of Emily and Joel (because of the height differences of Emily standing and Joel sitting).It would certainly be appropriate to incorporate a dolly, or a traveling shot. For this master a legitimate camera point of view would be an objective shot; the script doesn't indicate that the scene is from anyone's specific point of view.

For this master, the camera is set up for an objective long shot looking down the counter at Joel watching Emily waiting on customers. Because it's a long shot, both Joel and Emily are in full figure (see figure 1). Before Emily gets to Joel to take his order, we start to dolly in and end up on a medium shot of both of them just as the dialogue begins (see figure 2). Because it's a master shot, the scene will be shot in its entirety. The director may want to shoot many master shots different ways (high angle or shoot it from the reverse angle).

Fig. 1 Master shot: long shot

Fig. 2 Master shot: medium shot

Generally, however, there's simply not enough time in the shooting schedule in episodic television to get too fancy.

Actors have two principal technical considerations regarding master shots: first, the 180-degree rule; and second, continuity concerns, which I'll address later. Figures 3 and 4 illustrate the 180-degree rule. Imagine a 180-degree line from one end of what the lens sees to the other end (see figure 3). Unless it's a character's POV, all the objective coverage shots must be filmed from somewhere on this arc (see figure 4). The master shots establish a plane of perspective — the basic blueprint of what the audience is going to see.

WHAT'S IMPORTANT ABOUT
THE 180-DEGREE RULE?

An actor needs to know this rule to keep his eye line in sync with the 180-degree arc. The actor's eye line is where he needs to look during coverage. In our example, the lens would always be next to Joel's left eye during Emily's coverage so that her eye line, when she looks at Joel, is always to the left of the lens (see figure 5). The opposite is true for Joel; the lens would always be next to Emily's right eye so that Joel's eye line is to the right of the lens (see figure 6). This may seem basic, but it can become complicated at times.

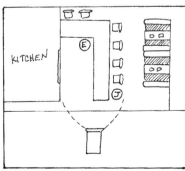
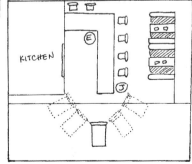

Fig. 3 180-degree rule   Fig. 4 180-degree rule

Fig. 5 Emily's coverage shot.   Fig. 6 Joel's coverage shot.

WHAT ABOUT THE COVERAGE SHOTS?

Once the master shot is filmed, we move on to the different coverages. Remember that all the coverage shots in this example are going to be shot somewhere on the 180-degree arc from where the master was filmed. Also, because we're now moving the camera for each new coverage shot, a new setup is required for each shot.

Let's pretend that Joel's character is a recurring lead role on this show. We'll shoot his coverage first. (Generally the star, or the more important role, gets his coverage shot first.) Our first coverage shot could be a close-up or a medium close-up from behind the counter or a high angle shot filmed from Emily's perspective (see figure 7). Because scenes tend to be broken down by action, this coverage will only accommodate the sequence before the dialogue starts. It's an objective shot whose purpose is to show Joel watching Emily going about her business. Coverage shots like these give the audience a sense of what the character is thinking. You can get fancy with these shots, but because of the need for economy in television, there usually isn't enough time. (For a shot like this where there is no dialogue, it's imperative that the actor playing Joel be thinking: See Principle 6.) It's up to the director, but depending on the type of shot being used, Emily could walk in and out of frame.

Once the dialogue starts, we'll shoot Joel's coverage as a POV shot from Emily's viewpoint. (This would be a director's decision, but it's pretty much a standard type of coverage shot.) We'll choose a high angle shot because Emily is standing over Joel; the camera will be

Fig. 7 Emily's POV: high angle shot   Fig. 8 Emily's POV: high angle shot

placed at the same height as the eyes of the actress playing Emily. If we remember the 180-degree arc from the master shot, we know that the camera has to be placed on Emily's right (see figure 8), so Joel will look just off to the left of the camera's lens (see figure 9). This becomes his eye line. Normally the actress playing Emily will stand with her head next to the lens so that the actor playing Joel can minimize the distance between the lens and her eyes. (The actress playing Emily may even need to walk to a designated spot next to the lens so that the camera can pick up Joel's eye line following Emily into position.)

You may wonder, since this is a POV shot and is supposed to see what the character is seeing, why Joel doesn't look directly into the

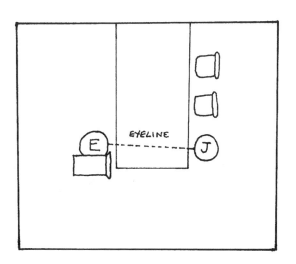

Fig. 9
Emily's POV;
Joel's coverage

lens as if the camera were Emily's eyes instead of looking beside it. This is a legitimate question. The reason is that most of the time the viewers want to feel like they are surreptitiously watching the action. It's disconcerting to have the actor look directly into the lens. Unless it's a conceit established early, most often you won't see characters addressing the camera. Watch coverage shots on television and in films. The characters are usually looking just slightly off the lens. Viewers accept that the actor is talking to another character. If the actor talked directly to the lens, viewers would feel as if he were addressing them personally.

If the above-described shot is what we want for this particular coverage shot, the entire scene will now be shot from this angle (or as much of the scene as the director wants). Just as the director could choose to shoot different kinds of shots for a master, there are any number of coverage shots the director could choose to get of Joel. The challenge for the actor playing Joel in this example is that he has to act as if the camera isn't there. He certainly can't stare at Emily during the entire scene; that wouldn't look natural. On the other hand, as he looks around (which is certainly natural), he has to be careful not to strike the lens (look directly into the camera). Doing so breaks the convention or illusion that the audience is vicariously watching something private. Never forget that in most cases the camera isn't supposed to be there.

Usually other actors you're in a scene with will stay and work with you when they are off camera, but not always. Using our example, if the actress playing Emily were a major star, she might not stay while the camera shot Joel's coverage. In this case, someone else would read Emily's part for the actor playing Joel. (This is actually quite rare.) Because the voices for both characters have already been recorded during the master, the off-camera actor does not need to be present for the on-camera actor's coverage. However, until you become a major star, you will always be expected to be present off camera for the other actor's coverage.

If you are ever confused about what your eye line is for a particular shot, don't be afraid to ask. I've seen highly experienced film actors ask, "What's my eye line for this shot?" The best person to ask is one of the camera operators. Because of the time pressure, don't try and show off how much you know by assuming you know your eye line. Everyone involved would much rather you ask than delay the shoot.

After Joel's coverage is finished, the setup is turned around to shoot Emily's coverage (see figure 10). This time, if we choose to shoot from Joel's POV, we'll use a low angle shot. Because of Emily's movement in this scene (compared to Joel's fairly static position), several setups may be needed for her coverage. For instance, the beginning of the scene, when Emily is waiting on other customers and walking up and down the counter, may entail various shots along the 180-degree arc to see clearly all her action, or even POV shots from the kitchen (see figure 11). There are also two moments when she starts to leave that may require different setups.

So let's say that we're going to need four different setups for Emily's coverage: the first for the action before the dialogue; the second for the beginning of the dialogue until she starts to leave with Joel's order; the third from Joel's line, "Hey, Em . . . " through her line, "I never thought you'd ask"; and the fourth for her last line. Any number of types of shots can be used for her coverage from medium to close-ups to over the shoulder and tracking shots. The challenge for the actress playing Emily is not only acting as if the camera isn't there, but also remembering to maintain her eye line, hit her spike marks, and stay in frame.

Hitting spike marks becomes even more vital when filming with one camera than when taping with three. Filming with one camera necessitates that each shot be carefully planned to make certain that

Fig. 10
Joel's POV;
Emily's coverage

Fig. 11
POV shot from
kitchen

the entire shot stays in focus. Depending on the scale of the shot, if an actor moves inches away from the area that the camera is focused on, the entire shot can be destroyed. Obviously coverage with a lot of movement isn't going to be filmed as tight (another word for *close*) as one with less movement. In other words, the coverage for Emily can be in close-up only when she is standing still talking to Joel. The actress playing Emily will have to be extremely conscientious about hitting her spike marks as she moves throughout her coverage. She will have to stop in a designated place, look up, turn, and see Joel without striking the lens. This could happen in the first part of the scene; for example, while she is waiting on other customers, she could look up at Joel indicating that she'll be there in a minute.

Because only one camera is used to capture everything, the process is very time-consuming. The scene with Emily and Joel requires a fairly simple setup. It has only two principal characters and the dialogue is about two-thirds of a page long. Still, at least four setups will be needed; more than likely seven different setups will be used. Imagine how much time it takes to shoot every scene this way! This gives you an idea of how precious time is even when shooting a simple scene. On an episodic television show, this scene would be shot in an hour or less. To accomplish this complicated task in just one hour, everyone on the set must be a consummate professional: each must know his or her job intimately and perform it flawlessly. Actors have to bear in mind that they, too, are expected to perform (in every sense of the word) their job conscientiously as well.

WHAT HAPPENS TO THE SET WHEN THEY TURN THE CAMERA AROUND?

Everything that the camera sees has to be prepared with set pieces, lighting, and extras. Conversely, everything behind the camera has to be cleared to make room for the camera and the necessary crew. For this reason, many episodic series are shot on a soundstage where all the walls of the sets are removable. Preparing everything within the camera's POV is called *dressing the set*. In our example, the area filmed during the master shot would have to be dressed with extras and set pieces and be lit. During the coverage shot, while Emily and Joel are speaking, an entirely new background needs to be dressed. For instance, let's say in the master shot two customers (extras) leave to pay their bill; they walk toward the camera and pay at the cash register where Joel is sitting. During Joel's coverage, we would have to see them paying at the exact time they did during the master shot. Repeating whatever happens in the master shot during the coverage is called matching the action or maintaining continuity.

WHAT IS CONTINUITY?

The term *continuity* means that continuous and logical action is established throughout filming: An action in the coverage shot must match the action established in the master shot. For example, if an actor opens a door with her right hand in the master shot, she must match that action in all subsequent coverage shots by always opening the door with her right hand. In fact, for matching purposes the actress would also need to stand in the same place and at the same angle. Smoking during a master shot presents a more complex situation: Not only must the actor smoke in the exact same places during coverage, but the cigarette's ash must also match. (One of the best pieces of advice I ever received was that you should never actually smoke during a shoot; for every cigarette "smoked" in a scene, five to ten cigarettes will be consumed during filming.)

Since scenes in episodic television and film are often filmed out of sequence, it's easy to forget what exactly has happened between the master shots and the coverage shots. There are innumerable stories of continuity gaffes in films. One of the most famous is the gladiator in *Spartacus* who wore a wristwatch. A more subtle gaffe occurred in *The Graduate*. Dustin Hoffman was supposed to be driving south, but because he drove north through a specific tunnel, he was really going in the opposite direction. Most film lovers are aware of many more. The mere fact that there are countless stories of continuity inconsistencies is a good indicator of how noticeable — and important — continuity is.

Continuity also embodies the collaborative nature of filmmaking. Almost everyone connected to shooting the film is involved — director, editor, script supervisor, actors, and others. Everyone on a set must be diligent about what happens during shooting so that during postproduction the editor doesn't have to work around continuity mistakes. Because shooting with one camera requires many different setups, maintaining continuity is important to avoid wasting time and money. In shooting film for episodic television or movies, time *is* money.

In our example of Joel and Emily, the coverage shots were filmed immediately after the master, so it wouldn't be that difficult to maintain continuity. But what if we shot the master and something unforeseen arose and we couldn't shoot the coverage for three days (or, in the case of a movie, three weeks)? In those circumstances, it would be understandable for everyone to forget all the subtle actions that were done in the master. Dealing with these challenges of continuity is, for the most part, the script supervisor's job.

WHAT IS A SCRIPT SUPERVISOR?

The script supervisor is the equivalent of a stage manager in the theater. For some reason in the film business, the script supervisor has traditionally been a woman's job; in fact, not too long ago the position was referred to as the "script girl."

A script supervisor's job is one of the most demanding and important on a film set. Besides the director, the director of photography, and the camera crew, the script supervisor is closest to the action on a set. The script supervisor is responsible for notating *everything* in the script that is pertinent. She writes down the actors' blocking; deviations of dialogue in the script (if an actor paraphrases in the master shot, it must be matched in the coverage shots); what the actors are wearing (it's her job to not only make certain that the actors are wearing the same clothes but also that they are wearing them in the same way); how the set is dressed at any given time; the scene's time of day; and, of course, the composition of the camera shots and each shot's point of view. Script supervisors are also responsible for noting which shots are to be printed. (Every time the director yells "cut; print it," the film must be developed. If the director yells only "cut," then that film will not be developed.) As you can imagine, this job is highly responsible and requires amazing organization. It's little wonder that the script supervisor takes a lot of Polaroid (or digital) photographs of the actors and the set.

WHY IS CONTINUITY AN IMPORTANT CONSIDERATION FOR THE ACTOR?

Even with the help of a script supervisor, actors need to take responsibility for their own continuity. This is a requisite skill that actors need to master to act successfully in episodic television or film. It's even more crucial for the actor to pay close attention to continuity when his performance is shot out of sequence. If continuity represents the collaborative nature of filmmaking, one of the actor's jobs in that collaboration is maintaining continuity in his performance. Actors must keep track of what they do physically, how they do it, and where they do it (where in their dialogue they pick up a glass, sit down, walk across a room, stop and turn, and so on). The director and editor are relying on the actor to understand how continuity works and, at the very least, be proficient at matching actions to the dialogue repeatedly over the time it takes to shoot a scene.

In the example of Joel and Emily's diner scene, the actress playing Emily has a much greater challenge in her continuity than the actor playing Joel. This is simply because she has more action. For instance, during the coverage shots in the first part of the scene, she will have to match her actions of delivering food and picking up dirty dishes that she established during the master shot as much as possible. A good way to maintain continuity is to keep movements economical and specific and to justify them. In other words, you should have a reason for everything you do.

Breaking down and analyzing the scene will help you determine movements that are justified and easily matched. In your analysis, you need to define the beats of the scene (beats are the small moments of action comprising a scene). You also need to determine the character's objectives (what the character wants to accomplish) for each beat within the scene. Let's say in our diner scene that Emily has two beats before the dialogue starts. In the first beat she is busy trying to get out the last orders at the end of the lunch rush. Like any good waitress working at a counter, she doesn't waste time, energy, or movement; she brings out more than one plate of food at a time, and when she's finished distributing them, she grabs dirty dishes to bring back with her. Her objective for this beat could be *to get food to the customers as quickly as possible and to clear the empty plates*. This objective will help her to remember where and in what order the food goes, as well as the order in which she picks up the empty plates. After she completes this beat, she sees Joel, which initiates a new beat. She may still have food to get out to other customers, but her objective has changed because she has a secret crush on Joel and she wants to impress him and free up some time so she can wait on him. Obviously the way she gets the food out now will change because her objective has changed.

Once the dialogue starts, I see four beats. The first starts with Emily's line, "Hi, Joel . . . " and ends with her line, "That's OK." The second begins with her line, "Did you want to order something?" and ends with Emily starting to walk away. The third beat begins with Joel's line, "Hey, Em . . ." and ends after Emily's line, "I never thought you'd ask." This final beat is when Emily comes back for her very last line. Beat changes are determined by different criteria: a change of subject, a new idea, someone entering or leaving, or an unexpected event. In our example, Emily's first beat ends and second one begins with her changing the subject; the second one ends with her starting to walk away; the third beat begins with Joel's new idea; the third beat ends with her walking away again; the fourth one begins with her returning and ends with the end of the scene. The actress playing Emily should have a different objective for each of these beats.

This analysis assists the actor in keeping track of continuity by matching the appropriate action with the objective for each beat. (Of course, the movement should also be appropriate for the character.) The actor can then more easily remember what he did and where he did it during the coverage shots. Let's go back to Emily's first two beats. If the actress chooses as an objective getting food to the customers quickly, that objective will determine how she carries the plates. If she has a crush on Joel, when she sees him (which is a beat change), she might choose to make herself look better by wiping a strand of hair from her eyes with the back of her hand. Later in the scene she'll more easily remember that she took out her order pad and pen when the beat changed on her line, *"Did you want to order something?"*

However, it's not enough to be able to successfully match actions. The actor must also be cognizant of emotional continuity.

What do you mean by emotional continuity?

There are two types of continuity: physical and emotional. We've been discussing physical continuity. Emotional continuity is maintaining what the character is feeling from shot to shot and being able to match it from the master shot to the subsequent coverage shots. The truly professional film actor will always consider her character's emotional life as an important part of continuity as well.

Let's continue to use Emily as our example in illustrating emotional continuity. The character of Emily certainly undergoes a change in the way she feels between the first beat of delivering the food and the second beat when she sees Joel. Later, her emotions also make a transition between taking his order and accepting his invitation for a date. Because she has so much physical continuity to keep track of, it can actually help the actress to connect her physical continuity to her emotional continuity.

During the first beat of the scene, Emily is not only in a hurry to get the orders out and clean up the plates, but she is tired of running around. Her emotional state should reflect this. The actress could connect her physical continuity to her emotional continuity by remembering the given circumstances and choosing the appropriate objective. For instance, if, in the master shot, the actress playing Emily chooses the following objective to correspond with the given circumstance: *to get food to the customers as quickly as possible and clear the empty plates,* she might want to add *despite the fact that I'm exhausted from working nonstop for two hours.* This will help her remember her physical continuity (of where the orders go) as well as her emotional continuity (exhaustion). However, her objective changes, as well as her physical and emotional states, when she first sees Joel. A physical action, such as wiping away a strand of hair, could remind her that she wants to *look better to Joel.* In this way the actress uses the action/objective to remember not only her physical but also her emotional continuity.

As an exercise in continuity, proceed through the scene in this manner with both characters. Make sure that you define the beats and employ logical objectives to correspond with the circumstances of the scene. I have also included exercises at the end of this chapter to deal specifically with the issues of physical and emotional continuity. Just keep in mind that when carrying out these exercises *don't choose actions that you can't match!* Don't make complicated physical and emotional choices. For example, stay away from frenetic or arbitrary movement. At the same time, be careful of emotional choices that change too quickly. Also avoid initiating movement or emotional changes in places in the script where it doesn't make sense, like in the middle of a phrase; use the script's punctuation, or make up your own.

The great paradox, of course, is that performances for episodic television and film have to appear spontaneous. At the same time, physical and emotional continuity are needed. If a physical action and emotional reality do not match, important parts of a performance generally do not make it into the final product. However, as long as you have separated the beats and defined the character's objectives, there will be consistency, and the physical and emotional moments will fit within the continuity.

PRINCIPLES OF EPISODIC TELEVISION

As you can see, there are many technical considerations when acting for one camera. Don't become discouraged if you think that there's too much to remember. Most of your education will be experiential: You'll learn by doing. Of course, one of the best ways to do this is to test yourself on camera in a classroom situation. As you experiment with the technical considerations of continuity, types of shots, and different coverages, use the following principles to help you learn to act for episodic television. As with all the other principles, consider them also as tools to help you audition for this genre.

1. Help to resolve the story line.

Soap operas are called serials, which suggests a continuing narrative. Nighttime dramas are called episodic television because each show or episode is a unique story. This difference affects the way dramatic shows and soaps are written and produced.

We've already discussed the importance of the story line in soap operas. The story line takes a long time to develop and often the resolution is nonexistent; the story goes on indefinitely. For the actor in dramatic episodic television, it's more challenging working with the story line because each show is produced over a ten-day period and the story is usually resolved within that one episode. If the development of a story line on a soap opera is luxurious, on dramatic television it's frantic. When acting on a soap, you need only know your place in the story line. When acting on a television drama, not only do you need to know your place in the story, but you also need to look for ways to resolve it. You need to be aware of how your character both tells and concludes the story.

In filmed television, there's a lot to be done in a short amount of time. One of the biggest differences between this genre and the others is that episodic television is more beholden to the pressures of time and money. Your work as an actor has to be economical. Because of shooting schedules and budgetary concerns, little time exists to discover your character's importance to the story during the actual shoot. (It's a lot easier to do this on a film set.) It's the actor's job, off the set, to recognize where his character fits into a story line. Don't wait for the director to tell you; don't wait to get onto the set to find out. When you study the script, analyze your character's function in the story.

An actor playing a regular needs to be keenly aware of his character's purpose in each episode. Even though the executive producer(s) may have ideas about where the main characters are going to end up over time, the individual actors playing the leads aren't necessarily going to know their potential futures; therefore, there's no reason to worry about it. Nevertheless, actors have a tendency to always want to develop personal story lines. This is fine if done privately — as long as it doesn't deter the actor from concentrating on the current episode. Actors must remember that the story is about the main characters. Every episode is a new story, and the leads must be attentive to their relevance in the story for that particular episode.

In many ways the actor playing a guest star, co-star, or featured part has a more difficult task. Often these characters exist only to further the action of a single episode. The actor must not only honor the character's raison d'être, she must also find a way to humanize a character that is essentially a plot device. The actor's challenge falls somewhere between playing a character's purpose and making that character a believable human being. This issue is dealt with in depth in Principle 4, but in short, the actor appearing for only a day or a week in an episodic series has to make strong intuitive choices for her character in addition to respecting the need to resolve the story.

Actors playing guest roles have little time on the set to become comfortable with the environment and the personnel, which presents a further hurdle. I've worked on many television dramas in which I had to come on the set, establish my character, and do my job without knowing anyone I was working with. The best way to handle this discomfort is to do your homework (know your lines and do the appropriate analysis) and feel secure with your place in the script. It's also a good idea to spend as much time on the set as possible. Michael Caine suggests that you hypothetically make friends with the set in his excellent book *Acting in Film*. Never discount the benefits of good preparation.

The more time you can spend preparing for your audition, the better off you will be. Very often for audition purposes you are only given the side or sides (the scenes) that your character appears in. If you're unsure of your place in the script from what you've been given, ascertain what you can and make a choice based on what you do know. Frequently if you're auditioning for a role as a guest star and the character is substantial, you will be given an entire script to look over. However, if you don't get one, don't panic; you can usually get an accurate idea based on the scene(s) you are given. If you really feel stuck and just aren't getting the needed information from the sides, don't be afraid to ask at the audition. The casting director should be able to answer your questions. Asking might just prove to them how alert you are.

In discerning how your character is significant to the story line, I recommend that you try this device: Determine the *event* of the scene when reading the sides; discover the overriding action happening in the scene. Much like *TV Guide*, be able to describe and summarize the action in one sentence. Once you can articulate what the action is, think of how your character relates to that event. Chances are you'll get closer to expressing how your character relates to the story line.

EXERCISES

- As you watch episodic television, try to verbalize every character's pertinence to the story line. In as few words as possible list each character's significance to the story. Did the actors help resolve the story line?
- Take a scene from a play or a television show. Try to find the event in the scene and how the characters relate to it within the scene.

2. Moment-to-moment work is essential for dramatic episodic television.

Developed and taught by Sanford Meisner, one of the pioneers of actor training in this country, moment-to-moment work is a technique for creating a character by existing fully in each moment of the scene. Doing this with every scene will ultimately create an entire performance. To use a simple example: If you build a brick house, you must have a blueprint and an idea of what the house is going to look like,, but you can only build it one brick at a time. The same applies to acting: The script gives you a blueprint of the character, but you must create it one moment at a time.

Many of our best actors (especially successful film actors) worked with Sanford Meisner and his devotees at the Neighborhood Playhouse in New York. Meisner's entire approach to actor training is all about being in the moment. His system is still taught today at the Neighborhood Playhouse and at many other places in the country. I highly recommend that you become acquainted with it and learn to incorporate the Meisner-based repetition exercises. I especially advise that you do the exercises on camera. They're helpful with assisting the student who is learning to work on camera because they force you to work in the moment. (I also suggest that you become familiar with Larry Silverberg's excellent books on the Meisner technique.)

The premise for working moment to moment is that great acting appears as if it's being done for the first time. Great actors effectively (and seemingly effortlessly) make an audience believe that they are the actual character, experiencing all these things. Originally, moment-to-moment work was intended for performing onstage. Though that's still true, it's even more appropriate for actors working on film. For our purposes, a moment is any part of a scene that is being filmed. The camera can see into the actor's soul. It's like a laser that exposes truth, and because of this, you have no choice but to concentrate on each moment.

From our earlier discussion of continuity, you probably understand the need for this principle. It's necessary as an actor to step into the script at any point during the shoot and know exactly what's going on. This can only be achieved if the actor focuses on the individual moments. It's the director's job to have an objective view of the entire script. The actor can only deal with what is going on during each moment (of course, he must always have an eye on the character's continuity). Therefore, actors are powerless to determine the result of their performance; they must implicitly trust the editor and the director. Because the editor and the director have control of what an actor's performance is ultimately going to look like, moment-to-moment work for the actor becomes extremely significant. In essence, every moment on film must be a complete performance so that the actor gives the editor and director something to work from.

The first way (and maybe the best way) to prepare to work moment to moment is to be thoroughly familiar with the script. This is especially true if you are playing a large role as a regular or a guest star. (If you are the only in one scene, you should be well versed in that particular scene.) Because of the time constraints of this genre, this is more important for episodic television than any other medium. Being well acquainted with the script will also help you during last-minute schedule changes. If a scene is scheduled to be shot outside and the weather turns bad, the director may decide to go indoors and shoot another scene. You have to be prepared for that, and a multitude of other scenarios. Find time to read the script as many times as you can. Knowing your part inside and out is one of the few things you *can* control. Even though a script supervisor is on the set to help you remember your place, don't rely on her too much; be absolutely sure where you are in every scene and be ready to work from there at any given time.

I'll give you an example. I played a guest star role on an episode of "Spencer: For Hire" years ago. It was a large part and I appeared in almost every scene. The episode was shot on location in Boston and, of course, was shot entirely out of sequence. To be ready for each day's work, I had to be well acquainted with the script. Although I had read the script a number of times before arriving on the set, the writers continued making changes throughout the shooting.

To complicate matters, I was also doing an Off Broadway play in New York, so I couldn't devote all my time to the episode. I had to fly back to New York in my spare time to do the play. (I'm not complaining; I was happy to be busy.) But every time I returned to Boston, new pages were waiting for me. I couldn't possibly memorize the entire new script (nor would I advocate that). Instead, once I received the call sheet for the next day's schedule, I spent every spare minute at the hotel working on the scenes scheduled for the next day. While I worked on the new scenes, I reviewed the earlier ones to remind myself what had already happened to the character so that I could feel comfortable working in the moment of each new scene.

Because of all this groundwork, I must have read the entire script a hundred times. (This is also a good way to memorize lines.) In fact, when it came time to wrap (the term for finishing up a shoot, as in "That's a wrap!"), I was the only one who realized I hadn't recorded a voice-over that my character was supposed to do. I had to remind the director, who was very grateful. Had I not noticed, it would've cost the production company a lot of money to bring me back in and record it during a separate looping session. (In a looping session, the actor goes to a recording studio and dubs the sound for a scene; I discuss this more in chapter 7.) My agent, however, wasn't happy I had spoken up because it meant I lost an opportunity to make more money, but doing this made a good impression on the director, and he eventually rehired me a number of times.

The other way of working in the moment is to free yourself so that you're immediately present and available to your partner. In other words, it's not about trying to duplicate something you've prepared; to be in the moment, you have to be absolutely spontaneous as if you don't know what's going to happen next — when in fact you do. Actors have a tendency to want to "get it right" or "do it the way I did it in rehearsal." What often happens, though, is that the acting simply looks well rehearsed, and that looks false. The audience pays to see a living performance, not a rehearsal. You have to convince yourself that you've never been in this situation before and that you truly do not know what is happening next. It takes years of training and work to get there, so don't worry; just start working toward that goal. Sanford Meisner, who taught many of our greatest actors, said it takes twenty years to become an actor. Of course, this included even working actors. But every journey has to begin somewhere; it's never too late to take the first steps.

When auditioning for episodic television, be thoroughly familiar with the sides so that you can be in the moment as much as possible. Even though you may know the script well, always carry the sides or script with you into the audition. The purpose of your audition is not to prove to the casting director or the director how well you memorize lines. If you come into an audition off-book, you may try to duplicate your rehearsed audition. You may find yourself only thinking of your next line instead of showing them that you have the same characteristics as the character you're reading for. Having the script in hand sends a subliminal message to the auditors that the audition they're seeing isn't necessarily a finished product.

EXERCISES

- I recommend the exercises in Larry Silverberg's wonderful series of workbooks, *The Sanford Meisner Approach*. Incorporate them into your curriculum on acting for the camera. Make sure you tape them and play them back for discussion.

- One of the best exercises in Silverberg's first workbook is the Group Story, in which a group of actors builds a story one word at a time. Use it to sharpen listening skills as well as to force you to be in the moment. Everyone sits in a semicircle, with the camera set up for taping as if it's a master shot. (The exercise should actually be done in a circle, but unless you can set up the camera in the middle of a circle just have everyone sit in a semicircle.) The group must tell a story one word at a time with no pauses, letting the story go where it wants to go rather than any one person trying to take the story where she wants it to go. The point, of course, is that no one in the group can control the story if it's being told one word at a time. As the story moves around the semicircle, each actor can't possibly predict where it's going to be when it gets to him. First, tell a complete story one person at a time around the semicircle with the camera panning the storytellers; then repeat it, making sure the group creates two main characters. Start the exercise again with yet another story. This time the group members should close their eyes, incorporate two main characters, and make sure there is a conflict. Then they should repeat the exercise one last time with their eyes open, re-solving the crisis.

3. In episodic television the acting needs to be straightforward and unaffected.

Because of the time constraints of episodic television, there is simply not enough time for subtlety. Acting choices must be made quickly, and your best bet is to keep them direct. Don't, however, think that this need for straightforwardness is a criticism of episodic television or results in inferior performances. You need only to look as far as the casts of "E.R." and "N.Y.P.D. Blue" to see how simple, honest acting choices can result in brilliant performances.

Most of this need for simplicity comes from the scripts. Usually, an awful lot of story is packed into a one-hour show. Watch a typical one-hour drama and you'll likely see no fewer than three or four story lines happening simultaneously. If the script for a one-hour drama is seventy-five pages long, in a ten-day shooting schedule you have to shoot seven and a half pages a day to complete filming! (Compare that with film, where it's not uncommon to take three months to shoot a script that's 160 pages long, which averages to just over two and a half pages a day.) There's just no room or time for subtlety in episodic television.

So if there's no time for subtlety, what do you do? Answer: Use yourself and keep it natural. Whether you are preparing a role for an audition or after you've gotten the job, the most important question you can ask yourself is: What would I do if *I* were in this situation? There's no reason to think that your reaction wouldn't be appropriate for any situation that arises in the story line of a dramatic episode. Always start by determining how you'd deal with the conflict even if it's never happened to you. Most of dramatic television is very action oriented and the stakes are always high. (By stakes I mean the risks involved.) This advice is especially applicable for actors hired to play guest star, co-star, and featured roles. Usually, most of the main characters are the heroes of the series. They're the ones responsible for resolving the particular crisis of the story. The guest stars et al. are frequently either the victims or the antagonists — the instigators of the conflict. It is incumbent on them to raise the stakes. Go straight to the heart of the action. If you get too intricate, you can always diffuse the stakes.

When you're preparing an audition for a drama series, bring as much of your perspective as possible to the part and keep it simple and honest. Remember the high stakes involved and be unwavering in your purpose. Characters in dramatic episodic television are arrows on a straight trajectory; there's no arc, just a projectile traveling toward a target.

EXERCISES

- Tape a game of charades, with one person performing the charade and three people watching. If you are working with more than one camera, have one camera get a master shot of the three-person team; the other camera should shoot a medium shot of the person doing the charade. Otherwise, tape only the performer. Make sure that there's a time limit. After everyone has had a turn performing a charade, play back the tape and discuss it. What kind of immediacy was achieved due to the time constraints? Were they able to be more or less natural due to the time limitations?

- In a class situation, have everyone write out a highly risky situation for two people: for example, two people afloat on a lifeboat in the middle of the ocean for a week, or a prosecutor grilling a murder suspect on the witness stand. Tape an improvisation with the primary intention being that both characters are to play the high-stake situation in a direct manner. Play the tape back and discuss it. Everyone should be willing to point out any performances that were too oblique or subtle.

4. Learn to trust your intuition and instincts when making choices.

An actor who trusts and use his intuition and instinct usually makes interesting and vigorous choices. As a teacher, I can't teach students to have instincts, but I can alert them to and help them develop the intuition and instincts they already have. Because episodic television demands economy, the actor who can trust and use his instincts is probably the one who gets the job. Actors who succeed in this genre tend to have excellent intuition.

One way to exercise those traits is to know yourself and what you're successful at doing and, even more important, what you're *not* successful at doing. Many actors make the mistake of forcing a response that's not appropriate. Overemotionalizing is an example of this. Too often actors go for the initial, obvious response because it feels good to them or because they think that's what's expected of the character; they want to go for the big emotional moment. They do this without considering what is really going on in the scene and without heeding their own intuition. For instance, if someone receives bad news about something, she may not necessarily respond by crying. A wide range of responses are possible. Often when someone hears bad news (depending on how bad it is), the reaction is one of shock. Most people in shock don't have the capacity to cry.

Overemotionalizing happens when actors get inspiration watching other actors instead of watching themselves or the rest of humanity. Get inspiration from yourself. Trust what you feel about what's going on around you, pay attention to your reactions, and make mental notes. I once heard a lovely definition of an actor as someone who has to remember *everything* that happens to him or her. Well, start to remember everything that you experience. Certainly your willingness to be vulnerable is a step in that direction. To open yourself up to the world around you in all its beauty and ugliness demands vulnerability. As it turns out, vulnerable people are often intuitive and instinctive.

You also need to know instinctively how people perceive you. This has more to do with choosing characters that align with your physical type (see chapter 2, Principle 2) than with who you really are. Casting according to type is more common in episodic television than in film; it all has to do with the expeditiousness and economy of the genre. You will be typed by how you look, and it's your job to live up to that image. The successful actor on episodic television knows this and fully plays it. If you look like a bad guy, it behooves you to act like one as well. This will also help you fulfill the previous principle. You need to assimilate this self-awareness so that it becomes instinctive. Some say that adhering to a type is the antithesis of good acting. But I feel the skill is being able to recognize what you need to do for each genre and to adjust accordingly.

Use auditions to help you expand your intuition and instincts. It takes real courage to act; yet in auditions, actors tend to be conservative in their choices. They are so eager to please the auditor that they don't acknowledge their own unique intuitive perceptions. The worst thing you can do in an audition is to try and get in the head of the auditor and figure out what she wants. What she wants is to have you solve her problem for her and be the one she's looking for. So, take a risk and start listening to and trusting your intuition and instincts. Chances are that if you go in a wrong direction, the director or casting director will tell you. But more than likely, they'll be thrilled. They'll realize that you're instinctive — and it's those actors who they usually take the time to direct.

EXERCISES

- As a way for you to look to yourself for inspiration, start keeping a journal. Record all your reflections and feelings about your daily experiences. Write down urges and thoughts that you have about everything. Go over the entries on a weekly basis so that you're forced to recall all the occurrences.

- Have everyone in a class situation be responsible for bringing in sides (scenes) from episodic shows or plays (the more obscure the better). Along with the sides, have each person delineate the types needed for each character. Be as specific as possible. Choose a casting director(s) in class who then assigns the sides to different students for audition purposes. Make sure that the actors who are auditioning are typed into the appropriate roles. Tape the auditions with one camera so that the person auditioning is the only person on camera. The goal for each auditioning actor is to let her intuition and instinct guide her in how she should audition for the role. (Be sure to adhere to the type that's indicated.) It's very important when you play it back to honestly assess the actors' success in making intuitive and instinctual choices. Were they doing what they believed to be right? Or did you feel they were complying with what they felt someone else wanted? How effectively did they merge the physical and internal type?

5. Know what the action of the situation is and actively play it.

Ninety-five percent of all episodic television is action-oriented. The shows have a dynamic story line usually accompanied by a high degree of suspense. The word *drama*, derived from the Greek *dram*, meaning "to do," implies action. Actors in nighttime dramas need to be alert and sensitive to the parts they play in the action.

Obviously the action is always found within the given circumstances; it's not enough just to describe the setting. You don't do "E.R." justice to describe the crux of its action as taking place in an emergency room. To really get to the heart of the action you have to describe the life and death circumstances that regularly challenge the physicians, nurses, and staff. Each character has a purpose in the action, and it needs to be as descriptive as the scene itself. Therefore, as you think about your character, find ways to effectively describe the situation that the character is in.

For example, pretend you're playing a mother whose son has been in an accident and you're waiting to find out how your child is. The scene calls for you to be looking through the window of the door to the emergency room where they're working on him. You might express her mental state in this way: "I'm out of my mind wanting to touch my son and see him laugh. If only I hadn't let him go to the store by himself; I feel so guilty for letting this happen to him. I wonder why my hands won't stop shaking."

Does this paint an active picture of this character's condition? The most significant part of this description is what the mother *wants*, and the key to making it interesting for both the actress and the audience is how active that choice is.

To play the circumstances actively, the actor needs to find an active *purpose* for the character's existence. What's the mother's purpose? What does she want? From what she says, her overriding desire is to touch her son and see him laugh. I think that's a fairly active objective. You could say the mother just wants her son to be OK; but that's probably not the most active choice that the actress could make. If you were watching this scene, what would you find more interesting? The mother who simply wants her son to be OK (which is certainly implied by the circumstances), or the mother who desires to touch her son and see him laugh? I know I'm going to be more drawn to (and heartbroken by) a mother who wants to touch her son and see him laugh. My point is that you must find a way to describe as actively as possible your relationship to the situation. In so doing, you have to choose objectives that are as active as the situation that the character is in.

This objective might not work for every actress, and that's OK. What's important is that each actor finds the active objectives that work for him. Once that happens, you'll be surprised where it can lead. For instance, where do the shaking hands come from? Have you ever been so nervous about something that part of your body involuntarily shook? I included shaking hands because her objective was so real to me that shaking seemed a natural consequence. If I had chosen to write, "I hope my son is OK . . . ," I doubt I would've added the shaking hands. If one creative idea in writing motivates another, imagine what can happen when the actress herself has a creative idea!

What if the scene is not such a clear-cut life-and-death situation? You then have to create an active purpose for that situation. Let's say that you're in a courtroom scene and you're being interrogated about something trivial. Two possible objectives are: "I want to answer the questions because I have to," or "Being in front of all these people scares me. More than anything I want to get off the stand! Let me answer the questions quickly so I can get out of here!" Which one of these objectives seems more active to you? For an actor which one sounds more interesting to play? Sure, a legitimate objective for the character is to want to answer the questions, but how interesting — and active — is that? Personally, I feel the more active choice is for the character to want to get out of there and to do that, he'd better answer the questions. In your own descriptions, if you paint the picture with vivid colors, it may inspire you in other ways that you hadn't thought of.

This kind of work has to start during the audition process. When you're preparing for the audition, make sure you can define the action of the circumstance and *describe* your character's relationship to it. Within your description it's critical that you acknowledge the character's *purpose* and *objective* in as active a manner as possible.

EXERCISES

- Take scenarios from *TV Guide* and distribute them randomly to a group of students (make sure you don't divulge the show they're taken from). Have everyone rewrite the scenarios so that the essence of the action is clearly stated. Everyone should read them aloud to each other and discuss if the action has been sufficiently articulated.

- Using the same scenarios, everyone chooses a character that fits their type. Write out two objectives, making sure that one is highly active and appeals to you. Improvise each objective and tape it. Play the objectives back and discuss which choices are more interesting to watch.

6. Your reaction close-ups are as important as your verbal close-ups.

Because so many shots used on episodic television are close-ups, your reactions when listening have to be as active as the close-ups of your speaking. I cannot stress the importance of this enough. During reaction shots, many beginning film actors are afraid of doing too much; therefore, they end up doing too little. As we discussed earlier, when they turn the shot around to get coverage of the reaction, a lot of actors feel that the heat is off because they don't have to speak. They end up not working hard enough in the coverage. Active listening is essential to successful camera acting.

The key to active listening is twofold. First, you have to always be in the moment (see Principle 2). Second, you should always be thinking. The camera has a way of picking up someone's thought process. As you watch a filmed performance, you intuitively know when someone is thinking. You also know when someone is not. If an untrained eye can instinctively tell, imagine how glaring it is to someone with a trained eye like a director or producer.

I'll give you an example. I once played a very successful real estate developer on an episode of "L.A. Law." The city of Santa Monica had passed an ordinance mandating that every new office building had to contain a work of art. My character did not like being told what to do and in protest placed an offensively racist piece of art in front of a new office building he was constructing. The city of Santa Monica then sued my character to take it down. What made the story line effective was that the black attorney with the firm (the excellent actor, Blair Underwood) defended my character's freedom of speech.

During the courtroom scenes, the director would repeatedly ask the actor playing the city attorney for more when his coverage was shot. He was wonderful while he was speaking his lines, but during his re-action shots, he was wooden. I sensed the director's frustration in getting the actor to do more. He hadn't had much experience and he was trying to avoid overreacting. The result was that he maintained a poker face throughout his reaction coverage.

When I finally saw the episode on television, I had far more camera time and coverage than he did. The other actor was left almost entirely out of scenes. He hadn't given the director enough to work with in his reaction shots; therefore, during editing he wasn't included in as many coverage shots as he might've been, had he been listening more actively.

Maintain an internal monologue that is somehow subtly manifested in your expressions. One of the best techniques for doing this is the Five-Step Reaction as described in chapter 1. Let's review it.

Step 1: Hear. This is eliminated if you're already in conversation with someone, but if you're not, then you need to give someone your attention before you can understand what he or she is saying.

Step 2: Listen. Make sure you acknowledge the difference between hearing and listening. A classroom situation provides a good example of students often hearing what is being said, but not listening. Listening implies comprehension.

Step 3: Form an opinion. This is the most crucial of the Five Steps. This is the step most people miss when listening onstage or on camera. When one is truly listening, one is instinctively forming opinions about what is being said. Never miss this step when listening during coverage because having an opinion about what's being said helps the wheels turn — and the camera always picks up the wheels turning.

Step 4: Want to speak. Generally when someone forms an opinion about what someone else is saying, he or she is motivated to respond. This desire is *active*. In fact, this and the previous step are really what make listening energetic. Forming an opinion and the need to speak are both active. Think about situations where you were totally engaged in what someone was saying, had formed an opinion, and couldn't wait to say something. That urge is interesting to watch and can be useful in a reaction shot.

Step 5: Speak. The natural conclusion of the previous four steps is this one. There's no stopping someone once they have the urge to speak.

For purposes of a reaction shot, pay close attention to Steps 3 and 4. You always want to be having an opinion about what the other character is saying, and having the urge to speak can bring an interesting immediacy to it. If you think about it, those are the shots that they're going to use anyway. In editing they cut to a reaction shot because they know the audience wants to know how the character feels about what's being said.

One mistake you can make when listening is to go to the other extreme and listen too hard. The actor who brings too much intensity to his listening is just as sterile as the actor who doesn't do enough. Unless it's done for a purpose, it's just bad acting. What's important is to listen honestly and realistically. In life we constantly comment to ourselves about what someone else is saying. What matters is that the camera is astute enough to pick up your thoughts. As long as you have them, the camera will notice.

In auditions you will be tested. Casting directors and directors are hyperaware of self-involved actors who don't listen. I've seen directors test actors to see if they are capable of listening. I've witnessed directors purposefully misdirect or give conflicting direction just to see if the actor is listening. Let's face it: If you don't have listening skills, how are you going to be able to carry out direction?

A sure way actors have of proving their inability to listen is in audition situations when they make the mistake of acting only on their lines. When the other character is speaking (very often the casting director or a reader in an audition) is often the moment actors take to look at their next line — and thereby lose an opportunity to listen and react. Instead, seize those moments to connect with the person reading opposite you — even if it means missing your cue and having to look down at the sides for your next line. Think of it this way: Reactions are vital during the filming, so why wouldn't they be during the audition as well? Since so much time is spent on reaction coverage, make sure your audition contains reactions as well. Remember the old saying: Acting is reacting.

- Everyone should prepare a monologue. In pairs, each person should perform his or her monologue. Tape the shot over the shoulder, making sure the person being taped is the *listener*. As you listen to the monologue, make sure that you have an internal monologue going on. Play back the tape and discuss the reactions of the listener. Were the reactions natural? Did they ever feel forced? Was the listener trying too hard to "show" he was listening? Could you tell what the listener was thinking?

- Working in pairs, everyone should prepare a scene. Tape the scene with one camera. Do not shoot a master, shoot only one actor at a time. (You'll end up getting a one-sided view of the scene.) When an actor is not speaking during the scene, she should try incorporating the Five-Step Reaction. Play back the tape and discuss it. Were each actor's reactions as active as when she was speaking?

7. Try to be loose and relaxed on the set and in the audition.

You must be mentally and physically relaxed enough on the set to adapt to almost any situation. The most successful actors on episodic television can modify what they're doing at a moment's notice, aren't thrown by changes to the script, and don't need a lot of rehearsal. It all has to do with the rigors of a tight schedule and an inherently fast pace. But, as much as I've talked about the pressures of working in episodic television, you've still got to be able to have fun!

Because most actors train for the stage, they become accustomed to working on scenes from great plays. It's important to learn your craft by studying masterpieces. However, when an actor is working on a scene from an Ibsen play, Ibsen isn't around constantly giving you changes. (During rehearsals for the world premiere of an Ibsen play, I'm sure he was around rewriting.) Unless they have a lot of experience with new plays, most stage actors are used to performing a fixed work and find it difficult, while working on television and in film, to adjust quickly to new lines and circumstances. Working on a dramatic episodic television show (as well as commercials, sitcoms, soaps, and films) is like working on a world premiere; the project is perpetually in motion, being reshaped and rewritten.

When you first get the script, it may be multicolored, let's say white, blue, and green. On the title page of the script it will list the dates and the colors of all the various editions. For example, the original script was finished on July 13 and was printed on white paper. Subsequently, the first revision was made on July 17, and those changes were made on blue paper. The most recent revisions were made on July 18 and are printed on green paper. Now you have a history of the changes, and the network saves paper by not reprinting new scripts every time it changes.

But changes don't stop just because the actors now have the script. The day after you get the script, you might receive an overnight package with a number of pink pages and a new title page. These are the newest revisions, which you have to insert in the existing script (if the writers rewrite the entire script, you'd get an entirely new script in pink, or whatever color is being used). This process continues even after filming begins. Finally, you end up with a rainbow-colored script. (You can also follow the specific changes on each page by looking for an asterisk [*] in the margins of each page. This asterisk indicates where individual lines have been changed on that page.) Sometimes these changes will affect you and sometimes they won't. If your part is large (let's say you're a regular or a guest star and are in quite a bit of the episode), then chances are most of the changes will somehow affect your character. Obviously, you can't let these changes upset you. You can't get so locked in to what you're doing that you can't readily and easily assimilate the various alterations.

Besides adapting to script changes, this principle also means having a relaxed and confident demeanor while you're on the set. I mentioned in Principle 1 how difficult it is for an actor who only works one day or one week to feel comfortable entering an environment where he doesn't know anyone. However, the actor needs to get over his fears as quickly as possible. How you do this is up to you. I suggest you get to your call time as early as possible and wander around the set. Introduce yourself to the assistant directors (there's always a first AD and a number of second ADs). If the director is not busy, try to grab a few moments with him or her. Your foremost task, however, is to introduce yourself to your fellow actors. This is relatively easy when it comes to meeting the other guest stars, co-stars, and featured players. They're in the same situation as you and will most likely welcome an overture to help increase their own comfort level.

If you have a scene(s) with a principal, try to introduce yourself whenever you (and he) have a moment. I caution you about barging into the principal's trailer, as this is not likely to make a good impression. You have to be sensitive to his privacy, as he generally has none. Ask someone who is normally on the set (like an AD) how he or she recommends you proceed. Otherwise, the best time might be immediately after the first blocking rehearsal of your scene. At that time it's appropriate to ask the principal if he has a moment to rehearse. I caution you, however, to keep it professional. You won't win points for asking the principal to have a cup of coffee while you try to impress or get advice.

If you can't rehearse with the principals or other guest stars, you must be self-confident enough to not let it get in your way. This is one of the greatest challenges actors face: the ability to appear self-assured when in fact they're not, the ability to seem relaxed when they're tense, and the capacity to look as if they're carefree when they're self-conscious. Experience certainly helps, and the more of it you have the more confident you'll feel. There are reasons actors have egos. You have to like and believe in yourself enough so that you can deal with all these situations.

Being a talented improviser might ultimately be the best protection in handling these uncertainties well. Actors who can think on their feet have an advantage when dealing with the demands of episodic television. It should be noted that my definition of improviser is not limited to improvising a scene from nothing. It also means an actor who can change the intention, characterization, situation, and even meaning of existing dialogue within a scene instantaneously if given the opportunity. As a student of acting, look for occasions to study improvisation or join improvisational troupes. At the very least, get into the habit of trying to act scenes in many ways. In an environment where you're constantly asked for modification, it's best to be prepared for anything.

EXERCISES

- Everyone pairs off and prepares scenes. These scenes should preferably be from plays that are being worked on in an acting class. Tape the scenes. Immediately after the scenes are taped, have someone recommend a complete change of circumstance, intention, or anything else that forces the actors to drastically alter their perception of the scene. (The recommendations don't have to align with the original context of the scene.) Without rehearsal, the actors should immediately re-enact the scene attempting to incorporate the recommended changes. Play the scenes back and discuss them. What's important is not the success of the scenes, but the ability of the actors to shake off their predetermined ideas and do something different.

- Using the same scenes from the previous exercise (or new ones, it doesn't matter), tape the actors performing them as they have prepared them. This time, however, someone off camera holds a "super remote control." This super remote control cannot only fast forward and rewind the scene, it can do it in slow motion and control the language spoken and the style of the scene — and anything else you want it to do. After the actors start their scene, the holder of the super remote control can arbitrarily use it at any time; for instance, she can shout "fast forward," and the actors must immediately fast forward the scene until told to stop. If the super remote control holder shouts out "Spanish," the actors must switch to Spanish. (Of course, the actors are not expected to know how to speak Spanish.) Play the scenes back and discuss how effectively and quickly the actors adapted.

EPISODIC TELEVISION EXERCISES

Experimenting with master and coverage shots is a good way to practice for episodic television. Use only one camera and play around with the different camera shots. Start out with the earlier Joel/Emily scene (or any scene of your choice). When shooting the coverage shots, make sure that you're especially aware of the 180-degree rule and the actor's eye line.

As you become more comfortable working with one camera and learn to deal with the different shots and coverage concerns, start taping scenes of your choice incorporating the principles of episodic television. Pay particular attention to working moment to moment, playing the situation actively, and trusting your instincts; most important, don't forget to shoot reaction close-ups of characters listening. Of course, you'll also want to concentrate on continuity in all the scenes you shoot. Exercises 2 and 3 below deal exclusively with continuity concerns.

EXERCISE 1

Everyone in class should pair off. The teacher (or a nonparticipant) should find story lines of actual episodic television from an issue of *TV Guide* (omitting the titles) and distribute them to the pairs. (I find that pairs work best. You can certainly incorporate more than two people, but you want to avoid groups.) For example, in one story line, lightning has apparently caused the deaths of five people in a small town. Two FBI agents get involved when a sixth death occurs under suspicious circumstances. (This is an actual *TV Guide* synopsis of an episode from the "X-Files.")

The person handing out the scenarios should make sure the pairs don't know which show it comes from. Pairs should also refrain from sharing their plot with the other pairs. Each couple creates an improvisation based on their *TV Guide* synopsis. The two objectives of the exercise are to create strong choices from scratch and to play the inherent action in each scenario. Tape the exercise with one camera. Shoot a master shot of the improvisation. Pairs are not permitted to watch each another's scenes as they are being shot. After all the improvisations have been taped, play back each scene without sound. Note: None of the pairs should know ahead of time that their scene will be played back without sound. Viewers must discern what's going on within each situation without relying on the dialogue.

My point is this: Because episodic television is so action oriented, you can turn on any show and watch it without sound and 90 percent of the time, you'll still know what's going on. You can tell what's going on by behavior alone because people are playing strong actions with high stakes. Even in a courtroom drama, you can tell who's winning and who's losing without turning on the sound. You just know.

It is important not to divulge the intention of this exercise before playback or its effectiveness will be diminished. It is interesting to watch the audience trying to guess what is actually going on in the scene; viewers will enjoy talking through the possibilities with one another in an effort to guess correctly. This is one way to demonstrate that if you do not act with strong enough choices, you will not be effective working in television. When you take away sound, it becomes even clearer how necessary it is to play the action strongly and how powerful choices need to be.

Finally play back the scene with sound to see how close the audience came to guessing what was going on. This exercise can be repeated more than once if time allows.

EXERCISE 2

This is an exercise for physical and emotional continuity. Everyone should write down a character and a situation where the character is engaged in something fairly active: for example, a short-order cook during a busy breakfast rush. Don't use the situation or character you yourself wrote; pass them around and use one written by someone else. Then hand out a copy of the Pledge of Allegiance. The actors should prepare it as they would a monologue and make choices to fit the character and situation they are given.

Shoot a master of the entire monologue. Then, to demonstrate continuity, go back and shoot the exercise out of sequence. In other words, for the master shot the actor recites the entire Pledge of Allegiance in one take. In the coverage, the "director" should ask the actor to start again, for instance, at "and to the republic." Continue this way for three or four takes. The challenge for the actor is not only to start where she was directed (out of sequence), but she must match specifically what she was doing at that point in the speech. She must try and match the master shot *emotionally and physically*. Play it back and discuss it.

For this exercise it is almost irrelevant what the text is. The advantage of using the Pledge of Allegiance is that everyone knows it; you don't have to think about it. The challenge for the actor, no matter what text is used, is to return to an exact moment with a matching action. Most important, it's a test to see if the actors can remember not only what they were doing, but also what they were feeling at any given moment in the scene.

Text and action don't need to fit — that's irrelevant for this exercise. This exercise is specifically aimed at strengthening continuity skills. Michael Caine says in *Acting in Film*, "The true professional film actor is not only familiar with physical continuity, but is familiar with emotional continuity. Not only do you need to know when you picked up the pen but you also need to know how to match the way you felt when you were picking it up."

This exercise is trial by fire, no question about it. No need for discussion about character development, motivation, or anything else that is directorial in nature. Dive in, shoot the scene, and then discuss it. The lesson is: *Don't choose actions that you can't match!* Don't make things too complicated. If your actions cannot be matched, they will not end up on film. Remember to keep physical movement and the emotional reality connected to the beats of the monologue.

EXERCISE 3

Repeat Exercise 2. Use the Joel/Emily scene, a contentless scene from elsewhere in this book, or a scene of your own choice. Shoot it as a scene for two people. Like the Pledge of Allegiance, the scene should be something the actors know extremely well and don't have to think about. The content of the scene is not what's significant. What's important is that there is physical activity and an emotional reality to the scene.

Shoot a master of the scene and then go back and shoot it out of sequence starting at different places in the scene. In the playback of the scenes, see if the audience can point out the consistencies (or inconsistencies).

SUMMARY

Episodic television is also referred to as nighttime dramatic series. The distinctions between employment categories in this medium are principal and extra. Principals have dialogue and extras don't. Like sitcoms, the billing classifications include series regular, guest star, co-star, and featured. Because it's filmed, episodic television (as well as motion pictures) are governed by the SAG, which determines the minimum payments actors can receive as well as rules concerning overtime and breaks.

Actors have to be attentive to the differences between the demands of working on multiple cameras (including the genres of sitcoms and soaps) and one-camera filmmaking (including episodic television, motion pictures, TV movies of the week, and miniseries). They should be familiar with master and coverage shots, with particular emphasis on the eye line and the 180-degree rule. Actors must also be somewhat familiar with types of shots and with what happens in postproduction, especially editing. The most important technical consideration is that of continuity. Because filming with one camera is generally done out of sequence, continuity ensures that the physical and emotional life of the character is logical and cohesive. The best way for an actor to deal with continuity is to do the appropriate analysis of the action and the beats of a scene.

The seven principles to be considered for auditioning and acting in episodic television are:

1. *Help to resolve the story line.* Because of the time constraints in nighttime dramatic series, there is a need for economy in acting. Always determine how your character helps resolve the story line.

2. *Moment-to-moment* work is essential. Because episodic television is shot out of sequence, it's imperative that actors always be prepared. At the same time, however, the acting must appear spontaneous. To accomplish this, the actor must always be in the moment.

3. *The acting must be straightforward and unaffected.* Acting choices must be made quickly and directly. There is no room for subtlety.

4. *Learn to trust your intuition and instinct.* Remember everything that happens to you, and look to yourself for inspiration. Be comfortable with yourself.

5. *Know what the situation is and actively play it.* Find the inherent action in every scene and choose dynamic objectives for your character to pursue.

6. *Your reaction close-ups are as important as your verbal close-ups.* When your reactions are being filmed you must always be *thinking*. Use the Five-Step Reaction process: 1. Hear, 2. Listen, 3. Form an opinion, 4. Want to speak, 5. Speak.

7. *Try to be loose and relaxed on the set and in the audition.* Because of the rigors of fast-paced episodic television, it is important that the actor be adaptable and have good improvisation skills.

CHAPTER 7
FILM

Since the early part of the twentieth century, films have permeated America's collective consciousness. They made us laugh during the Depression, they inspired us and gave us hope during World War II, they raised serious questions during the Vietnam War, and they've helped change the way we think about everything since then. Above all, they have always entertained us when we needed it most. Films have been an integral part of every generation for almost a hundred years. Motion pictures have had a profound effect on American society, and have been instrumental in defining our culture and the way we live. They have been around long enough to witness the end of the industrial age and have been influential in ushering in the information age. For better or worse, our movies reflect us to ourselves and to the rest of the world.

We refer to films as flicks, movies, motion pictures, moving pictures, or just plain pictures. The term *film* can imply an arty, less economically oriented motion picture, whereas *movie* usually suggests a more mainstream product. Whatever you want to call them, they are an American paradigm. Though countries all around the world produce films, often it is American motion pictures that are the most popular and emulated. Our movies are not only Hollywood's version of the American psyche, they also express our fascination with success, glamour, fantasy, hero worship, and storytelling. Movies define who we are as much as fast food, big cars, and musical theater. Movies are a staple of our cultural diet. For decades, "going to the movies" has been a common and enjoyable form of entertainment for many. I would go so far as to suggest that for some going to the movies is the only entertainment outside the home.

Because movies represent such a significant option for our entertainment dollar, they perfectly exemplify the corporate-minded culture of our country. The American motion picture business is big business. Movies earn a lot of money for the studios that produce and distribute them, and they have a significant impact on our gross national product. The revenues generated by domestic release in theaters, as well as the residual earnings from television, videos, and DVDs, pale in comparison to what our movies make throughout the rest of the world; so much so that I've heard it said that our country's biggest export is the motion picture.

Ironically, even though our movies are unique American ambassadors, both culturally and economically, it was really the French and Russians who were the early pioneers of the medium. The French invented motion pictures, and the Russians developed the art of filmmaking. One of the earliest Russian directors, Sergei Eisenstein, has had an enormous influence on current American directors, such as Martin Scorsese and Steven Spielberg. In the art of film acting as well, one of the earliest influences was the Russian director Lev Kuleshov. In the early 1920s, Kuleshov experimented with how editing affects the audience watching a film, which became known as the *Kuleshov effect*. This experiment has had a profound effect on the idea of acting on film.

In addition to the Kuleshov effect, this chapter discusses what to expect when auditioning for film roles; the differences between working in episodic television and film; the film schedule for a typical day; and, of course, exercises for all eight principles.

WHAT IS THE KULESHOV EFFECT?

As a novice film director in 1923, Lev Kuleshov experimented with the relationship between the filmmaker and the audience. In this experiment he brought one of the great actors of his day into the studio and filmed a close-up of the actor's expressionless face. He then went out and shot such disparate subjects as a bowl of soup, a woman in a coffin, and a little girl playing with a doll. Kuleshov then edited the images so that the shot of the actor's face was immediately followed by the image of the bowl of soup, which then cut to another shot of the actor followed by the image of the woman in the coffin, and so on.

Kuleshov then showed the final edited version to an audience. Afterward, he asked audience members what they had seen. They reported that they had witnessed a brilliant performance by the actor. The audience believed that the actor was first looking at a bowl of soup, then at a woman in a coffin, and finally at a little girl playing with her doll. They made assumptions about his thoughts and feelings. They were certain he was hungry while looking at the bowl of soup, sad to see the woman in the coffin, and happy watching the little girl playing with her doll. The actor, however, did not know about any of the images and therefore couldn't possibly have had any of those thoughts and feelings. Stimulated by Kuleshov's juxtaposition of the images, the audience members supplied their own emotional content to the scene.

For actors, this experiment is important because it demonstrates how potent and influential editing is. It should also prove to the actor that when working on camera, the goal of his performance should not be to manipulate an audience; the audience needs to be allowed to endow a scene in the way they want. Of course, since this experiment, the results of the Kuleshov effect have been disputed for various reasons. For one thing, audience members are not necessarily going to accept an actor's blank expression as a sufficient expression for their own emotions; also, because of technological advances, audiences today are more discerning.

Ultimately, the Kuleshov effect teaches us that there is a fine line between how much "acting" an actor can and can't do. This issue is interwoven into a number of the principles of film acting in this chapter. But before we get to the principles, let's discuss some of the practicalities of working in film.

HOW MUCH MONEY CAN YOU MAKE WORKING IN FILMS?

Working in film falls under the jurisdiction of SAG. The minimum pay scale for acting in films is the same as working in episodic television (see chapter 6). If you are playing a small part, you will be paid a day rate because you will probably only work one day. If you work longer than eight hours, which SAG defines as one workday, you will get overtime. (This is discussed in chapter 6.) Should they not finish your scene during the day you are scheduled to work and they call you back for another day, you would make another day's salary at the same minimum or negotiated rate. If your role is larger, you might be paid a week's rate; again, this is a negotiated rate. (SAG has minimum rates for a week's work as well.) If your role is large, they might give you a "run of the film" contract that essentially puts you on hold for the length of the shoot. In that case, you would be guaranteed a set amount for as long as they are filming the movie. This could be broken down by a certain amount per week or a set figure for the entire period. In these cases, however, you would still make overtime if you worked longer than eight hours in a day. That amount would be prorated based on your actual rate. (In some cases, I have doubled my day or weekly rate just in overtime.)

With the exception of the SAG minimums I've given you, the sky's the limit — actors can make whatever they can negotiate. For instance, an actor can make the SAG minimum of $617 for a day or $10,000. (If you're just starting out, however, I doubt that the studio is going to give you $10,000 for a day's work.) In the end, it all depends on how badly they want you and how good your agent is. Agents are responsible for negotiating salaries. Agents are also responsible for contracting where the actor is billed in the credits. If your character is important to the film, you might be billed at the beginning of the movie, after the title of the film. Stars generally get their names in the credits before the title, called "above the title." If your name appears alone, it is called a single card; if your name is one of two names to appear, it's a double card; if it's one of many, it's a shared card. If you have less than a lead role, the only billing you'll receive is in the cast list at the end of the movie. The entire cast is listed in this way, usually by order of appearance. As in television, extras never receive billing.

Mistakes made during shooting or discovered in postproduction can provide opportunities for making more money. For instance, you might be brought back to reshoot scenes for any number of reasons. Let's say that you're working one day on a film. They shoot your scene, and you finish and go home. But during the rushes or dailies, they discover that something went wrong technically. They would call you back to reshoot your scene. If this happens, of course you would get paid for another day's work. You can also make extra money for looping, which we'll discuss momentarily.

WHAT ARE RUSHES AND DAILIES?

If a director likes a shot, he'll say "print it" at the end of the take. This phrase means the director wants the film developed. Doing this saves those scenes that the director likes and thinks might be used in the final version of the movie. (For scenes that aren't developed, the film is thrown away. You might think this is wasteful, but the film itself doesn't cost nearly as much as the developing process.) At the end of each day's work, the director, producer(s), director of photography, actors, and anyone else important to the project view all the scenes that have been saved and developed. These clips are called rushes or dailies. The dailies are literally the raw footage minus all the elements that will go into the final version, such as music, special effects, and so on. It is from the dailies that the editor chooses what goes into the final film.

WHAT IS LOOPING?

Looping refers to dialogue added after a movie is shot and edited. For example, let's say the director and the editor choose one particular shot of a scene between two people for the final version. But there may be a small problem with the sound quality. Perhaps during that particular take a plane flew overhead and obliterated the entire dialogue or perhaps just one line; other than that, the take was perfect. This doesn't happen often; the technicians usually detect a plane flying overhead or some other disturbance during the shot, but sometimes things are missed. It could be something as insignificant as the actor not articulating or the sound person not getting a good take.

Fortunately, this can be easily fixed with looping. The actor (or actors) is brought in for a looping session, which is conducted at a recording studio. The actor wears a headphone and watches, with script in hand, the scene play on a screen. First, the actor watches the scene silently, so she knows when to insert the dialogue; then the scene is replayed and on a designated cue, she reads her line into the microphone.

It sounds easy, but it's an art itself and can be quite difficult; when you dub the line, you have to be perfectly in sync with the movement of your mouth on the film. (This method is also used for dubbing a movie into English or another language. Generally, though, in those cases, the movement of the mouth does not have to match the sound exactly.) To ensure that the line is in sync, sound engineers cue the actor with a series of beeps. The beeps are timed to correspond with the exact moment when the actor needs to read the line. For instance, the actor may need to say the line on the fourth beep: *beep . . . beep . . . beep . . .* [line]. If the actor does it perfectly, the line will be in sync with the movement of the mouth. Like anything else, practice makes perfect. By the way, the actor is paid his daily rate or a pro-rated amount of his weekly or overall rate for the looping session.

WHAT IS THE CASTING PROCESS FOR FILMS?

One of the biggest differences between episodic television and film is time. More time is devoted to making a film, and the casting process often takes longer. (Films also tend to cost more money.) There are exceptions, but casting usually takes several months. Films are more of a director's medium, and casting is one of the director's paramount concerns; it's been said that 90 percent of a director's job is casting.

The casting process for movies is similar to that for episodic television. It usually entails a studio committing to doing a particular project and then hiring a director and a casting director. The director and casting director meet extensively to give the casting director an idea of the type of actor the director wants for each of the principal roles. (Many times a studio's commitment to a project is predicated on not only a director already being part of the deal, but also the promise of one or two stars who are interested in doing the film.) Based on what he has been told by the director, the casting director creates character descriptions and sends out breakdowns to managers and agents in New York and Los Angeles. (Depending on where the film is being shot, sometimes the breakdowns are sent out to actors' representatives throughout various parts of the country.) Agents then submit pictures and résumés of the clients that they feel fit the character descriptions. The casting director screens the pictures and résumés and chooses the actors that he wants to bring in to audition for the film. I'm not sure what percentage of actors whose pictures and résumés have been submitted are chosen to be seen, but my guess is that less than 10 percent of those actors actually get an audition.

This is a fairly simplistic description of how the casting process works. It doesn't take into account that a primary function of managers and agents is to court the various casting directors. Managers and agents are constantly wooing casting directors so that their clients will be given preferential treatment when it comes time to cast a film. In addition, managers and agents (those who are conscientious, anyway) are seeing plays, watching television, viewing student and small-budget films, and attending showcases trying to discover talent. A lot of factors come into play when it comes to finding the right actors to read for characters in films. There is no sure-fire method for casting. In addition, I should mention A, B, and C lists and packaging, a recent development in film production, which all play roles in the casting process.

WHAT ARE A, B, AND C LISTS?

A, B, and C lists are made up of actors who have done quite a bit of work and have a certain cachet. If you're just starting out as an actor, these lists won't mean much to you; but it's always good to know that they exist. For more seasoned professionals, being on these lists is vitally important; moving up on them is even more so for some.

These lists help casting directors categorize actors. Obviously, the A list represents the crème de la crème of this country's or the world's acting pool. This list is comprised of what we might call movie stars. Many actors, whether or not they admit it, want to be on the A list. The A list can be the director's (and casting director's) first choice in casting a role. In fact, play this game (as I'm sure you already have at some point): Pretend you're a casting director and imagine recasting your favorite movie. Think of your first choice for a particular role: If you could cast any star, who would it be? Basically, this is the same thing casting directors do. Your first choices would constitute your A list. This list is pretty standard throughout the industry and, of course, changes based on who's hot. But it's not a hard-and-fast rule; occasionally directors don't depend on any list and cast an unknown actor in their movies.

The B list represents the actors who are not quite movie stars but who are very recognizable. Often, these actors are the director's or casting director's second choice when actors on the A list are not available or are not interested. C list actors are less recognizable than B list, but still noteworthy talent and are the director's third choice.

However, directors and casting directors don't automatically go to the B or C lists for second or third choices. A director might choose a C list actor as his first choice, and an actor on the A list could be his second choice. These lists have more to do with name recognition and popularity than talent or suitability for a particular film.

A, B, and C lists are limited to a handful of actors and are an elite group. Most actors would consider it a distinction to be on any of them. Unfortunately, some actors are not satisfied with simply making a list; they only want to move up. However, actors who end up one-hit wonders or who become unwanted will descend or be removed from the lists.

WHAT DO YOU MEAN BY PACKAGING?

Because of the corporate sensibility of the entertainment business, management companies and agencies are behaving more and more like large corporate entities. The big agencies especially are now offering their clients everything from individual management and legal representation to business consulting and public relations. It was once common for only actors to have representation; now everyone has it. It is normal now for agencies to represent screenwriters, directors, cinematographers, and others in addition to actors. As a result, agencies are becoming one-stop shopping for studios interested in making motion pictures and TV programs.

Of course, these agencies use this power as a negotiating tool. For example, a studio is interested in a script written by a screenwriter represented by KDL agency. The studio contacts the writer's agent at KDL and expresses interest in buying rights to the script. The agent then offers a package deal: He tells the studio executives that they can produce the script only if they also hire a director, certain actors, and a cinematographer, who all happen to be represented by KDL. If the studio agrees to do this, it becomes a package deal for the agency. In many ways, the agency has all the leverage and consequently the power.

Some people think that packaging implicitly means that the agency becomes a producing entity. In fact, there is widespread debate over the conflict of interests involved in agencies that produce their own projects. This is the inevitable result of packaging, which resembles typical corporate consolidation. I hate to think, however, that it might someday mean that an artist can't work unless he is part of a mega-agency or able to be part of a package deal.

HOW DO I AUDITION FOR MOTION PICTURES?

The actual audition process for a movie is very similar to auditioning for episodic television. (Remember that in all auditions, an enormous amount of work has already gone into getting the audition before the actor even walks in the door.) First you read for the casting director. If the casting director is familiar with your work, you might end up bypassing that step and going straight to the director and (sometimes) the producer. Unlike television, however, many times an actor is put on tape for a film and the tape is sent off to the director. This generally happens as a type of callback when the director can't be there. Whichever method is used, the most important thing an actor can do is to be prepared.

Actors need to think of auditions as opportunities that can't be wasted. The path to success in this business is for you to be sufficiently prepared so that when an opportunity does arise, you are ready to capitalize on it. Since the only way to get a job is to audition for it, start to envision an audition as the sum total of all the hard work that you've put into your career. Whether it is the training you've received, the hustling you've done to get an agent, or the showcases and work you've done for free — for most actors it is all these things — the audition is the natural extension of the constant groundwork an actor must do to get people to recognize her work. So when you receive the call for the audition and get the script, or the sides, and you have done the appropriate preparation, the audition becomes your moment to show off how perfect you are for the project.

The audition process generally happens faster in television than in film. In television, the work usually starts soon after the audition, but not so in films. Though it can certainly happen, don't expect an immediate phone call after you audition for a movie. I've been cast in a motion picture close to a year after auditioning for it. Now that particular case may be a bit extreme, but it does happen. You can also expect any number of callbacks as well. I've even read for one role, only to be called back for another. The point is, you never know what's going on in the mind of the director. My advice is not try to figure out what the director is thinking. I know I've wasted opportunities because, instead of doing my work, I spent too much time and energy trying to figure out what the director wanted. As tempting as it may be to do this, don't. Become zenlike about the entire audition process.

WHAT ARE THE DIFFERENCES BETWEEN EPISODIC TELEVISION AND FILM?

As I've already mentioned, the major difference between working in television and working in film is time. Both television and film adhere to tight working schedules, but the pace is much slower in film. An episodic television drama has to shoot seven to ten pages a day to complete a script in ten days. Generally, a film shoots much less — usually two to three pages a day. In film, you have more time to shoot the entire project, but don't make the mistake of thinking that time can be wasted — it can't. Time is money and what television and film have in common is the enormous cost of shooting.

Having more time does mean you have more freedom when it comes to making acting choices, however. For one thing, a director usually tries to build in rehearsal time, whereas in television you basically get nothing. Rehearsal enables you to experiment with acting choices. Most of the principles of film acting deal with this to some extent. Many actors opt to work in film rather than television because of the slower pace allows them much more room for creative choices.

Another difference is that television is more text oriented whereas film is more visually oriented. So much more can be created with film than with television. Although a good script is essential to storytelling whether on television or at the local multiplex, when you are bound to words you cannot establish the subtle, intricate moods that great films are capable of. In film, moments are constructed visually, shots are composed like paintings, and metaphor can be expressed through camera angles, light, and color. Because of this, movies are more of an art form for the director, the cinematographer, the actor, and even the writer than other genres.

Film also depends more on special effects than television, and additional time is needed to accommodate the current technology. To create these special effects, the film has to be shot in a studio in front of a blue screen, and this poses particular challenges for the actor.

WHAT'S A BLUE SCREEN AND WHAT ARE THE CHALLENGES FOR THE ACTOR?

Most special effects (also known as FX) are added digitally in post-production. Special effects have become as necessary for some movies as a soundtrack. It would be financially impossible to physically produce, while the film is being shot, the special effects common in today's movies. Harry Potter's magic, the fight sequences in the *Star Wars* series, and Spiderman's flying would cost outrageous amounts of money to film. In fact, it would be impossible to create on the set what they can now create in a computer in postproduction.

Scenes that use special effects are filmed in a bare studio in front of a blue (or green) screen. These colors happen to be most receptive for the special effects process that is added later. The actor working in front of a blue screen usually does not know what the scene will ultimately look like; he has to *imagine* everything. The actor is merely told what his action is, or more likely, what or who he is reacting to. In the completed film, an actor may be seen fighting a monster or an alien. But during the actual filming, the actor fights only with an idea — an imaginary monster or alien. Tommy Lee Jones and Will Smith do amazing jobs of acting with invisible scene partners in *Men in Black I* and *II*. Only when all the effects are added in postproduction do these scenes end up looking realistic. As an actor in a scene with special effects, you must convince yourself of things that aren't there and be able to pretend that you're believably acting with them. If you can't, you won't be able to convince an audience that they exist. (I deal extensively with imagination in Principle 3.)

WHAT IS A TYPICAL SCHEDULE FOR THE SHOOTING OF A FILM?

The best way to get an idea of a typical schedule is to look at a call sheet, which is the schedule for each day's work. It is completed by one of the assistant directors. The format for the call sheet is almost the same everywhere. It is a two-sided piece of paper that relays, on a daily basis, all the information that the cast and crew need to know about the schedule. Each day the call sheet is distributed on the set for the next day's schedule. If you haven't appeared on the set, it will be sent to you before your first day of work. Once you get the job, you will get a call sheet for each day that you work. Besides your script, it's the most important piece of paper that you'll receive.

The back of the call sheet, which does not concern us here, is exclusively used for information pertaining to the crew. It lists the call times for all crew members and all the props, as well as special equipment needed for that day. At the bottom, an advance schedule for the next day is often given.

Let's look at the front of a call sheet for a hypothetical movie called *The Wonder* (see figure 1).The upper left-hand corner is self-explanatory: it lists the studio making the film, the producer, and the director. In this area, the sheet might also list the first assistant director and contact numbers. The upper right-hand corner states the *crew call,* which is when the crew is expected to arrive and begin setting up. The day and date are important because this call sheet is for that day only. The weather forecast is listed as a convenience for everyone; sunrise and sunset is for the benefit of the director of photography and the lighting crew. Just above the grid is the *shoot day,* which gives you a good idea of where the production is in the overall shooting schedule. By looking at this call sheet, you know that the filming is projected to last 104 working days. Obviously, the crew is in the first week as this is the fourth day of filming.

Reading the grid, along the top, you see Set, Scenes, Cast No., D/N, Pages, and Location. *Set* and *scene* represent the locale and the scene numbers that appear in the script. For example, we know that scenes 17, 18, and 12 take place in Michael's restaurant. Just below where the set is listed there is a brief description of what happens in the scene. *Cast No.* tells you how many cast members are in the scene. Every principal is given a number; usually stars and leads have the lowest numbers and smaller roles have higher numbers. Atmosphere means the same thing as extras; they're not given numbers — the number that appears after *Atmos* represent how many extras will be needed for that scene. Back at the top of the grid, *D/N* indicates whether the scene takes place during the day (D) or at night (N). (I address later why the scenes in Michael's are listed as *N* when they're

	21st Century Productions Producer: Frank DeAtley Director: Shelley Wardlaw	"The Wonder"	CREW CALL: 6A DAY: THURSDAY DATE: MAY 23 WEATHER: SUNNY SUNRISE: 5:57A SUNSET: 8:58P

SHOOT DAY 4 OF 104

SET	SCENES	CAST NO.	D/N	PGS.	LOCATION
INT: MICHAEL'S REST.	17	1, 2, ATMOS(15)	N	1 4/8	**LOC. #1**
Lucy and Lou eating					Bab's Grill
INT: MICHAEL'S REST.	18	1, 2, 50, ATS (15)	N	2/8	Mission Bl.
Lou asks for the check					
INT: MICHAEL'S REST.	12	1, 2, 48, ATS (15)	N	2/8	
Lucy and Lou are seated					**LOC. #2**
EXT: PARKING LOT	30	7, 8, 9, ATS (8)	D	4/8	Ming Garage Centre Ave.
Bill, Karla & Fred plot					**LOC. #3**
EXT: STREET	34	7, 8, 9, ATS (6)	D	3/8	Centre Ave.
Bill, Karla & Fred on street		**TOTAL PAGES: 2 7/8**			

NO.	SWF	CAST	CHARACTER	MAKEUP	ON SET	REMARKS
1	W	SAM GERROL	LOU BARRET	6A	7A	P/U 5:30A
2	W	MEGHAN HENRY	LUCY BARRET	6A	7A	P/U 5:30A
7	SW	JACK SHANNON	BILL FERITE	3P	4P	P/U 2:30P
8	SW	ERIKA PANGLOSS	KARLA FERITE	3P	4P	P/U 2:30P
9	SW	DELROY HOLMES	FRED ZAP	3P	4P	P/U 2:30P
48	SWF	NAOMI SKOWBO	HOSTESS	1P	2P	P/U 12:30P
50	WF	DAVID KEMP	WAITER	10A	11A	P/U 9:30A

STANDINS/ATMOSPHERE		SPECIAL INSTRUCTIONS	
2 STANDINS: LOU, LUCY	6:30A	MAKE UP:	
3 " ": BILL, KARLA, FRED	3:30P		
ATMOS TO INCLUDE@		PROPS:	
6 FEMALE PATRONS/REST.	6:30A		
6 MALE PATRONS/REST.	6:30A	FX:	
2 FEMALE WAITRESS/REST.	6:30A		
1 MALE BUSBOY/REST.	6:30A	WARDROBE:	
2 MALE TOUGHGUYS/P -LOT	3:30P		
2 MALE ATTENDANTS/P -LOT	3:30P	GRIP/ELEC.: SC: 17, 18, 12 --	
4 FEMALE FRIENDS/P - LOT	3:30P	**(DAY FOR NIGHT)**	
3 FEMALE PASSERSBY/STREET	5:30P		
3 MALE PASSERSBY/STREET	5:30P	SOUND:	
TOTAL ATMOS: 34		DRIVERS:	

Fig. 1. Call sheet, front side

scheduled to begin shooting at 7:00 AM.) *Pages* tells how many pages are in the scene. All movie script pages as well as TV, miniseries, and movies of the week are broken down into eighths. (In a script, a scene can be as short as an eighth of a page, or as long as two pages. They are generally not longer than two.) Therefore, we know that scene 17 is a page and a half long. At the bottom of the Pages column is the total number of pages scheduled to shoot that day. *Location* informs us where the filming is taking place. Today, the film crew is shooting at three locations: Bab's Grill on Mission Boulevard (which really exists and would be rented by the studio to stand in for Michael's restaurant); the Ming Garage on Centre Avenue, which will be the parking lot; and the sidewalk on Centre Avenue, which will portray the street.

The next row is in bold and headed No., SWF, Cast, Character, Makeup, On Set, and Remarks. *No.* refers to the number each actor has been assigned for the duration of the movie (only the numbers of the actors pertinent for that day are listed). Sam Gerrol and Meghan Henry, the stars of *The Wonder,* are given numbers 1 and 2. The hostess, Naomi Skqwbo, and the waiter, David Kemp, are smaller characters and their numbers reflect that. *SWF* is an acronym for start, work, finish. This is an easy way for everyone to see the actors' employment status. Because our two stars each have a *W,* we know they are in the midst of working on the picture. *SW* implies that Jack Shannon, Erika Pangloss, and Delroy Hughes are starting work today (their numbers indicate they are secondary leads). We know that Pam Skowbo, the hostess, is only working one day because she is listed as *SWF* (start, work, finish all in one day). This indicates that she does not appear in any more of the Michael's restaurant scenes, unlike the waiter, David Kemp, who has worked before. However, because of his *WF* we know that this is his last day as well. *Cast* is a list of the actors' names, and *Character* lists the roles they are playing in the movie. *Makeup* refers to the time the actors report to makeup; essentially, when they show up for work. *On set* indicates when they need to be finished with makeup, in costume, and on the set ready to go. Although there is usually a rehearsal, unless told otherwise, the actors still need to be in makeup and in costume and report to the set at the given time. *Remarks* is generally reserved for any comments about the actors that the crew needs to know. In this case, as on most call sheets, this lets transportation (as well as the actors) know how the actors are reporting to the location. When a film shoots on location and the actors are from out of town, as in this case, they are housed at a local hotel and picked up and dropped off every day of the shoot. (I talk more about this in chapter 8.)

Let me point out that the *On set* part of the call sheet is a good indication of the director's planned schedule for that day. Notice that the two stars are called at 7:00 AM, and the waiter is called at 11:00 AM. This means that the director is planning to take approximately four hours to shoot scene 17. That may seem like a long time, but notice that scene 17 is one and a half pages long. That represents about a half day's work. The director is planning to take two hours to shoot scene 18 because the hostess's call time is 2:00 PM. (There will probably be a one-hour lunch break between scene 18 and 12.) The cast and crew also know that they are to finish up Michael's scenes and move to the next location by 4:00 PM, because that's when the actors are called for the scenes at the parking lot. This way everyone knows that they have to be ready to start by 4:00 PM at the new location. The final street location would be very close to the parking lot because scene 34 is called immediately following scene 30. The fact that the extras needed for that scene are called at 5:30 PM indicates that the director probably plans to start the street scene at approximately 6:00 PM.

Let's take a quick look at the last part of the call sheet. Under *Stand-ins/Atmosphere* the call times appear for those cast members. Stand-ins usually have a higher status than extras. They are normally hired for the duration of the shoot and are paid a daily rate that is slightly more than what the extras earn. They literally stand in for the principals after rehearsals and before the actual filming begins while the crew is lighting and focusing the camera for the shoot. As you can see, all five of the lead principals have stand-ins, and their call times are listed. Below that is a description of the atmosphere: what they do, what scenes they are in, and what time they are called. The assistant directors are responsible for dealing with the stand-ins and atmosphere. At the bottom is the total number of stand-ins and atmosphere needed for that day. To the right are Special Instructions. This is reserved for the various crews. Any and all special considerations needed for that day's shoot are given to the different crews; for example, special makeup requirements, such as a prosthesis. Note the special instruction listed for the *Grip/elec* (these are the electricians responsible for power and lighting on the set). You'll notice that scenes 17, 18, and 12 in Michael's are to be shot Day For Night. This means that in the script those scenes are meant to take place at night. Since they are filming those scenes during the day, the electricians will need to create the illusion that it is night. This is done by lighting the scene a special way and blacking out all natural light from the outside.

WHAT IS A TYPICAL DAY LIKE ON A FILM SET?

One of the best sources I can refer you to regarding what a typical day on a set is like is the excellent *The Camera Smart Actor* by Richard Brestoff (published by Smith and Kraus). I recommend that you read it, especially chapter 6, "The Next Shot's in the Glass." In it, Brestoff creates a scripted scenario following a newcomer's first day on a set. He covers everything you need to know about what to expect on your initial day of work.

You now know that when you're called onto the set to work you're already in makeup and costume. As I've mentioned, there is usually a rehearsal. Compared to the other genres, this rehearsal can be fairly comprehensive. I've been on film sets in which the director has cleared the set of all crew members and rehearsed just with the actors. During this rehearsal, not only will the director block, but the rehearsal can become rather in depth regarding analysis, character, and motivation. Once the director is satisfied with where the scene is going, she will invite the crew to join the rehearsal. It's at this point that the director goes over with the DP (the director of photography, also known as the cinematographer) what she is looking for technically (camera angles, lighting, and so on). After the DP watches a rehearsal and has a fairly good idea of what she needs to do, the actors are dismissed and the stand-ins (who normally watch the actors rehearse) step in. (The principals are called "first team," and the stand-ins are the "second team.") At this point, the crew takes over and prepares the technical aspects of the scene for filming.

This is where it can start to become difficult for the principal actors. You've rehearsed, you've gotten a good idea of what the scene is about, and you've begun to understand what the director wants in the scene; now you have to step aside and wait so the scene can be set up for the actual filming to begin. This wait can be long (anywhere from thirty to sixty minutes), and you have to find a way to keep up the momentum that you've created for yourself as your character in the rehearsal. (The first three principles are meant to help you with this.) Be aware of the abundant distractions that await you. First, there is the "crafts table," where food is always available for the cast and crew. It's very easy to head over there and start eating. There is also the distraction of socializing with your fellow actors. I don't mean to suggest that you shouldn't talk to your colleagues, but keep in mind that your work is yet to be done. There is also the temptation to dissipate your energy by walking around or just hanging out, but you really want to save your energy for the actual shooting. Until you've filmed your scene, you haven't accomplished what you were paid to do, so do whatever you need to do to maintain your concentration, focus, and energy. I recommend that you stay in your trailer (all principals are given dressing room space in a trailer) to rest and concentrate while you await your call.

When the location is prepared for shooting and you're finally needed, the second AD (one of the assistant directors) will come get you and escort you there. (A word of advice: You should never leave the area unless you notify an AD of where you can be found. If you want to continue working in this business, don't ever be the one responsible for keeping the production waiting. Remember that it's costing the studio thousands of dollars a minute to produce the film; don't you be the one wasting their money.) Once you're on the set and they're ready to begin, the first AD will announce, "First positions." *First positions* is equivalent to *places* in the theater; it means that you are physically where you're supposed to be when the scene starts. Every time the director goes back to the beginning of the scene, the first AD will always instruct the actors to get into first positions.

A major distraction on the film set is the tremendous amount of commotion that goes on. I've always compared a film set to an operating room. No matter how busy and populated an operating room can get, it has only one focus — the patient who is being operated on. The set of a motion picture is its own universe completely focused on what the camera is shooting. Everyone on the set is there to serve the scene that is being filmed. Dozens of necessary crew members work extremely hard preparing the set to look just right. It takes many talented people to shoot a film — not only the actors, but also the crew. The actor should never lose sight of the crew's effort, time, and commitment in preparing the location for the scene. However, like a surgeon, the actor must be able to completely block out all the other people and the hustle and bustle to concentrate on his task. The actor must, in essence, maintain privacy in the most public place.

Now that you have an idea of some of the practicalities of working in film, let's clarify some of the intangibles of what might help you secure work and what you do once you get it. Although it's important to know about the casting process and what a typical day is like, all that information is going to be rather useless if you are not ready to practice the art of acting.

PRINCIPLES OF FILM ACTING

Let the following eight principles help you create the kind of privacy that you're going to need when you get onto a movie set, despite the inherent distractions. They are meant to stimulate the way you think about acting in motion pictures. My recommendation is to take your time incorporating these ideas. Film is an acutely gratifying medium in which to work. More than any of the other genres we've dealt with, the process of working in film is much less rushed and allows more thought to be given to the acting. Let these eight principles assist you in the way you think about auditioning for films as well. Have fun, use them as you see fit, and also try out the exercises that accompany them.

1. Make friends with the camera.

You've heard the phrase: "The camera loves that actor!" Besides good looks and striking bone structure, great film actors have a special relationship with the camera. It's a symbiotic connection that is riveting to watch. It's difficult to define, but maybe it's an actor's ability to make audience members feel as if they can't take their eyes off them. Think of brilliant film actors — Robert De Niro and Katharine Hepburn, for instance — they have a mystique on film that makes them irresistible. This is probably not something that an actor can produce at will, but it's as if remarkable film actors have been in front of a camera all their lives. This may be a quality that cannot be learned, but I believe it all starts with feeling completely comfortable. So we might as well begin there.

Why is it that we can be brilliant in front of our bathroom mirrors or in the presence of those we know extremely well, and why is it that we become self-conscious in front of others? I'll bet it all has to do with feeling comfortable in a situation because we aren't afraid of being ridiculed. We tend to accept ourselves completely in front of a mirror because we trust it, and our truest friends have earned that designation because they accept us. Generally, we also tend to fall in love with people who accept us as well. (Or at least we hope they do.) As a film actor, you must be able to create that kind of trust and acceptance with the camera. The camera has to become your best friend.

Remarkable film actors are able to be completely at ease and natural on camera. However, none of us are born with the ability to be at home in front of a camera. How many times have you been told to "be natural" when someone is taking your picture, only to become tense as a result? You probably became alarmed thinking you must be coming across as unnatural. You then likely felt grotesque as you pursued "being natural." You cannot *try* to be natural in front of the camera — that is the result, not the means. You must *be* completely natural; you cannot manufacture it.

The process of being natural starts with establishing a relationship with the camera. This is not easy to do. The scene in front of the camera may be intimate, but the distractions behind the camera are innumerable. The actor first needs exceptional powers of concentration, shutting out everything and creating a bond between him and the camera. The actor establishes a private world consisting of him, his fellow actors, and the given circumstances, and the only one allowed to see this world is the camera. The camera is a private audience, and everything is done for the benefit of that audience.

Concentration is a technical skill usually learned early on in the process of becoming an actor. Just as one must become technically proficient at playing scales when learning to play the piano, actors in film must be proficient in the art of concentration. This skill must be practiced every day. You might want to practice by reading with the television on, or having a intimate conversation in a crowded place, or try something as simple as studying your hand while ignoring everything going on around you.

Of course, the irony of this principle is that though we tend to make eye contact with our closest friends and loved ones, actors on film usually do not make overt contact with the camera. So what I'm asking you to do is to create a relationship with the camera even though you're never going to look at it. In a sense, the camera becomes a sort of private friend who is always watching you.

Have you ever had a friend, family member, or lover who so permeated your consciousness that you felt she was always with you, watching you? No matter where you went or what you did, you found yourself always trying to impress her, to gain her approval. In many ways our society uses the omnipotent, invisible observer as a behavioral guide. It could be God, Santa, parents, or the police who are always part of our consciousness to help us live responsible lives. The film actor allows the camera to infiltrate his consciousness in a similar way and modifies his behavior accordingly. Let the camera become a ubiquitous presence in your life. As you go about your daily life, pretend that you're on camera. Besides developing your concentration, always imagining that you're being filmed will also help you become natural in front of the camera.

You need to bring that relationship with the camera to the audition. Sometimes auditions for film are taped like commercials; in that case, the only person at the audition will be the casting director. The tape is then sent to the director and the producer, and when they watch it, they will certainly note if the actor is comfortable and appears natural on camera. When the director is at the audition, the best thing you can do is to completely concentrate on what you are doing. You could also pretend your best friend is at the audition and you are doing everything for her. Believe me, the director will want someone impressive to watch. Think of the moments when you are the most compelling, and by all means bring that person to the audition.

EXERCISES

- Establish an extremely high-stakes activity (breaking a code, defusing a bomb, etc.) and improvise enacting it. Whatever you choose, make sure that it's a life-and-death situation (it works best if it's something that requires the person doing it to be stationary); be sure to include a time limit for the activity. Shoot it with one camera. The person operating the camera should do everything possible to distract the person doing the activity. This exercise tests the concentration of the person doing the activity. Before playing back the exercise, ask the actor how cognizant he was of the camera (as well as the person operating it) and if it distracted him in any way. During the playback, notice how well the actor concentrates on his activity. Chances are that if the stakes were high enough, the actor would be totally engrossed in the activity and unaware of the camera. It's this kind of concentration that is needed when working on camera.

- As you go about your daily life, assume that you are being watched at all times by your own private audience. Without overdoing it or drawing attention to yourself, imagine that you are showing off for your private audience. At the end of the day, think about your behavior and what, if anything, you did was altered by the idea that you were being watched.

- Whether you're doing a scene, monologue, or exercise, secretly experiment with the idea of your own private audience as you tape it. In other words, incorporate a private audience as you see fit. Imagine different people in your life whom you would want to impress (even people from your past or historical figures). See if you can determine what people work best for you and observe if anything happens to your performances as a result. It's best not to divulge your choices to others. Keep your private audience private.

2. Always find the focus of your character and zero in on it.

Concentration must have a purpose. Let's call it a focal point. Having that focal point is what makes concentration active. Focus is, literally, the object of concentration. If you are reading a book while music is blaring from the stereo, the focal point of your concentration is obviously on what you're reading. Focusing gives the actor the tools necessary to concentrate appropriately as the character. You need to achieve focus at the beginning of every scene before the director yells, "Action!," and it must be still active when the director calls, "Cut!" Also, having a strong focus will help you concentrate through the long hours of shooting.

When a scene is about to be filmed, you should always be ready for "Action." Think of it as a windup and a pitch in baseball. You have to be finished with the windup and be ready to let go of the ball by the time "Action!" is called. Just before filming begins, the assistant director calls, "Sound." When the sound is ready to record, the sound person replies, "Speed." "Camera" is then called, and when the camera operator is ready, he says, "Rolling." Only then can the director give the command, "Action!" Actors don't receive the same courtesy. The actor must be up to speed by the time "Action!" is called. To get yourself up to speed, you must find the focus of the character by placing yourself in the given circumstances of the scene.

It is always a good idea to begin your action in the moments before the director's cue. Many times the director will talk you through what's just happened before she calls for action. For example, if you are playing a short-order cook at work, the director might remind you of what happened in the previous scene, and you would want to start cooking fifteen seconds before action is initiated. Doing this will automatically give you an action, which will focus you and put you into the scene. Otherwise, the audience gets the sense that it has caught you during an "inhale" — the moment right before an activity — rather than where you should be — in the midst of an activity.

Staying focused is important because of the long stretches of time between takes. It takes time to set up each shot, and actors end up waiting — either standing around or sitting in their trailers — for long periods. It's difficult to blithely jump in and out of focus at will. You may be shooting a long, tension-filled scene — perhaps four or five pages — over a two-day period of time. You must always be ready to dive back into any moment of the scene at any time. That is intensely demanding on an actor's concentration and emotional instrument. You need to find an anchor for yourself so that you can get back into character at will.

Conversely, it is dangerous to complete a take and, at the moment the director says cut, drop out of character and start joking with crew members or fellow actors. Sometimes the director keeps the camera rolling after a scene is supposed to be finished just to see what happens. Often, great moments in film occur unintentionally when the actors stay in character and continue improvising a scene.

Occasionally, inexperienced actors think the scene is over when the dialogue stops (and most of the time it is); but it is never the actor's job to make that call. Only the director can cut a scene. So, until you hear cut, keep going. This also holds true for line problems. I've seen many actors alienate the director (and get taken aside) for asking for a cut when they've forgotten or fumbled a line. Again, even if you think you have really screwed up, wait for the director to stop you — don't do it yourself.

There are two golden rules of film acting: *Never start the scene until the director yells action* and *never stop acting until the director yells cut.* Breaking these rules are rookie mistakes and will let everyone on the set know that you are new to acting on camera. They will sometimes forgive the excited impulsiveness of a beginner not waiting for the action cue, but will not so easily forgive stopping the scene before cut is yelled. If you want to prove how professional you are, adhere to these rules.

Acting in film requires an enormous amount of energy. Maintaining the necessary focus demands an even greater amount of energy. When you think about the pace of shooting a film and the mandatory waiting time between shots, you realize how amazing it is that actors can keep up the kind of focus demanded of them. So not only is it necessary to have energy, it's just as important to conserve it. If you spend too much time between takes chatting, joking around, socializing, or eating, you will dissipate your energy. By the end of the day when you're called on to film coverage of your big scene, you won't have any energy left, and your work will suffer. Never take your energy for granted — and never underestimate the amount of energy you will need to focus yourself for each shot.

In an audition, the best way to put this principle into practice is always to be focused and concentrating when you enter the room. Unless the director or producer initiates conversation, don't spend a lot of time chatting with everyone. If it's appropriate (and, again, if it's initiated by someone else), make small talk only after you've wowed them with your talent. In other words, earn the idle chatter by doing your work first, but let the director take the lead. After seeing you read, many times the director will want to get more of a sense of who you are. He might ask you about yourself or what you think about something. Even if you think it's irrelevant, get into a discussion. You never know — it just might be the conversation with the director that gets you the job. If nothing else, it is usually a sign that the director is interested. But more than anything, he wants to see how well you can focus on the task at hand. Whatever you do, maintain your focus, whether it's the audition or a conversation with the director.

EXERCISES

- Tape a scene of your choice. Attempt the scene two different ways. The first time, tape it with absolutely no preparation. Immediately before action is called, be thinking of something else or talking with someone off camera. Then tape the scene a second time. This time devote as much time as you think necessary to focus in on your character before you start taping the scene. Try starting an appropriate physical activity thirty seconds before you start taping. Play back both scenes and see which one appears more focused. You might find the take where there was no preparation more spontaneous, but I doubt the performance will be as clear otherwise. Let's face it, depending on the type of role you're playing, there may be times where you don't want to spend too much time focusing before the director announces "Action!" That's OK, but it takes a certain amount of experience before I would recommend someone do that. For now, just try focusing.

- You'll need a director for this one. Tape a two-person scene of your choice. Shoot a master shot of the scene. There should be a director off camera who calls action to start the scene and, more important, cut to end it. The director should let the actors keep going when they get to the end of the scene and delay cutting the scene as long as possible, just to see what the actors do with it. Play it back and discuss the effectiveness of the improvisation after the scene was supposed to end.

3. Enter into the world of the scene as much as possible.

This principle is unique because everyone accomplishes it differently. Not only do you need to concentrate and focus on a film set, you also need to do whatever is necessary to help you maintain the reality of the situation.

Many of the greatest American film actors have accomplished this by adhering to the method school of acting. The method asks for the actor, to the best of her ability, to become the character within the situation. This style of acting is commonly attributed to Constantine Stanislavski. Nothing could be further from the truth.

Stanislavski developed what he termed a system of actor training, not a method. He was the founder of the Moscow Art Theatre at the turn of the nineteenth century. His teachings have changed the way acting is taught, and he is generally considered to be the father of modern acting. Before Stanislavski, acting was histrionic and laughable by today's standards. Many acting teachers have since based their teaching on *one aspect* of Stanislavski's system and developed it as their own. Method acting, or the method, was developed by Lee Strassberg and taught at the Actor's Studio. It became so popular that many people have since assumed that Stanislavski's system is the same as the method and that learning the method is the same as learning the Stanislavski system. That is not true.

While I have respect for it, I don't necessarily agree with the basic tenets of method acting. For one thing, I think it's impossible for actors to literally become a character. But whether it's the method or some other technique, the actor must find some way to stay in character and maintain the necessary focus over long periods of time. Imagination is a viable alternative to method acting.

Imagination is one thing actors need plenty of. After all, isn't it tacitly implied that acting is pretending? Films (as well as television and theater, for that matter) pretend that what is going on is real, when it's not. More important, the audience is asked to pretend to believe what it sees, even though audience members know it's not real. Actors and audience alike need imagination to help them suspend their disbelief. In many ways, imagination is a prerequisite for pretending.

Think of imagination as an ethereal rumination. But for imagination to be useful, it needs fuel to take flight. The actor provides the necessary fuel by analyzing the situation and the character and asking appropriate questions. Keep the questions basic: Why am I here? What happened to me to get me to this point? Where do I want to go? What do I need? What is this other person to me, and how do I want to change him? How do I feel about what's happening to me? If you do this for every scene you're in, you will not only be doing the necessary analysis, you will also be sparking your imagination forcing it to come up with answers — and the answers will help you create your circumstances and become intimately acquainted with your character.

Only you can determine how much of this work you need to do to be ready to shoot the scenes that you are in. It's not difficult to do this if you are only in one scene. But if you're on the set a full day (a day can last twelve to fourteen hours), a week, or throughout the entire shoot (which could be months), you're going to have to develop your own system to do this. Experiment with your imagination by asking the questions I've listed and by coming up with your own. One of the most effective ways of doing this on a film set is to use yourself as the basis for your character and imagine what *you* would do if you were in the same situation. Find the part of your own personality that is most like the character you are playing and explore the questions and answers from that perspective. Above all, keep exploring different ideas so that you can stay fresh within the world of the scene. For your audition you need to enter the world of the scene by imagining as much of the given circumstances as possible. Here's an example:

Years ago I auditioned for *Pulp Fiction*. I read for the part of Mr. Orange (the role that eventually went to the wonderful Tim Roth). I was asked to read a scene at the beginning of the film when Mr. Orange is in the back seat of the getaway car after being shot. The only people at my audition were Quentin Tarantino (the film's writer and director), the casting director, and the reader. I chose to play the scene on the floor in a corner of the room. I imagined that the pain of being shot in the stomach would be excruciating. I writhed around on the floor in tremendous pain. When I was done, the casting director said she thought I might have gone a bit overboard, but I defended my choice by saying, "Well, imagine how painful it would be to have hot lead in your stomach." Tarantino, who I could tell was excited about my audition, interjected, "Oh no, he's right. The pain would be agonizing. That was perfect. Do it again!" I found out later that he really liked my audition, but that they needed a "name" for the role — someone with name recognition from the A, B, or C lists. (There was talk of me playing Mr. Brown, but Tarantino ended up playing that role.) Imagine my surprise later, when I saw the film and watched the scene played just as I had performed it at my audition. Through my imagination I brought a reality to the scene that other actors may not have; by fully pretending to be a part of the world of the scene I drew my audience in. Ultimately, I felt complimented that I may have had something to do with a great moment in the film.

- Have everyone bring in scenes from films. They can be transcribed or found in the published version of the film. Avoid popular scenes; use scenes from lesser known films. Distribute them to other members of the class. (You shouldn't end up with the scene you brought.) When you get your scene, stimulate your imagination by asking yourself these questions: Why am I here? What happened to me to get me to this point? Where do I want to go? What do I need? What is this other person to me and how do I want to change him or her? How do I feel about what's happening to me? If these questions provoke other questions, so much the better.

- After you have done your homework, shoot the scene. However, don't film the scene where it is supposed to take place (for example, if it takes place in a kitchen, shoot it in the living room). Tape the scenes in a class or lab setting with boxes representing chairs, tables, or beds. The objective is to force you to create the world of the scene and as much of the environment as you can by using your imagination. When you play it back, have group members comment on how effective you were in making them believe that you were who you were supposed to be, where you were supposed to be, and so on.

4. Look for opportunities to incorporate humor into a role.

Humor does not merely consist of telling jokes. Actually, humor means the ability or faculty of discovering and expressing the ludicrous or absurdly incongruous. It also implies unpredictability; a person with a sense of humor may be said to possess a variable nature. Such a person is often dynamic, interesting, and even eccentric. Having a sense of humor is a requisite quality for an actor. Think of the great performances you've seen on screen; I'll bet many contained humor. What intrigues you about your favorite film actors? Besides looks, these actors likely have qualities that distinguish them from almost everybody you know, and one of those qualities is humor.

Certainly, possessing a sense of humor also implies an ability to make people laugh. Humor can be both unique to a situation or culture and universal in its appeal. What one finds funny, another may not; while some things make everyone laugh. Humor can be witty and charming; it can also be sarcastic, ironic, dry, self-deprecating, and satiric — among many things. There are as many kinds of humor as there are people, but all of us have a need to laugh and be charmed. This is one reason we go to the movies.

Because a lot of time is spent shooting film, this principle is readymade for film acting. Whereas the acting in episodic television needs to be straightforward, in film the actor has the time to explore and build his character and develop subtleties of humor and other personality traits. And it's the discovery of those qualities that makes performances riveting and unforgettable. This is one reason many actors want to work in film more than other media: There is more time to develop multidimensional characters.

The problem is that no one can be taught to have a sense of humor. In many ways this characteristic, like instinct, is something you either have or you don't. I do believe, however, that it can be nurtured. One way to do this is to assume that every character you play has a sense of humor, even if you think that you personally don't. As an actor your task is to find it in every character. This is easy to do if you are fortunate enough to be playing a role that is written with abundant humor. It's even more imperative, though, to find it in roles where none is apparent. I'm sure you'd be hard pressed to find the humor in Hannibal from *Silence of the Lambs*. However, if you've seen Anthony Hopkins's brilliant performance, you saw how much humor he brought to that character. Many actors make the mistake of hastily assuming that if a character isn't written with a sense of humor, he hasn't got one. Sometimes it's up to you to unearth it. Just make sure that it's shrewdly incorporated. In other words, not every role is going to be performed with the kind of zaniness that Robin Williams inventively brings to some of his roles. Each person needs to look for the kind of humor that appeals to her and that she feels comfortable doing. Explore other choices that feel more natural to you.

This exploration begins with the audition. One of the first things you should look for in a character is his sense of humor. If it's apparent in the writing, great. If not, you need to create it. Ask yourself what makes the character interesting to you. If you need to, privately create something interesting about the character; you don't need to share this with anyone else. Many times a sense of humor manifests itself in obscure ways. What's important is that you bring something to the character that will make the character interesting and exciting. Many times a director will cast an actor because she brought a sense of humor to a character where none seemed to exist.

EXERCISES

- While watching a favorite film, pay attention to the actors that get your attention. See if you can determine the amount of humor that they bring to their characterization. In what way does their sense of humor add to their performances? Does it make them more interesting to watch?

- If you are working with a class or a group of people that are familiar with each other, try to honestly assess one another's sense of humor. Really try to articulate what it is about each person in the group that makes him or her intriguing, funny, and charming. As you do this, be sure to include examples of the person's behavior that makes you think this. Develop improvisations based on the examples that are given. See if you can recreate the sense of humor attributed to you.

- For this exercise, use contentless scenes (like previous ones in this book) or scenes from films that are fairly generic in the sense that there is nothing overtly funny about the situation or the characters. (For example, two people at a bus stop talking about the weather.) As you prepare to shoot your scene, see if you can discover some kind of humor in your character. The humor that you find should be kept secret from everyone. Tape the scene twice. For the first take, try not to bring any of the humor to it; then tape it again incorporating the humor that you discovered. See if you can tell the difference in the scenes. Even if the humor that you found in your character is something that is secret, the point is that even for the most innocuous situations, a sense of humor will make the character more interesting to watch.

5. Always include the use of opposites in your acting.

I believe the basis of all great film acting (or any acting, for that matter) relies on the ability of the actor to play opposites. Playing opposites means making a choice that is diametrically opposite to the initial obvious action. For example, if a scene calls for a sad response by a character, instead of crying — the obvious choice — the actor would smile — a choice that is certainly *not* obvious. Or the character may say, "I have to go," but then stays. Playing opposites makes a performance complex, subtle, and much more interesting to watch. Obviously, playing opposites is not appropriate all the time; it may appear that you are not taking the situation seriously or making an unsuitable comment about your character. But I think that you should always experiment with playing opposites. Directors will quickly let you know if the choice you're making is the wrong one.

Proficiency in playing opposites has been the essence of great acting for a long time. It goes as far back as William Shakespeare. Because Shakespeare's language is essential to understanding his plays, an actor must first comprehend the language to play the character. Shakespeare uses figures of speech in his plays to guide the actor through the language. One figure of speech is *antithesis*. Antithesis is the direct opposite of something else: hot is the antithesis of cold, love is the antithesis of hate, up is the antithesis of down, and so on. Shakespeare used this device to bring intellectual and emotional complexity to his characters. In *Romeo and Juliet* for example, Romeo says in act 1,

> Here's much to do with hate, but more with love:
> Why, then, O brawling love! O loving hate!
> O any thing, of nothing first create!
> O heavy lightness! Serious vanity!
> Mis-shapen chaos of well-seeming forms!
> Feather of lead, bright smoke, cold fire, sick health!

There's antithesis in every line! Shakespeare gives the actor playing Romeo a pretty good clue that there's a lot going on with the character. (He's madly in love.) An actor playing the role will need to be sensitive to antithesis in both the language and the character. Whether you call it antithesis or playing opposites, the idea has been a good acting strategy for a long time.

Great actors still bring intricacy to their acting through antithesis. The difference is that today actors can use behavior as well as language to express it. In life, people continually act out opposites. Many times we say one thing only to mean another, or we start to do one thing and end up doing something else. In movies, observe how frequently opposites are used. How often have you seen a movie in which the male and female leads start off fighting and end up falling madly in love? Opposites are even present in the stereotypical characters of the bad guy that you love to hate and the loser that you hope will win. In both society and movies, opposites play a key role in our cultural subconscious. We're attracted to opposites.

Opposites also enable audience members to instill their own emotions into the characters. If an actor overemotes, the audience feels left out and unable to become deeply involved. Imagine a scene in which a policeman informs a wife that her husband has just died. The actress could scream and cry passionately, or she could play opposites and try hard *not* to cry. Her reaction would be one of shock; she might even smile slightly, as if to thank the policeman for taking the trouble to come and tell her. Which one of those two reactions would you find more effective? The second would affect me more profoundly; watching her struggle with this horrendous news would be much more moving, and it may be a more realistic reaction than getting overly emotional and sobbing uncontrollably. If the actress emotionally overreacts, I, as the audience, have no room to feel for her; she's monopolizing all the emotion and not letting me share in any of it.

All the other genres we've discussed up until now have demanded that the actor be direct in his acting. You generally don't have the time to develop detailed characterizations in commercials, soaps, sitcoms, industrials, or episodic television. Working in film is extravagant by comparison because the actor can cultivate a richer performance. In film the actor does not have to immediately settle for what might be expected; there is room for experimentation.

A film set is not a laboratory, however, where the actor is free to take superfluous risks and spend as much time as he wants to create an interesting character. Self-indulgence is never acceptable when working in film. Financial considerations always need to be taken into account. Don't think that because more time is devoted to filming a motion picture, the producers don't watch the bottom line. They watch it like a hawk. If the actor is doing nothing but wallowing in her choices, the producers are probably going to fire her.

What I *am* urging you to do, however, is to give yourself permission to look a bit more in depth at your characters and reconsider obvious choices. This is best done as homework while you're at home preparing. Get into the habit of at least entertaining the idea of playing the opposite. When your first impulse is to do one thing (whether it's an emotion or an action), experiment with an opposite emotion or action just to see what happens. Once you get onto the set, bring your ideas with you to rehearsal. The worst thing that can happen is that the director will tell you that the choice is wrong. Of course, you need to adapt and be able to change your choice if need be; but if you experiment with opposites, you just may end up creating more interesting and spontaneous characters.

One place to start is in the audition. Be careful, though; don't use the audition to do your homework. Do your homework for the audition as thoroughly as you would for the job — even more thoroughly because you'll probably have much less room for experimentation. Also, don't make the mistake of announcing to the casting director or director that you're experimenting with playing opposites. Just do it. The people at auditions are not interested in hearing you talk about your "process." They want to see the perfect person for the part walk through the door; it's your job to be that person. Playing opposites may be the way to get the job.

EXERCISES

- Pay attention to how often people play opposites in life. Do this by noticing your behavior, as well as that of others. Learn to recognize your objectives and those of others and see if you can tell when you and others use opposite tactics subconsciously to achieve a desired goal. As an actor you should always be on the lookout for this kind of "backwards" tactical behavior in life. It is rich material for playing objectives in unexpected and unusual ways. Sometimes the most interesting choices are often 180 degrees from the direction we expect.

- Everyone should pick a short scene and fully rehearse it with a partner. While you do the homework on your character, make sure that you pick an objective and a tactic for achieving that objective. Once you have figured out your tactic, practice playing an opposite one. That is, practice playing an opposite action from what you normally would do to gain your objective. For example, if you really want to leave, pretend to want to stay. If you really want someone to pay attention to you, ignore him or her. Tape the scene as a master shot using one camera. During the playback, discuss the use of opposites and how this is very much like what we do in life.

6. Learn to use Michael Chekhov's veiling technique.

Perhaps the first person to teach acting specifically for the camera was Michael Chekhov (1891–1955). Chekhov was playwright Anton Chekhov's nephew and was initially part of Stanislavski's studio at the Moscow Art Theatre. He eventually made his way to the United States and became famous for his teaching and acting and for his character roles in Hollywood films. He wrote a classic book on acting called *To the Actor*, which is included in the excellent book *On the Technique of Acting* (edited by Mel Gordon and with a preface and afterword by Mala Powers). In the afterword, Mala Powers writes a detailed essay on Chekhov's techniques for acting in film. I urge you to read this admirable book.

One of his finest techniques for film acting is the idea of "veiling" an emotion. Chekhov believed that instead of decreasing your emotion in front of a camera, you should increase the emotion and then veil it. Chekhov urged the actor to let the emotion build to a climax and then to imagine a veil coming from above, below, or from the side and covering the face or the entire body of the actor. The veil acts as a gossamer filter that tempers the emotion. To use another metaphor, think of boiling a pot of water; your emotion is the water you are going to heat. Once it starts to boil, you then reduce the emotion to a simmer. The veil has the same effect as lowering the heat. It filters or softens the emotion, thereby keeping it from overwhelming what the camera sees. It is a purely imaginative tool that the actor uses to maintain the intensity of the emotion and, at the same time, keep it from becoming too powerful for the camera. By using this technique the actor purifies the emotion without forsaking it altogether. If the veiling is done correctly, the emotion that remains is, in a way, more genuine and will better fit the performance on camera.

Often actors working in film make the mistake of thinking that because the camera sees every move and emotion and magnifies it, that they shouldn't do anything at all. As a result, their performance is devoid of any emotion whatsoever. A performance can become so small that not even the camera can pick it up. On the other hand, unrestricted emotion in front of a camera can appear uncontrolled and, therefore, come across as overacting.

For an audition, an actor should rehearse the veiling technique as a preparatory device. When you practice your sides at home, try overdoing your role emotionally and then imagine a veil descending over you as you do it again.

What's most important about this principle for audition purposes is that if you audition in front of the director (as opposed to a camera), you have to imagine that you are acting in front of a camera. Bring the appropriate intensity to the reading, as you would if you were on camera, and not as if you were onstage. After all, the director will be looking for a performance that is appropriate for the camera, not for him in person. Remember that when you audition for anything that's going to be on camera, you have to keep in mind the size of your audience. The camera can get in very close, so you have to act accordingly. Even if you're accustomed to auditioning for theater jobs in large rehearsal rooms in front of a lot of people, if you find yourself in the identical situation auditioning for film or television you must still pretend that a camera is in front of you. The veiling technique can help your performance have vitality without appearing too broad, yet keep you from obliterating your performance by being totally void of emotion.

EXERCISES

- Use a monologue that you are familiar with. Everyone doing this exercise should select an emotion with which to play the monologue. Make sure it's *not the appropriate emotion*. For example, if it's a monologue where the character is sad, don't choose that emotion for this exercise. The purpose of this exercise is for you to do a monologue with which you are familiar, but to perform it without repeating the same feeling that you normally use.

- When performing the monologue, the actor should be taped in a medium close-up. The actor should attempt to do the monologue with as full an emotional value as possible. In other words, let the passion get to the boiling point and tape it so that it's over the top. As soon as the monologue is finished, cut. Then immediately retape the entire monologue, slightly increasing the emotion while placing an imaginary veil over it. Remember to picture the veil enveloping you — either completely or just in front of your face. It can descend from above or rise from below. It can be different colors or however you choose to visualize it. You can endow the veil in any way you like, according to your individual psychological needs or desires. That it is at least translucent enough to see through is what's important. Remember to shoot the second take immediately after the first one so that the actor has the sense of how the veiling affects what's happening with her performance. To guide the actor through the steps, it's important for there to be someone coaching the actor through this process.

- Play it back and discuss the differences between the two takes. When I've done this exercise I've noticed that if the actor has succeeded in visualizing a veil, it's interesting how even though the actor has increased his emotion during the second take the ultimate effect is a more underplayed yet intense, controlled, intimate, and personal performance.

- Try this exercise again using a different monologue. This time use a suitable feeling for the monologue. Try not to let its appropriateness deter you from fully playing it and enabling you to visualize a veil during the second take. (The danger of using an emotion that fits is that actors tend to bring prescribed ideas of how a monologue should be played to the process; they also tend to rely too heavily on the words of the text. Because of this, they are usually not as successful in taking the emotional risk needed to get the most from this exercise.) After the playback, discuss the differences between doing the exercise with the inappropriate feeling and with the appropriate one.

- Do the same exercise again using two-person scenes instead of monologues. Like the first exercise, have the two people perform the scene with unsuitable emotions for the scene. First tape the scene with both actors playing the scene emotionally over the top, then immediately tape the scene again with both actors increasing the emotion and at the same time veiling it. Tape the same scene a third time and use the pertinent feelings. After the playback, discuss the effectiveness of both scene partners in being able to veil. Also take note of the difference between using opposite emotions and those befitting the situation.

7. You must always have an inner monologue.

Also called subtext or stream of consciousness, an inner monologue is literally the character's thought process. Because of its intimacy, film tends to capture this extremely well. While many great lines from movies have entered our collective vocabulary, we also tend to remember great moments when nothing was said. It's as if we can read the character's mind. Watch the last scene from *Monster's Ball*. Halle Barry's inner monologue was absolutely amazing and, for my money, was the deciding factor in her winning the Academy Award for best actress. Her inner monologue brought the audience so vividly into her mental state it was almost frightening. To me it was crystal clear what she was thinking and ended the movie so much more brilliantly than any dialogue could have.

"Always be thinking" should be every film actor's mantra. This principle is similar to Principle 6 in the last chapter on episodic television: they both deal with what happens when the actor is not speaking. But, though similar, the principles are actually very different. Television relies more on the text, whereas film is much more visually oriented. Television appeals to the sense of hearing and film to the sense of sight. Much of this is also purely economic. Television is faster paced and the product has to be completed more quickly. The pace of film is slower, allowing the production process to be more detailed.

This principle is also the natural extension of the previous ones about veiling and entering the world of the scene. If veiling is an active choice that the actor makes about manifesting emotion, having an inner monologue is an active choice about what the actor is thinking when he's not speaking. The actor *chooses* his character's inner monologue; it doesn't happen naturally or accidentally.

Being involved in the world of the scene is a sure method for creating an inner monologue. Most of us walk around talking to ourselves. Whether it's what we think of the person we're with or a song that we can't get out of our heads, we usually have an inner monologue going on. In life, our inner monologues always revolve around what is happening in our lives. Actors need to duplicate that behavior in the characters that they play; they need to create inner monologues that reflect the lives of their characters. Because of the camera's ability to peer into the soul of the actor, the object of its scrutiny can never be vacant.

You can certainly have a character-related inner monologue at the audition, whether or not you're saying lines. But I would wager that most actors when they're not speaking at auditions are thinking something like: "I wonder how I'm doing." "She seems to like me." "I wonder how he liked that line reading." "I really need this job." "I wish this reader wasn't better than me." The casting director and the director will pick up on that. What they would rather see is a fleshed-out character. As part of your preparation for the audition write out your character's thought process and learn it as you would study and learn your lines.

EXERCISES

- Prepare a scene as if you were auditioning for one of the roles. Write out your character's thoughts next to the other character's dialogue. (If it helps, follow the Five-Step Reaction sequence that I've diagrammed for you in Principle 6 of the last chapter.) Tape the scene as a single shot in a medium close-up of only the person who is auditioning. (In other words, shoot the entire scene while taping only one person.) Play it back and see if you can tell what the character's inner thought process is. Did it help the actor's audition?

- Everyone should pick an activity that has to be done within a certain situation. For instance, folding laundry at the laundromat. (Make sure that dialogue is not needed for the scenario to work.) Write out a detailed script of what the character is thinking as he folds the clothes. Write it as if it were a monologue that was going to be said. (Of course you're not going to verbalize it.) Don't share it with anyone else. Remember to make it specifically related to one idea; don't have a myriad of thoughts. Tape it with one camera in a medium close-up. When you play it back, see if the audience can figure out what the character is thinking.

- Try the first exercise for Principle 6 in the last chapter on episodic television. Make sure you follow the instructions.

8. Always play love and/or seduction in every scene.

This may be the most important principle for acting in film. I believe that every great film contains performances infused with love and/or seduction: the characters themselves bewitch each other and in turn bewitch the audience. Seduction or the quest for love is always present in remarkable performances. This quest is everyone's desire to be part of something bigger than he or she is — something outside him- or herself — and is at the heart of almost every great artistic work. This love may not manifest itself in the traditional boy-girl sense — the more usual forms of love or seduction that lead to sex or marriage. Not all characters are interested in sex. (Of course, Freudians would argue otherwise.) This love can just as easily exist between mother-child, friend-friend, and even humanity-society. All of us are seeking approval and acceptance on some level.

Love goes through various stages. At first, someone in love can't bear being parted from his beloved. The object of his love overtakes him psychologically and emotionally: He is swept off his feet, knocked head over heels. It's as if he were obsessed. Then, like gears changing, a shift occurs in the relationship, and love enters a new, less obsessive stage. Seduction, on the other hand, involves physically wanting to be literally part of another person. What they both have in common is an object of attention; the attention must be directed toward someone else. And that's what it boils down to.

As an actor, you must give yourself completely to another person; in essence, you are asking that person to become part of you. This intensity between characters creates an odd sort of conflict. Observing and vicariously feeling this mesmerizes the audience. Hypnotism might be a better word than love; in every scene each character wants to transfix the other character. The very essence of movies is hypnotic: Think of people sitting in a movie theater, waiting expectantly for something to happen — their eyes riveted to the screen, their mouths open. They look hypnotized. They look like they are being seduced. Whether you call it hypnotism, love, or seduction, there is something both magical and visceral about watching movies.

Perhaps the finest way to achieve this intensity is to literally seduce, love, or hypnotize your scene partner, even if it's not implied in the scene. (Remember opposites?) You might not want to use the words *love* or *seduction* or *hypnosis;* that's OK. You have to do what's right for you. This principle is going to be different for everyone, but you have to strive to create a synergetic relationship with your scene partner, because when you encapsulate it, acting is really about affecting another person. For an actor to create the kind of conflict that audiences find interesting, she has to involve herself in a relationship — a connection with another human being. Who we are is measured a great deal through relationships, and how we interact, respond, and feel about those relationships defines who we are.

You can certainly try to do this when you audition. Too often actors treat the person they reading with as an obstacle. They either ignore him or compete with him. Instead of discounting him, try to seduce or hypnotize him, or get him to fall in love with you. If it's a love scene where your character is trying to do that anyway, it's easy — all you have to do is play the given circumstances. But if love or seduction has nothing to do with the scene, give it a shot. It just might make the director take notice that something interesting is happening — and isn't that the whole idea? Just don't be overt about it. The director might question your choices if you're reading for a role where the character is at the grocery store asking another character where the milk is kept, and it seems as if your objective is to get the clerk to go to bed with you. Rather, make the effort to really connect with the person reading opposite you. You want something more than information — you want them to experience life with you on a deeper level.

EXERCISES

- Prepare a role in a scene as if you were going to audition for it. Make sure the scene is not overtly seductive or even about love. As you prepare for the audition, rehearse using objectives that are obvious to the scene; then practice using objectives like — "to charm the other person into falling in love with me," or "to mesmerize the other person." (Feel free to find your own objectives along similar lines.) Tape the audition with the person auditioning the only person on camera. Tape it first playing what you consider the obvious objectives; then tape it again playing the alternate objectives. When you play it back, discuss the version that worked the best. Which one was more interesting? Did the idea of love or seduction add an element to the scene that otherwise would not have been there?

- This exercise requires someone providing scenes to groups of two actors. When I do this exercise, I use three distinctly different scenes — the early scene from *Fargo* when Marge, the police chief, has arrived on the scene of the murdered state trooper and Lou, the patrolman, is explaining to her what he's done so far; the scene from *The Cutting Edge* when the two leads, Moira and D.B., first meet on the ice; and the scene from *The Shining* during the interview between Mr. Halloran and the boy regarding room 237. As you can see by my examples, these are scenes where love or seduction would be deeply subtextual, if present at all. Using the same criteria, pick similar scenes. Everyone should prepare these scenes finding the love or seduction in each of them. Tape each scene and include coverage if you have the time. When you play them back, discuss how the scenes were affected by the choices the actors made. What element, if any, was added to the scenes because of this?

FILM EXERCISES

Exercises are important to anyone learning the art of acting or to anyone trying to improve. You can never do enough. Don't get me wrong; it's also important to be working as an actor or involved in scene study and performance of scenes and monologues. Like musicians or athletes, actors need exercise; you've got to constantly be stretching those muscles.

I've already given you lots of exercises to try out with each of the principles, and I hope that you've found them helpful. Here are a few more that you might want to experiment with. Every time you do an exercise, always have a reason for executing it. Doing exercises for their own sake isn't helpful. Even if the goal isn't illustrious, the intention of an exercise should be to help you with something that you feel you need work on. Tape these exercises with one camera.

EXERCISE 1

This exercise combines Principles 6 and 7 — veiling and having an internal monologue. Two actors will do the exercise (let's call them Person A and Person B). However, only Person A will be on camera and should be taped in a medium close-up. (Actually, Person B is only there to assist Person A.) Person A picks an emotion. (It should not be shared.) Both actors will begin a Meisner-based repetition exercise. The purpose of the repetition exercise is to ensure that the actors are totally in the moment and are not forced to be thinking of their next line. Again, I urge you acquaint yourself with and incorporate the Meisner repetition exercises on camera. Person A will increase the intensity of his emotion during the repetition, until someone off camera asks him to "veil" it. At that point, Person A stops the repetition (while Person B continues it) and imagines a veil covering himself. While Person A engages in veiling his emotion, he should continue to listen to his partner and think an unbroken sequence of thought.

Let me give you an example. Say that Person A has chosen hate as the emotion. Person B is going to start the repetition. (If you haven't done the repetition exercises before, keep it simple.) Person B looks at Person A and says "You have red hair." (Person B can only say that if it's true. An important aspect of the repetition exercise is that whatever is said has to be honest.) Person A repeats "I have red hair." Both continue repeating those two lines while Person A lets the emotion of hate grow. The moment someone off camera says "veil it," Person A stops saying "I have red hair" and veils the emotion while incorporating an internal monologue. Person B should continue repeating "You have red hair." As Person A veils the emotion, he should think an unbroken line of thought as Person B continues saying her line. When the person off camera feels that Person A has had a chance to veil the emotion and maintain an adequate internal monologue, she should stop the exercise.

Think of the repetition as a primer for Person A. If his emotion is growing (like pot of water starting to boil), it will affect the way he says his line. Once Person A is asked to veil the emotion, the filtering replaces the text. As he veils his feeling, Person A must continue listening to Person B and maintain an internal monologue. It's important for Person A to not *do* anything more in this exercise. For instance, he should try and let his facial muscles remain as relaxed as possible throughout the exercise so that the veil can achieve its full effect. The reason for this is that veiling is an internal process meant to have an external effect; it won't work if it's the other way around.

When you play the exercise back, have the audience guess Person A's emotion. Then see if the audience can recognize Person A's internal monologue. Also, try and have the audience notice what kind of effect the veiling had on his performance. Ask the audience if the veiling altered the emotion and, if it did, how.

EXERCISE 2

This exercise combines the use of your imagination, emotion, and internal monologue. Think of it as an exercise in acting in front of a blue screen. (When *Jurassic Park* was filmed, the actors needed to convince us that they actually saw dinosaurs that weren't really there.) Each actor participating in the exercise should imagine seeing something that would result in a strong emotional reaction. (For example, witnessing a murder might motivate a feeling of panic or outrage.) They should write out and "memorize" a one-paragraph thought sequence in reaction to the incident. Since the object of the exercise is to use your imagination and not to recall something from your own life, make sure that what you choose to "witness" is not something that you've seen before.

The actors should be taped individually with one camera in a medium close-up. On the action cue, the actor should imaginatively see the scene unfold in front of him and react to it by internally reciting the monologue.

During the playback, have the audience attempt to guess what that the actor was witnessing and her thought process based solely on her reactions.

EXERCISE 3

This exercise develops the actor's confidence regarding the internal monologue. Everyone should write a monologue of approximately two paragraphs. It *must* be specifically about another person. (This other person is going to be imaginary.) The actor should memorize the monologue.; however, it's only going to be said internally.

The actor should be taped with one camera in a medium close-up. The actor should deliver his internal monologue (without speaking) directly into the camera's lens.

During playback, the audience should attempt to answer these questions: Who was the actor talking to? What was their relationship? What were the circumstances surrounding the internal monologue?

Finally, ask the audience how much of the internal monologue can they literally comprehend.

SUMMARY

Films have defined American society for almost one hundred years. In fact, they are our biggest export. The Kuleshov effect was an experiment by Russian director Lev Kuleshov conducted in 1923. It was the first investigation done to prove that, if given the chance, an audience will fill in the actor's emotional disposition with their own. The lesson for actors is that they don't need to "telegraph" anything when working on camera. It also proves the power that editing has on an actor's performance.

The pay scale for acting in motion pictures is the same as it is for episodic television, and because it's film, falls under the jurisdiction of SAG. Movies can also be lucrative when it comes to overtime and being called back for looping. The biggest difference between television and movies is that more time is scheduled for film and the pace is generally slower. This increased amount of time creates room for more complex and subtle characterizations. The casting process also takes a lot longer in movies. Because of the proliferation of special effects in motion pictures, actors need to be comfortable working in front of a blue screen. To do this successfully, actors must have good imaginations.

Call sheets are important because they tell you everything you need to know about each day's schedule. A typical day includes rehearsal along with quite a bit of time for the crew to set up each shot. The challenges for the actor include not wasting energy during this downtime as well as dealing with possible distractions because of all the activity that takes place on a film set.

There are eight principles for film acting:

1. *Make friends with the camera.* The best way to feel completely at ease is to have great concentration.

2. *Find your focus and zoom in on it.* Focus gives concentration a purpose. Always be ready for action, yet never start until it is called; never stop acting until you hear cut. Focus also will help you during downtime.

3. *Enter the world of the scene.* You need to do whatever is necessary to stay within the milieu. Imagination and analysis will help.

4. *Look for opportunities to incorporate humor.* Besides being funny, humor implies variation of character. Subtlety is routine in film, therefore find humor in every role.

5. *Always include the use of opposites.* Playing opposites is a choice the actor makes to diametrically oppose an obvious action with the opposite one. Playing opposites brings intricacy and complexity to all acting.

6. *Use Michael Chekhov's veiling technique.* Chekhov believed that you should increase the intensity of the emotion, then veil it. The imaginary veil helps to filter the emotion without losing it altogether.

7. *You must always have an inner monologue.* Film captures what you are thinking. Therefore, you should always be thinking. This has to be a conscious choice.

8. *Always play love or seduction.* Whether you define it as love, seduction, or hypnosis, you must always figuratively be pursuing it. Your acting should always be directed toward someone or something else.

CHAPTER 8

WORKING ON LOCATION

Being on location means filming in a setting that is not part of a controlled environment, such as a soundstage or the back lot of a studio. The word *location* comes from the Latin word *locus*, which means "place." But whenever you hear that you are working on location, you should automatically assume that travel is involved, whether the location is down the street, across town, halfway across the country, or around the world.

For an actor, being on location may be the most rewarding experience of working in front of a camera. Whether it's for a movie or television, it is always thrilling to arrive on location for the first time. Before you go, however, there are certain things to consider. In this chapter I discuss how working on location differs from working in a studio (whether on a soundstage or on the back lot), travel arrangements, the amount of money you make per diem, and, of course, the principles.

WHAT, IF ANYTHING, ABOUT LOCATION WORK SHOULD I BE AWARE OF FOR AN AUDITION?

The only thing that might be brought up at an audition is your availability. You may be asked, "If you get this job, are you free to leave for two weeks of shooting in Italy?" Usually, however, it's assumed that you are, and your agent will probably determine that with you even before you go out on the audition.

Because working on location is so common, I would recommend that you prepare yourself by getting and maintaining a passport. You may get a job and, because you're a last-minute replacement, have to leave for the location with very little notice. In that situation, having a valid passport will obviously work in your favor. You would kick yourself if you lost an opportunity for a job in a beautiful location just because you didn't have a passport.

YOU MENTIONED A SOUNDSTAGE AND A BACK LOT. WHAT ARE THEY?

A soundstage and a back lot are both part of a studio's real estate. But before discussing them, I must establish an important caveat: When I talk about studios, I'm talking about Los Angeles–based work. Granted, not all the filming done in this country takes place in Los Angeles, but a lot of it does. (Also, not every film, episodic television program, movie of the week, or miniseries is connected to a studio, even if it is shot in Los Angeles. Many are produced independently and are only shot on location in and around Los Angeles or someplace else.)

If you've ever looked at an aerial shot of Warner Brothers Studios, you probably saw what appears to be acreage full of airplane hangars. Those are all soundstages, which tend to dominate a studio's property. Soundstages are large, self-contained facilities that can usually hold a multitude of sets. A back lot is literally land where a studio can shoot outdoor scenes in the appropriate environment. You can see what a soundstage and a back lot look like by taking the tour at Universal Studios, for instance, or renting the film *The Truman Show*.

Both a soundstage and a back lot are self-contained controlled environments and provide tremendous versatility. A production can make exclusive use of a particular soundstage or back lot and store its scenery and equipment there, to which the crew have unlimited access. In addition, these facilities provide all the power that is needed, and they have none of the complications that come with working on location, such as permits, police presence, onlookers, and so on.

Because of a soundstage's size, anything can be put into it. It can be made to resemble any place, including outdoors. (However, if an outdoor scene is filmed on a soundstage, it is usually done for economic reasons; otherwise it would be filmed on location or on the back lot.) A soundstage is dedicated to a particular production as long as the production is shooting. As I mentioned in chapter 4, sitcoms are all shot on soundstages. So, for instance, if a sitcom is being shot on a soundstage at Universal, that soundstage will belong exclusively to that sitcom as long as it is in production. The same is true for an episodic series or a motion picture.

Almost every studio also has a back lot. The initial idea behind the back lot was to get more realistic-looking exterior shots. For instance, during the heyday of Westerns, studios had back lots that represented the rugged terrain of the West and the generic streets of western towns. Back lots can also represent a typical small town or an island in the middle of an ocean, among many things. Studios often permanently maintain small-town main streets on the back lot for ongoing episodic series to use; that way the set is available to the series (or motion picture) for filming at any time.

Because soundstages and back lots are self-contained, every production at a studio is similar to a little community. Each production has its own crew, personal wardrobe, and makeup trailers, and it is exclusively housed in that particular soundstage or section of the back lot. If you find yourself working at a studio, I urge you to walk around when you have the time. It's fun to see what other kinds of productions are being filmed and the different kinds of activities that are happening. The studios themselves are like little cities: Besides soundstages and back lots, they contain offices for producers and casting directors, commissaries, snack bars, gift shops, workshops, screening rooms, recording and looping studios, editing and postproduction facilities, and so forth.

Soundstages and back lots are versatile because of what can be done on them (which is substantial), and because everything there is temporary and can be adjusted to fit any requirement. I'm sure you've seen pictures of scenery on a back lot or a soundstage — buildings that are represented by their exterior façades only, or interior sets with temporary walls that look like sets on a stage. The sets are designed so that they can be easily and economically built and torn down. To shoot different coverage shots or to achieve different lighting effects for a scene, the crew must be able to move the scenery around relatively effortlessly. On a soundstage or back lot, everything appears real, yet nothing is. In fact, the only reality on a soundstage or a back lot is its impermanence.

At one time, movies and television were almost exclusively shot on a soundstage or on a back lot. Working on location is a much more recent phenomenon. But recent or not, location work has become an important option for films and television. There are now three options for filming: a soundstage, a back lot, or on location. But to appreciate fully what it's like to work on location, one must have a good idea of what it's like to work in a studio or on a back lot. In fact, many times productions will combine the use of locations with a soundstage or a back lot and shoot on two or more within the same film or television program. Therefore, it's important that an actor have a good idea of what it's like to work in all three environments and to understand the differences between shooting on a soundstage, on a back lot, and on location.

WHAT IS THE DIFFERENCE BETWEEN WORKING ON A SOUNDSTAGE OR BACK LOT AND WORKING ON LOCATION?

The biggest difference is that a location is authentic, whereas a soundstage or back lot is not. When you watch a film or television series, it can be difficult sometimes to tell where it's being shot. Generally, if there is a recurring interior environment (like the entire emergency room on "E.R."), you can assume it's on a soundstage. The same is true for a recurring exterior environment. If a program uses the same exterior, it is probably filmed on the back lot. This is especially true for exteriors that are supposed to be "period" (taking place in a different period of time). You can almost always tell when something is filmed on location, either by how it looks or how the location is incorporated into the shot. For instance, for a scene shot in a grocery store, if the characters leaves the store and ends up on a real city street, you can be pretty certain it's on location. A location's greatest asset is its reality: You don't have to pretend. As realistic as a soundstage or a back lot appears, the actor still needs to imagine that she is in the real setting. Let's look at this and other differences between working on location and at a studio.

Reporting to work at a studio is equivalent to a home game in sports. Whether you're working on a soundstage or on the back lot (which is kind of like being on location at home), you are considered to be "in town." You will be given a call time at which to report to the studio as well as a trailer outside the soundstage or near the back lot where you are working. (Trailers are like dressing rooms on wheels; they can be used at either a studio or on location. Only actors playing principal roles get a trailer.)

Similarly, working on location is equivalent to being on the road at an away game. Even if the location is down the street from a studio, travel is involved. Every time a production leaves the studio, equipment and everything else has to be brought to the location.

Though there are overall challenges involved with location work, the advantages of being on location far outweigh the inconveniences. (I deal with the individual challenges for the actor in the principles.) The biggest advantage to working on location is the reality of the location itself. A soundstage or back lot can duplicate an environment, but nothing can come close to actually being there. When you are on location, you don't have to pretend you're somewhere — you are there. The problem is that the "reality" usually belongs to someone other than the production company. For instance, if you're shooting in a real diner, you have to remember that it's someone's actual business. Just as the house where the fictional hero lives is really an individual family's home, and the school where many of the scenes are going to take place is a real school where students' attend classes. You get the idea.

So what happens to the real tenants when shooting takes place? Locations are scouted for appropriateness, and once found, permission has to be obtained and permits issued. The owners of the businesses, homes, and private property are paid handsomely for the use of their property and possessions, and in effect, they agree to hand them over for as long as they are needed. With the promise to make all repairs, the production crew is basically free to do whatever they want with the location for the duration of the shoot as long as the property is returned in the same condition it was in when they got it.

When productions use a public site, such as a school, street, park, or sidewalk, they must secure permits and pay the appropriate fees. The conditions for the use of these kinds of spaces are usually more restrictive, and in those circumstances, productions don't have the kind of freedom that they have when filming at a private establishment. For example, if a production wanted to shoot on a public street, they would need to clear all vehicular traffic (except their own), and they might only be able to shoot during specific times of the day or night. Sometimes productions take their chances and shoot whatever is happening during the moment at the location, but generally not. (When they do this, they lose control of the environment; they have to hope that people aren't going to stare at the camera or start shouting from their car as they drive by.) Often productions are only allowed to shoot during specific times when a location is least used. Obviously if a production was going to shoot at a school or a courthouse, they might be restricted to shooting only during the summer or in the middle of the night when these places are not in use.

Whenever a production shoots on location, police must be present. The police are usually hired from the local department, and the production must pay their overtime salaries. (Because so much filming is done in Beverly Hills and the productions sometimes use officers in small roles, it used to be said that the best way to get into SAG was to join the Beverly Hills police department.)

The police are there, ostensibly, to protect all the equipment and for crowd control. I deal with the possible distractions to actors from a crowd in the second principle, but when it comes to a crowd's presence on a location, there is sometimes a love/hate relationship with the production. Depending on the star of the project or where the location is, curious onlookers are always hanging around. I personally think they add to the atmosphere, but I do know some actors don't appreciate them. It can be difficult for an actor if he feels the crowd is interfering with his concentration. But for the most part, onlookers are as natural to a location as the elements.

WHAT ABOUT HOUSING AND TRAVEL ARRANGEMENTS TO AND FROM THE LOCATION?

SAG has rules within its contracts regarding travel and housing. Different rules apply depending on where the location is, what specific type of contract you are working under, the type of transportation you are taking to and from the locations, and where you live when hired. I'm not going to go into all the variations, but I will discuss the most common situations. If you are a SAG member, you can obtain all this information free by contacting SAG and asking for a copy of the SAG Codified Basic Agreement. If you're not a SAG member, you can buy it for a nominal fee.

Let's say you live in the greater Los Angeles or New York

metropolitan areas and are working on location within what SAG calls the "studio zone." The studio zone in Los Angeles is a thirty-mile radius from the corner of La Cienega and Beverly Boulevards; in New York, it is an eight-mile radius from Columbus Circle. If you are traveling within those zones, you are expected to drive (or take public transportation) to and from the location. However, depending on what kind of contract you're working under, you are generally re-imbursed at thirty cents per mile for the travel. If you live within the Los Angeles and New York areas and are hired to report to a location outside the studio zone, the producers have to provide you with transportation and pay you for getting there. (I discuss this in greater detail later.) If you live outside both Los Angeles and New York, the producers have to provide you with transportation as well (they also must pay you to travel). If you have to fly to a location, it is part of SAG's contract that you fly first class. SAG now offers a budget plan to producers that enables them to fly groups of actors coach class as long as they are on the same commercial or charter flight. This applies as long as no one (including other cast members or crew) is being flown at a higher class.

If you travel to a location where you have to stay overnight, the producers must provide you with housing for as long as you are at that location. Unless the producer notifies both you and SAG of it being otherwise, it has to be single accommodations. Depending on how long you are on location, you are usually put up in an apartment, a hotel, or a motel.

Do I get paid for traveling to a location?

SAG requires the producer to pay an actor for her time when she travels to and from a location as part of a day's work. The exception to this is if you are living in the Los Angeles or New York area and are traveling within the studio zone; then you would travel to the location the same day that your contract for work begins. In this case you are essentially commuting as if you were going to the studio, and as I've mentioned, you are paid thirty cents a mile both to and from the location. For example, if you live in New York and have to be on location in Hoboken, New Jersey, at 8:00 AM, you would receive thirty cents a mile both ways, but you are responsible for getting to the location on your own. If you live in West Hollywood and have to be in Anaheim (which is within the studio zone) by 8:00 AM, you would receive thirty cents a mile for the round-trip and be responsible for getting to the location.

On the other hand, if you were to drive to a location outside the studio zone, you would be paid thirty cents a mile while you were in the zone. Then, once outside the specified radius of the studio zone, you would be paid the prorated amount of a day's wage for the time you spent traveling. Let's say you were to drive from Santa Monica to San Diego, a distance of approximately 120 miles. Once you pass the studio zone — 30 miles from LaCienega and Beverly — you would essentially be "on the clock" and start making the prorated portion of a day's wage. So, in addition to the thirty cents a mile for 30 miles, you could be paid close to two hours of work depending on how fast you drive. If, for instance, you were to drive (or take public transportation) from New York City to New Haven, Connecticut — approximately 90 miles — the same thing would apply. After you left the eight-mile zone, you would be paid the corresponding day's wage for however long it took you to get there. Forget trying to stretch out how long it takes to get from one place to another just to make the extra money. Believe me, the producers know how long these trips are supposed to take.

The same goes for flying. If flying to a location takes most of a full day (eight hours) you will be paid a day's wage for traveling. If your flight is short and you end up flying and working in the same day, after a combined eight hours of travel and work, you would make overtime. For example, you are flying from Chicago to New Orleans. The moment you get on the plane the clock starts. Let's say that when you land in New Orleans, they pick you up and take you directly to the location on Bourbon Street and you start shooting. After eight hours *from the time you got on the plane*, if you're still shooting (even with breaks), you would start making overtime. But if you took an international flight — say you flew from San Francisco to work on location in Paris — you would, of course, make a day's pay for the flight. However, if the flight took longer than eight hours, you would not make overtime for the extra time spent traveling. It boils down to this: You make overtime on a travel day only if you travel and film on the same day, but you don't make overtime for only traveling. But remember that these are only minimum requirements. As long as the producer honors the basic SAG rule that actors must be paid for travel time, all this is negotiable between you and the production.

One other thing I should mention is that while you're on location, the production is responsible for transporting you from your lodging to the work site. Every day that you are called, you will be picked up at your hotel and taken to the location. At the end of the workday, you will be driven back to the hotel. One thing they will not do, however, is to shuttle you around to shop and sightsee. If you think you're going to have some free time when you're on location, I recommend that you rent a car.

What else is provided while I'm on location?

Besides lodging and transportation, you will receive a per diem allowance for food. The current rate per person is $12 for breakfast, $18 for lunch, and $30 for dinner. In essence, on top of your salary you make $60 a day for food. Not bad, huh? Of course, when you are working on location, you are fed on the set during the required meal breaks. A caterer is always on hand to provide breakfast, lunch, and dinner. (This is sometimes also true when you're working at the studio.) If your call time is 6:00 AM, you will be fed breakfast; if you're still on the set when everyone breaks for lunch, you'll be able to get that as well. The same applies for dinner. If you are on the set from 6:00 AM until 9:00 PM, you'll end up being fed all three meals. In this case, you wouldn't receive the per diem. If you were on location for a week in Santa Fe, New Mexico, for instance, and had one or two days off from shooting, you would receive the per diem. (In that case, I would recommend that you rent a car and go sightseeing.)

It's been my experience that meals provided on location are outstanding. Producers usually hire excellent caterers, and you are usually given a wide variety of choices. The other perk on a set (both on location and at a studio) is that a craft table is always available. A craft table is an area kept stocked with coffee, bottled water, soft drinks, fruit, nuts, muffins, candy, and all kinds of goodies for the cast and crew. Believe me, you've got to be careful — it's not hard to put on weight when you're working.

A clause in the SAG contract affects actors who live in Los Angeles, Chicago, and New York (places that have a major SAG branch office) and are hired to work in another one of these cities. This clause stipulates that these actors who live in these cities should be paid extra. Although they may not be by definition "on location," they are still out of town. (According to SAG it mostly benefits New

York actors who are hired to film in Los Angeles.) Let's say an actor who lives in New York is hired for a part in a film that is shooting at Paramount Studios in Los Angeles for a month. Now, Paramount Studios is definitely within the studio zone, and an actor living in Hollywood would certainly not be on location. But in a sense, the actor who is being brought in from New York is on location because he's away from home. SAG has stipulated that this actor will receive $75 per day in addition to his salary for the "inconvenience" of being out of town. In addition, he would also be flown from New York to Los Angeles, housed (Paramount would probably rent him an apartment or a hotel room), picked up and dropped off on days he is working, and given a per diem. As good as this sounds, I don't advise you to move to New York with the hope of being hired to work in Los Angeles. Many talented actors live in Los Angeles, New York, Chicago, and across the rest of the country, and producers usually find who they want living in the cities where they are shooting; they don't make a point of capriciously spending money if they don't have to. This clause does not apply to actors living in other parts of the country. For instance, if a SAG actor living in New Hampshire were hired to film in Los Angeles (or anywhere else), he would automatically be paid as if he were out of town on location.

PRINCIPLES OF LOCATION WORK

Before you pack your bags and prepare to travel, let's look at the six principles for working on location. They are designed to be used in conjunction with the principles that apply to the genre in which you're working. Unlike the principles in the rest of the chapters, however, they don't apply to the audition process. Nor have I included many exercises in this chapter. Instead, actors should use these principles during actual location shooting.

1. Always stay in the area of the location.

I mentioned in the last chapter on film that it is important for the actor to stay on the set during shooting. It is even more imperative that when working on location you never leave the area on days in which you are called for filming; in fact, you should assume that the set itself encompasses the entire region of the location. It's hard enough for the assistant directors to keep track of everyone when a film or TV crew is working on a soundstage; imagine the logistical nightmare when filming outside one. The best thing you can do is literally to stay somewhere on the set or in your trailer.

However, if you are absolutely certain that you're not going to be needed for a while (sometimes a very difficult thing to determine) and you want to explore the area, make sure that you notify one of the second assistant directors. Even though you might not be called for some time, she may advise you against it. If that happens, I would urge you to abide by her recommendation. You have to understand where she's coming from. If for some reason the director changes the schedule and wants to shoot a scene that you're in, the assistant director is responsible for your presence on the set. If you're not there, both you and the AD get in trouble. So if she tells you that you shouldn't leave, she's partially protecting herself — and you should respect that regardless of the motivation behind it. Besides protecting herself, she is also protecting you.

A huge part of being a professional actor has nothing to do with talent. It has to do with the work ethic. Many actors lose jobs because they don't possess the discipline necessary to be a professional actor. Frankly, if an actor gets a reputation of having a poor work ethic, she will find it difficult getting work in the future. Part of an actor's work ethic is to be where you are supposed to be when you are supposed to be there — even if that means enduring excruciatingly long periods of monotonous waiting. Location work can be frustrating because it's tempting to have a good time while you're there. Just imagine being in some exotic location shooting a film. You could be working in a place where you wouldn't be able to go even if you had the time, making more money than you ever thought possible. Your first impulse would be to go out and enjoy it, right? Well, you have to consider that your primary responsibility is to the people who are paying you. Believe me, if you're working on the film long enough, you'll have plenty of time to go exploring on your days off.

When you're first starting out, you cannot afford to acquire the reputation of someone who is irresponsible. There are too many unemployed, talented, and *responsible* actors waiting for just such an opportunity. If you're smart, you won't give it to them — especially over something as frivolous as wandering away from the location.

2. Avoid wasting energy on the natural distraction of location settings.

Let's face it: Working on location is glamorous. Imagine being on location in Times Square with hundreds of people standing around watching. (For an actor it's always thrilling to be in front of an audience.) An actor's natural instinct is to want to show off for an audience. However, this can be dangerous because of the inherent distractions built into this scenario. More than likely, a scene being shot in Times Square is not supposed to be taking place in front of anyone. The actor may have to play the scene as if he were completely alone. Especially on location, it takes enormous concentration to stay focused on what you are doing. A film set attracts a lot of curious onlookers; people are naturally drawn to the process of filmmaking. Many times crowds are interested in seeing a movie star, or they may think there's a chance that they will be discovered. Whatever the reason, crowds are a natural part of being on location.

Strutting around showing off, getting into conversations with people in the crowd, or flirting with all the girls or guys around you will end up draining you of energy. Instead of letting the situation get the best of you, try to feed off the energy of the crowd, allowing its energy to nourish you.

Many actors initially train in the theater where the focus is on stage work. Part of the appeal of being onstage is the communal interaction with an audience. There's something special about the actor/audience relationship in theater. If you've ever acted onstage (or even spoken before a large group of people), you are probably aware of the adrenaline rush that hits when you walk out there and have all those eyes looking at you. It can benefit the actor, inspiring and energizing his performance. That has to be one of the reasons why Al Pacino and other theater-trained film actors keep returning to the stage. Part of the excitement of theater is that a performance exists only because an audience views it live.

You don't get that same kind of rush working in television or film. (Especially as the workday gets longer.) In television and film, the performance is not intended for the onlookers. A performance is ready for an audience only after all the filming, editing, and postproduction are done. Other than the crew, nobody is supposed to be present while you are working in front of a camera. (Unless, of course, you're appearing on a sitcom.) When you're on location, you need to take advantage of the crowd by making it work for you. If the onlookers give you an adrenaline rush, by all means let it empower you. Don't let the onlookers distract you; feed off their energy. Let them motivate you and help you sharpen your focus, but don't perform for them.

Not only can the crowds be distracting when you're on location, but sometimes the location itself can be a significant distraction. Years ago, there was a television series called "The Nasty Boys." (It was produced by Dick Wolf, who created the brilliant "Law and Order.") The plot revolved around a group of undercover Las Vegas policemen who disguised themselves like ninjas to fight crime. Part of the series was filmed on location in Las Vegas. In one episode I was hired as a guest star and was cast as a corrupt political campaign manager. I had, literally, auditioned for and gotten the job on a Friday afternoon and was flown to Las Vegas that evening. That night I was on location on the Las Vegas Strip. The first scene we shot depicted a huge campaign rally where the gubernatorial candidate was assassinated while making a speech. It was a crucial scene in the episode and important for developing the story line and my character. As usual, filming was time-consuming; there were dozens of extras and, of course, curious onlookers. In addition to all that, a casino was right next to where we were shooting. In between takes, after letting the AD know where I was, I would wander off to the casino. All night long during shooting it was extremely easy for me to hop over and play the slot machines during breaks in the filming. So, despite the crowds, the slot machines ended up distracting me more. I became more interested in gambling than I did in my work. During the weekend of filming, I would find ways to gamble during breaks in shooting. I wasted a lot of energy and my concentration certainly suffered by letting the casinos interfere with my acting.

As a result, I ended up losing my entire per diem at the slots during the course of the weekend. Fortunately they don't pay your salary at the same time, or I probably would have lost that, too. (Thankfully we ended up shooting the majority of the episode in Los Angeles) The point of the story is that the location itself distracted me. (I don't mean to imply that it was the location's fault; it wasn't.) Not only did my work suffer, but so did my wallet.

Remember that it's the *actor* who is on location, not the character. Characters, like all of us, tend to focus on what they are doing and what they want instead of being aware of where they are and who's there. The only time it would be appropriate to be distracted by the crowd or the location is if the crowd were part of the shot or if the environment itself were an obstacle for your character. For example, in the film *Memento*, the lead character is suffering from an acute form of amnesia. *Everything* to him is new, interesting, and distracting. The actor who played this role, Guy Pearce, masterfully took advantage of every opportunity to react to his surroundings. In his case, he used the location in a manner appropriate to the film's material. You can be distracted by the crowds or the location itself, but only if your character is. (Personally, I would rather have had my character lose money playing the slot machines instead of me.)

3. Always take time to become acquainted with the location.

In his excellent book, *Acting in Film*, Michael Caine talks about getting to the set early and becoming acquainted with it. This is invaluable advice that applies especially to working on location. When you're on location, there generally isn't enough rehearsal (or any sometimes) for most actors to feel comfortable. What's enjoyable about working on location is that you are in the actual space. You don't have to approximate it like when you're working on a soundstage. If the scene calls for a mountaintop, you're there; if it calls for you to be at the beach, you're there.

However, you don't want to be playing what I call "catch up" with your location. You don't want to be appear to be learning about the location while the camera is rolling. Take the necessary time as part of your preparation to become accustomed to your surroundings. This is especially true if your character is supposed to be acutely familiar with that environment. It isn't as relevant if your character has never been to that place before. In that case, you're lucky because you can become accustomed to the environment along with your character.

In many ways, this principle has a lot to do with continuity. For example, let's say that you've been cast in a film where all five of your scenes take place at a beach. But instead of scheduling the scenes sequentially, the director has scheduled the last scene to be shot first. So even though your first day on the film will be your first day on location, the first scene that you're doing will actually take place in the film at a later point in the script. You've got to act as though your character has been there for a while. The best-case scenario would be for the director to rehearse all five scenes in sequence before shooting any of them, but you can't rely on that. You might very well have to become familiar with your environment on your own.

If you get to the location early and get used to it, you'll naturally appear as if you've been there awhile. However, it is not enough to get there early and merely walk around. (Of course, if that's all you're able to do, make the best of it.) As long as you don't get in the way of the crew setting up, visualize yourself in the scene while imagining what happened before. Take yourself mentally through the previous four scenes, imagining exactly where they took place. By doing this, you will automatically be making character choices about the location. After all, what you ultimately want to do is to establish a relationship with your location. Because the camera doesn't lie, the only way you can convince the audience that you're acquainted with the beach is if you really are. The more you do this, the more believable you will appear in the location. And having a relationship with the location leads us to Principle 4.

4. Let the location inspire you.

The great Italian director Bernardo Bertolucci once said, "Find things about the set that will serve to make your performance more full and complex." I have to believe that he was referring to being on location as well. Working on location is exciting, stimulating, intriguing, and inspiring. There is no substitute for the real thing when it comes to helping the audience willingly suspend its disbelief. For the actor, there is something delightful about being able to "live" in an environment similar to one that she may have imagined when she reads the script. On a soundstage, you have to pretend that the environment is real. On location it *is*. Because of that, it's easier for everyone involved — actors, the director, the director of photography, as well as the rest of the crew — to also suspend their own disbelief.

Let the location be your ally in the choices that you make about your character. Using the example of the beach, you can use the environment to assist you in learning things about your character. For instance, being on a beach is certainly going to influence the way you walk. While exploring the location and mentally improvising the scenes, ask yourself how your character might walk on the beach in a manner that exposes who he is. For example, would your character plod heavily weighed down by the sand? Or does he dance across the top of the sand dunes, or kick sand between every step? Other ways a location can inspire your character are sensory. Feel the warmth of the sun and imagine what your character feels about it. If there is a breeze, how does that affect your character? All these questions will hopefully initiate new ones and lead you to discover and make interesting choices about aspects of your character.

Often you will be on a location at a place that represents a personal space for your character: her home, for instance. Although it is an actor's job is to convince others to believe in a particular reality, it can be difficult to do this when you yourself are unsure of exactly what that reality is. Chances are that you haven't spent any time there, and you'll have to make quick decisions about it when you do get there. For example, what do you do when you find yourself in a location that is supposed to be your character's bedroom? A bedroom is the kind of place where if most people were blindfolded, they'd still manage to navigate through it perfectly well. The actor needs to convince us that she as her character is able to do the same. I also imagine that most of us could go through our bedrooms and give detailed accounts of every item in it, including facts about where we got them, how long we've had them, and so on. Knowing every detail about something we own is a way we bond with it. It is in this way that we tend to personalize our possessions, especially those things that mean the most to us. An actor will help her character appear intimately involved with her surroundings if she personalizes everything necessary about the location itself and what she finds in it.

The best way to personalize your environment is to endow every pertinent item within the location. Endowing something is simply creating a detailed story about it. For instance, if the location is supposed to be your bedroom, the choices you make will be more fascinating and specific if you can answer questions about where you got it or who gave it to you, how long you've had it, what it means to you, and what kind of private association it has for your character. Essentially, you should be able to subconsciously endow all the relevant articles on the set. Just make sure that the endowments are convincing to you. Doing this, hopefully, will inspire your performance and will automatically result in a personalization of the objects. Even if no one ever knows what you've come up with, the consequence of this kind of "endowed personalization" will create a believable relationship between the character and his habitat.

The same idea is also true if the location is a place where your character is employed. For example, you could find yourself on location in an office where your character has supposedly worked for much of her career. In a relatively short amount of time you must be able to walk into that environment and not only feel like you belong, but also appear as if you've been working there for a while. A way to help you achieve this might be as simple as knowing where everything is on your desk. But even that is going to be difficult to do if you don't get to the set early and scope out the location in detail from the very first time you're there. The kind of familiarity you must achieve can only be attained when you have personalized everything about what's on the desk as well as the office itself.

I can understand your panic right now if you think all this has to be done before you even start shooting. You are probably thinking, "I've got to get to the location twenty-four hours in advance to do all this!" Don't worry; it's impossible to achieve all this in its entirety before filming begins. Although you should still get there early and do as much as you can, don't forget the enormous amount of time that you're going to have during the actual shoot. You can continue this work in between shots, and it will help keep you from getting distracted by everything else. Just remember to be accessible to the location so it can inspire you. What's also important is to discover new things about it. If you do, those discoveries will create new opportunities for inspiration.

EXERCISES

- If you are working in a classroom situation, tape a two-person scene with one camera as if you were filming a scene on location. Bring props for the scene that have never been used in the space before and that are unfamiliar to the actors. Make sure to address the issues of the given circumstance of the scene and imagine that you are actually there. The most important thing for the actors to do is to personalize the objects for the scene and endow them with stories before shooting starts. During the playback, notice if the actors' comfort level and believability were enhanced by their relationship with the props.

- Each pair of actors should choose a two-person scene from a source of their choosing adhering to the following criteria — the characters should be familiar with each other and be living together. The scene should take place at the characters' home. (They should be intimate or related somehow. They could be lovers, brother/sister, wife/husband, etc.) Take a camcorder to someone else's (not one of the actor's) home to shoot the scene. The challenge for the actors is to establish not only a believable relationship with each other, but also to establish a relationship with their environment. During playback, discuss if the audience believed that the characters were familiar with their surroundings and how that helped or hindered the relationship between the two.

5. Your acting has to be as real as the location you're in.

The previous two principles have touched on this, but I think this is important enough to warrant its own principle. As I've discussed, being on location is thrilling because of the authenticity of being where you say you are. However, there is a risk to this. It's easy for a location to upstage a performance. Can you think of performances that didn't measure up to the location, and as a result, something was innately false about them? An actor can never forget that her performance has to be as honest as the location in which she's working.

You can do this by steadfastly playing the given circumstances. For your acting to be as truthful as the location itself, you need to pay attention to the last principle; but not only must you be inspired by the location but your acting must also be inspired by the *truthfulness* of the given circumstances. An actor has to understand that he needs to expand his idea of the given circumstances to include the environment where he is working. Many young or inexperienced actors assume that the given circumstances consist only of what they've rehearsed and what's in the text. The given circumstances should also encompass the world that they find themselves in. For example, I've seen inexperienced actors completely ignore something that randomly happens onstage (or on camera). It's usually something inadvertent, a mistake made by someone other than the actor. For instance, an actor onstage who completely ignores a piece of furniture that falls and breaks during her scene. Everybody in the audience turns to look, but not the actor. Inexperienced actors sometimes panic in these situations because they don't know how to handle something that's unrehearsed. They figure that if they ignore it, everyone else will too. After all, I'm sure we can all empathize with the urge to believe that if you ignore something long enough, it will eventually go away. The problem is that this doesn't work during a performance. The audience wants to see the character react to it; and if she doesn't, the audience is reminded that what they are seeing is not real. Accidents happen in life and we react to them; when they happen during a performance, actors must react as well. (We probably shouldn't think of them as accidents; instead, we should really consider them as moments of reality.)

The same goes for working on location. Actors can't ignore things that happen in the environment where they are working. If an actor chooses to ignore something that happens during a scene, he does a disservice to his character. In these cases, it's usually the actor's choice to decide that he's going to ignore a mistake when, in reality, his character would probably have reacted to it. If the wind is blowing in a scene, you've got to acknowledge it. If you don't, the audience will think there's something wrong with you. Don't get me wrong; I'm not advocating that you start to ad-lib lines based merely on the weather. You don't want to say, "Wow, it sure is blowing out here!" in the middle of a scene if it has nothing to do with the script. What is important is your behavioral reaction to the wind.

All of us can think of classic scenes where an actor on location reacted to what happened during the moment — the famous scene in *On the Waterfront* between Marlon Brando and Eva Marie Saint is an example. Marlon Brando as Terry Malloy, a shy dockworker, is trying to express how he feels when he inadvertently puts on Eva Marie Saint's glove, which he was holding. A favorite one of mine, a moment from *It's a Wonderful Life*, is subtle but perfectly illustrates the integration of actor and location. Jimmy Stewart is meeting his brother Harry at the train station. Stewart's character, George Bailey, has been at home running the business waiting for Harry to come back from school and take it over — freeing up George so he can pursue his dreams. Harry arrives at the train station with a new wife unexpectedly in tow. In one long, uncut take, Stewart goes through a series of reactions about the news of his brother's marriage and recent job offer. Toward the end of the shot, he walks over to where his new sister-in-law is standing, and an extra accidentally bumps into him. It happens quickly. In the close-up, Stewart reacts to the jostle but never misses a beat. The jostle doesn't detract from his performance; he brilliantly stays in the moment, maintaining both his concentration and his objective. The bump is an insignificant moment, really, but because of the way Stewart plays it, it adds much to the reality of the scene.

However, sometimes rules must be broken. There are three exceptions to this principle. The first one is simple; do what the director asks you to do. In rare cases the director may not want you to react to the environment. For instance, if the scene is especially tense or emotionally full, the director may feel that it would be inappropriate for you to acknowledge the wind; in that case, you shouldn't. My advice is to keep reacting until the director asks you not to.

The second exception concerns continuity. The continuity of a scene has to be a primary consideration. Let's say that you're doing a pick-up shot of a scene that has already been filmed. (In a pick-up shot, the director goes back and shoots a small section of a scene after the scene has been filmed in its entirety.) This could happen well after the scene was previously shot. In this case, for continuity reasons, you must duplicate everything about the original shot, including repeating the original given circumstances of the location. For example, perhaps on the day you initially filmed a scene, the weather was hot and hazy and you chose to acknowledge and play that reality. Since you've already established the weather, you must re-create the feeling of a hot and hazy day in subsequent pick-up shots — even if the weather becomes cool.

The third exception is more complex. Sometimes locations are meant to represent a completely different place; the location is standing in for somewhere else. Often locations are picked for what they look like and not necessarily for geographical accuracy. Certain cities in the United States and Canada are frequently used to represent other places. Because of its topography, for instance, Pittsburgh has doubled for Seattle, San Francisco, and Detroit.

Other substitutions are done for economic reasons. You might be on location shooting a scene on the streets of Los Angeles on a warm, sunny, 80-degree day. However, the script calls for a street in Minneapolis on a brisk clear winter's day. If the majority of the film is being shot on a soundstage in Hollywood, or if the rest of the film is supposed to take place in Los Angeles, the producers are not going to pack up an entire crew and travel to Minneapolis for one or two scenes.

When this happens, it can be challenging for the actor. There you are dressed in a heavy coat, scarf, hat, and gloves trying to imagine you're on a street in Minneapolis on a cold winter day, while you're actually sweating to death on the corner of Highland and Gower in Hollywood. Conversely, you could be on location in Chicago in March while the scenes are supposed to take place in the summer (you may even be asked to swim in Lake Michigan and pretend it's 90 degrees outside). March in Chicago can be windy and cold, but under sunny skies it could certainly pass for summer. Obviously, in both cases you can't react honestly to the location. Instead, you must realistically portray the given circumstances that you're asked to play.

The time of day that you shoot on location will also not often match the time called for in the script. For the sake of convenience, they may have to shoot either very early in the morning or very late at night. Many times the location can only be used in the early morning or late evening hours when it's generally quieter and more accessible to a large crew. (For example in *Vanilla Sky*, the opening sequence depicts various parts of New York City that are completely deserted. Those scenes could only have been shot very early in the morning when the city was relatively quiet.) I've regularly shot very early and very late when on location. For actors who keep regular hours, these late night and early morning shots can be difficult.

I mentioned in the last chapter that occasionally scenes are shot day for night (scenes shot during the day that are supposed to take place at night). Although day-for-night shots are usually done indoors, they may also be done on location.

Then there are disaster films, which may require working in 500,000 gallon water tanks or running in and out of burning buildings. (Usually, however, stunt performers tackle these scenes.) But whether these scenes use the absolute reality of your location or are hypothetical, in all instances you must uphold the integrity of your character by always playing the given circumstances.

6. Location work is fun. Enjoy it!

The previous five principles establish the parameters for working on location. I hope they will help you anticipate conditions, avoid making mistakes, and give you ideas that will make the experience easier for you. Having said all that, what's most important is to have a good time. Nothing is as rewarding as working on location. Especially if you've spent years toiling away onstage or in a classroom pretending to be someplace you're not. There is something liberating about acting in the real world. Make sure you enjoy it!

I've always thought of location work as a working vacation. You get to travel free of charge to places that you haven't been, you get free lodging, you're well paid, and, on top of all that, you get to act! What more could you want? But besides these obvious reasons for savoring the experience of location work, one of the most significant aspects of it goes back to the fundamentals of why people get into acting in the first place — the sense of community that acting gives you.

Unless you are a regular on a series, sitcom, or soap opera, location work is the closest you'll ever get to working as part of a "company" in the television or film industry. When you work on a soundstage at a studio, most everyone is commuting to work. Everyone involved lives at home and reports to work at the beginning of the day and goes home at the end of the day. Nothing is wrong with that, but it can sometimes feel somewhat disconnected; especially for someone who is hired to be there for a month, a week, a few days, or even one day. Creating drama is a collective and participatory art, and because of that, I think it's important that there be a team attitude. When you're on location, though, everyone is pretty much in the same boat; most everyone on the set is from out of town. Because of this, there tends to be even more of a collective spirit about the shoot. Everyone's primary reason for being on location is to do the work. Because everyone is away from home, the cast and crew tend to focus more intently on the workplace; they get to know each other more and there tends to be much more of a community spirit for everyone involved.

So, keep in mind that going to the trouble of applying Principles 1 through 5 will ultimately culminate with the result that you're going to have a huge amount of fun working on location. It will be well earned, because having that kind of fun is certainly the reward of hard work.

LOCATION EXERCISES

It's now time to go on location. For the following exercises you are going to need a camcorder or a digital camera that has a good microphone. Be prepared to use your own lighting if you travel to dimly lit places, but you should be able to use whatever natural light exists. It would be best for you to provide your own power source to plug in your camera and lights, but if you don't have one you'll need to get people to let you use theirs. Most important, in order to shoot these exercises on location, you're going to have to persevere and try to get people to cooperate with you. Whatever you do, make sure to get permission before you start shooting on someone's private party. Also, remember that the point of these exercises is not to achieve technical expertise; you are trying to simulate the reality of being on location for the actor. I urge you to especially adhere to Principles 4, 5, and 6.

EXERCISE 1

Actors should have two-person scenes prepared. (These scenes can include more people.) These can be scenes that were used for episodic television or film assignments. The actors, a "director," and a "crew" should go out and find a location that is different from the one that is asked for in the scene. For example, if the scene is supposed to take place in someone's living room, go out and find a convenience store to be used as the location. Make sure that the location has the potential for lots of people who could possibly play unwitting extras. It could be a bowling alley, a shopping mall, or a coffee shop. The director should shoot a master shot of the actors playing the scene in this "foreign" location and see what happens. If the director finds that the crowds are unwilling to interfere with what is going on, she might get some of the "crew" to encourage members of the crowd to walk through the scene and to interact with the actors. In this situation, it's very interesting to see what happens when unexpected things are thrown at the actors.

When you play back and discuss the scenes (which should not take place at the location), try to determine if the environment helped or hurt the actors. Are the actors able to bring the same kind of honesty to their work as the location provides? Ask the actors for their reaction to playing their scene in this alien situation. Did it or the "extras" distract them? Were they able to be inspired by the location?

EXERCISE 2

Actors are given two-person scenes in which the weather plays an integral role. In *Fargo*, for example, the outdoor scenes occur in winter with the temperature at minus 30 degrees. However, here's the catch: The scenes must be for weather conditions the *opposite* of actual conditions outside (summer scenes should be done during cold weather and winter scenes during warm weather). Therefore, scenes from *Fargo* would be suitable only if it were warm outside, and a scene from *Apocalypse Now* only if it were cold.

Shoot master shots of the scenes. They must be shot outdoors and the actors must realistically play the given circumstances that are provided by the text. They must play the heat even though it's really cold; likewise, they must play the cold even though it's warm.

Play it back and discuss whether the actors brought believability to the scene in spite of the location's contrariness. Did they convincingly portray the given circumstance of the script? Ask the actors if playing in the opposite conditions had any effect on them or their performances.

SUMMARY

Location work can be the most rewarding work done in front of a camera. One of the reasons for this is that being on location always implies travel because it takes place away from a studio. The challenges in working on location are that you are always in someone else's space, which you have to make your own, and working in public places such as schools, streets parks, and so forth can be more restrictive because of limitations on when you are able to shoot. But the positive reasons overshadow the negative ones because, overall, the most wonderful thing about being on location is the fact that you are in a more realistic atmosphere than you would be working on a soundstage or back lot at a studio.

Depending on your contract, SAG provides for transportation to and from the location and housing. If you travel outside of the studio zone, you are paid a portion of your daily rate, or an entire day's rate if you have to fly a significant part of a day. If you fly to a location and work in the same day, you would make overtime after eight hours. No overtime is paid for flying over eight hours. Besides transportation and housing you are paid a per diem for meals or fed on location.

There are six principles for working on location:

1. *Always stay in the area.* You can't afford to get in trouble for not being where you're supposed to be; therefore it's best to stay on location.

2. *Avoid wasting energy.* The crowds and the location itself can be distracting. Learn to use the energy of the crowd to your advantage and focus on your work.

3. *Always take time to become acquainted with the location.* Get to the set as early as possible so you can become accustomed to it.

4. *Let the location inspire you.* By personalizing everything on the set you will create a believable relationship between the character and his habitat.

5. *Your acting has to be as real as the location.* It's easy for the reality of a location to upstage an actor. To keep this from happening, you must include the location as part of the given circumstances. The exceptions to this would be if you were directed not to, if it threatened the continuity, or if the location was standing in for someplace else.

6. *Location work is fun. Enjoy it!* Enough said.

BIBLIOGRAPHY

Abbott, Leslie Abbott. *Acting for Films and TV*. Belmont, CA: Star Publishing Co., 1994. This is a good book and somewhat like a textbook. It has some good exercises and deals with film and television. For me, the scenes are the best part of the book.

Adler, Stella. *The Technique of Acting*. New York: Bantam, 1988. The only original member of the Group Theatre personally to study with Stanislavski. This is an invaluable book on understanding Adler's interpretation of Stanislavski's system.

Atkins, Greg. *Improv! A Handbook for the Actor*. Portsmouth, NH: Heinemann, 1994.

Barr, Tony Barr. *Acting for the Camera*. New York: Harper and Row, 1997. This is a revised edition of the original version published in 1986. The newer edition contains exercises by Eric Stephen Kline. A fine book, this was the only book for a long time on camera acting. However, it doesn't deal with the challenge of auditions.

Brestoff, Richard. *The Camera Smart Actor*. Lyme, NH: Smith and Kraus, 1994. This is an excellent book. It is especially good for the "day in a life chapter" of what to expect on the set for the first time. It contains a wonderful bibliography and glossary.

Caine, Michael. *Acting in Film*. New York: Applause Theatre Book Publishers, 1990. This is the most famous film-acting book on the market written by the well-known and excellent actor, Michael Caine. It is the companion to his wonderful video of the same title. Anecdotal in style and invaluable for anyone interested in Michael Caine's process and experience.

Chekhov, Michael. *On the Technique of Acting*. Edited and with an introduction by Mel Gordon; preface and afterword by Mala Powers. New York: HarperCollins, 1991. This contains the complete edition of Chekhov's *To the Actor*. It's especially useful for the afterword "Michael Chekhov in Hollywood" in which Mala Powers describes Chekhov's methodology on acting for the camera.

Cohen, Robert. *Acting Professionally*. Mountain View, CA: Mayfield, 1990. This book is an invaluable resource for an actor thinking about starting a career. A no-nonsense practical guide on the business side of a life as an actor.

Fridell, Squire. *Acting in Television Commercials*. New York: Crown Publishers, Inc., 1986. Possibly the best book on acting in commercials, this is written by a very successful commercial actor. There are a lot of good tips. It contains information about auditions, but the book is only specific to commercials.

Gordon, Mel. *The Stanislavski Technique/Russia: A Workbook for Actors*. New York: Applause Books, 1987. This book is incredibly well researched. Gordon offers extraordinary exercises that were initially practiced by students learning Stanislavski's system.

Grotowski, Jerzy. *Towards Poor Theatre*. New York: Simon & Shuster, 1968.

Hagen, Uta. *Respect for Acting*. New York: Macmillan, 1973.

Harmon, Renee. *How to Audition for Movies and TV*. New York: Fireside, 1991.

Hayes, Vangie. *How to Get into Commercials*. New York: Harper and Row, 1983.

Hindman, Kirkman, and Monk. *TV Acting*. New York.: Hastings House Publishers, 1982.

Silverberg, Larry. *The Sanford Meisner Approach: An Actor's Workbook*. Volumes 1–4. Lyme, NH: Smith and Kraus, 1994. A tremendous resource explaining Meisner's repetition exercises. A very accessible series of books, Silverberg simply and clearly puts the Meisner technique into practice with a wonderful collection of exercises.

Spolin, Viola. *Improvisation for the Theater*. Evanston, IL: Northwestern University Press, 1963.

Stanislavski, Constantine. *An Actor Prepares*. Translated by Elizabeth Reynolds Hapgood. New York: Theatre Arts Books, 1936. A book every actor should read and study. Written late in his life, it's Stanislavski's attempt to document his system.

———. *Building a Character*. Translated by Elizabeth Reynolds Hapgood. New York: Theatre Arts Books, 1949.

———. *Creating a Role*. Translated by Elizabeth Reynolds Hapgood. New York: Theatre Arts Books, 1961.

Shurtleff, Michael. *Audition*. New York: Bantam, 1978. For the longest time this was the only book on auditioning. Many more are available today, but this one is still one of the best. Shurtleff, for many years a very successful casting director, offers some incredible tips.

THE AUTHOR

JOHN SHEPARD has been an actor for twenty-five years and has worked extensively in every genre that he writes about in this book, including location work. In addition, he has performed on Broadway, Off-Broadway (New York Shakespeare Festival/Public Theatre, Manhattan Theatre Club, Theatre for the New City and Soho Rep.), and he has toured. He has also acted at some of the country's leading regional theaters including Yale Rep, Long Wharf Theatre, Actor's Theatre of Louisville, Mark Taper Forum, Huntington, City, and the Oregon Shakespeare Festival. He lives in Pittsburgh where he acts, directs, and teaches. He has taught acting for the camera at the University of California, Irvine, University of Wisconsin-Stevens Point, University of Illinois, Urbana-Champaign, and he is currently at the Conservatory of Performing Arts at Point Park University, where he is chair of the Theater department.

THE ILLUSTRATOR

DAVID DROXLER was born and raised in Delaware County, Pennsylvania, southeast of Philadelphia. He has studied art since childhood, receiving multiple awards and recognition. David went to the Conservatory of Performing Arts at Point Park College where he majored in acting and was a student of John Shepard. He is currently travelling the country as a working actor. This book marks his first published work as an illustrator.